Advance Praise for
Student-Centered Pedagogy and Course Transformation at Scale

This book breaks new ground by describing how Purdue University embarked on embedding a culture of teaching across the institution and succeeded in engaging faculty and influencing teaching and course design at scale. The book shows how, with leadership from the top, coordination between different centers in the university, and a model that respects faculty's agency, the reach and impact of faculty development can be transformed.

"One major lesson from IMPACT is that [its] features can be intentionally cultivated for any major campus initiative to improve learning and teaching."—**George D. Kuh**, *Chancellor's Professor Emeritus of Higher Education, Indiana University*

STUDENT-CENTERED PEDAGOGY AND COURSE TRANSFORMATION AT SCALE

STUDENT-CENTERED PEDAGOGY AND COURSE TRANSFORMATION AT SCALE

Facilitating Faculty Agency to IMPACT Institutional Change

Chantal Levesque-Bristol

Foreword by George D. Kuh

STERLING, VIRGINIA

Published by Stylus Publishing, LLC.
22883 Quicksilver Drive
Sterling, Virginia 20166-2019

Library of Congress Cataloging-in-Publication Data
Names: Levesque-Bristol, Chantal, 1973- author.
Title: Student-centered pedagogy and course transformation at scale : facilitating faculty agency to impact institutional change / Chantal Levesque-Bristol ; foreword by George D. Kuh.
Description: Sterling, Virginia : Stylus Publishing, LLC, 2021. | Includes bibliographical references and index. |
Identifiers: LCCN 2021005571 (print) | LCCN 2021005572 (ebook) | ISBN 9781642671018 (paperback) | ISBN 9781642671001 (hardback) | ISBN 9781642671025 (pdf) | ISBN 9781642671032 (ebook)
Subjects: LCSH: IMPACT (Program : Purdue University) | College teaching--United States. | Student-centered learning--United States. | Effective teaching--United States. | Educational change--United States. | Organizational change--United States. | Education, Higher--Aims and objectives--United States.
Classification: LCC LB2331 .L474 2021 (print) | LCC LB2331 (ebook) | DDC 378.1/250973--dc23
LC record available at https://lccn.loc.gov/2021005571
LC ebook record available at https://lccn.loc.gov/2021005572

13-digit ISBN: 978-1-64267-100-1 (cloth)
13-digit ISBN: 978-1-64267-101-8 (paperback)
13-digit ISBN: 978-1-64267-102-5 (library networkable e-edition)
13-digit ISBN: 978-1-64267-103-2 (consumer e-edition)

Printed in the United States of America

All first editions printed on acid-free paper that meets the American National Standards Institute Z39-48 Standard.

First Edition, 2021

To Dustin and Dylan. My constant muse and inspiration. You both inspire me to become the best version of myself.

Mom and Dad. For your unconditional support and love.

Alice. For the guidance.

CONTENTS

FOREWORD

Build It Right, They Will Come, and All Will Prosper

As I write, colleges and universities in the United States are in the grip of COVID-19 uncertainty. One of the hard truths about higher education likely to persist long beyond the COVID pandemic is that the quality of learning and teaching will receive far less attention than other more easily measured indicators that have little to do with the quality of the undergraduate experience. You know them—rankings correlated with perceived institutional prestige, externally funded research productivity, number of faculty honored by external organizations, and so on.

However, akin to a trim tab and the ship's rudder working together to steer a large ocean liner, a much-needed, long-awaited, albeit slow, turn is under way as more faculty use student-centered pedagogy to enhance learning and personal development. Multiple factors are contributing to this welcome turn, not the least of which are escalating tuition costs and worries about whether students are prepared to live an economically self-sufficient, socially responsible life after college.

Espousing the value of deep, relevant student learning and effective teaching is one thing. Creating the institutional conditions that encourage and reward the use of promising approaches to scale and sustain such work is quite another. This is what sets Purdue University's Instruction Matters: Purdue Academic Course Transformation (IMPACT) apart from many well-designed faculty development and institutional improvement efforts.[1]

IMPACT is a massive, complicated, multiyear campus-wide initiative with many moving parts aimed at improving the learning and teaching of Purdue undergraduates. Fundamentally a comprehensive faculty development effort, the focus is on redesigning course-level instruction and related activities based on promising pedagogical practices. In addition to the hundreds of participating faculty members, other moving parts include continually evolving instructional formats and varying physical classroom and online settings. To their credit, IMPACT personnel employed an implementation strategy that made it possible to respond in a timely manner to the inevitable challenges that emerge with such a large, complex initiative and adjust the work accordingly going forward. Did I mention COVID-19 (see chapter 10)?!?

As you will soon discover, there are many reasons IMPACT merits attention by institutional leaders, faculty developers, and others. Consider just three data-informed observations:

1. IMPACT boosted the use of empirically derived effective learning and teaching practices institution-wide by involving hundreds of faculty across the 12 colleges on the West Lafayette campus who voluntarily participated in faculty learning communities focused on incorporating engaging pedagogical approaches in their courses.
2. Students in IMPACT-designed courses had higher end-of-course final grades and lower drop/fail/withdraw rates compared with their counterparts in non-IMPACT courses.
3. Student-centered instruction was front-loaded to help students start strong, when in fall 2016 95% of first-year first-time enrolled students took a redesigned IMPACT course.

It's All About the Culture

The road to excellence in any endeavor begins and ends with culture (Collins, 2005; Peters & Waterman, 1984; Schein & Schein, 2017). This is because culture exerts a powerful though largely tacit influence on how people think and what they are rewarded (or sanctioned) for among many other facets of university life (Kuh & Whitt, 1988). IMPACT leaders recognized this and—undaunted—set an audacious goal: to change the culture of a major research university to embrace engaging pedagogical practices (chapters 1, 9). I am persuaded that three culture-bending levers (Kuh, 2013) that characterize IMPACT's operating principles and activities are instrumental to its effectiveness. The first is an equity-minded commitment to betterment, an impulse that animated IMPACT from the outset. IMPACT staff focused on measurable improvement on multiple student learning and related indicators (chapter 7) that were aligned with the institution's strategic plan (Purdue University, 2020). They also were committed to continuous quality improvement. Toward this end, IMPACT staff used quantitative and qualitative data to document the quality of the work and identify ways to tweak the approach to improve both faculty and student performance (chapter 7).

The second cultural lever is the initiative's campaign orientation. To be sure, IMPACT had to be conceptually and theoretically sound (chapters 2, 3). At the same time, it also needed to be a vocal champion and locus of effort for improving learning and teaching that can only be realized over years of effort, fueled by an institutional vision of inclusive excellence enacted by collective will and action. To do this at scale, IMPACT did two things. First, IMPACT personnel and senior campus administrators periodically publicly endorsed IMPACT's important mission-centric purposes. This stands in stark relief from faculty development work that too often operates on the margins of institutional life and receives little attention by the reward system (chapter 9). Second, IMPACT staff annually aggressively recruited participants to join the semester-long faculty learning communities where much of the course design activities occurred and continually provided information that individual faculty could use to challenge and support students to devote effort to educational activities that enrich learning (chapters 6, 7, 9).

The third cultural lever was nurturing a collaborative ethos. Meaningful collaboration is a function of effective working relations among those responsible for implementing IMPACT and prospective faculty and academic staff participants. Cultivating a collaborative ethos is not possible absent respect, trust, and competence, which are products of confidence about goals, agreement between espoused values and the means used to achieve desired ends, and a willingness to continuously assess performance. Coordinated by Purdue's Center for Instructional Excellence—led by the author of this book, Chantal Levesque-Bristol—IMPACT benefitted from full-throated support from such influential institutional partners as the president's office, the office of the provost, technologies at Purdue, libraries faculty, the Evaluation and Learning Research Center, and distance education (chapters 1, 9). As the initiative ramped up, IMPACT prioritized and promoted the use of discipline-friendly educationally effective practices (chapters 4, 5, 6), prompting deans and numerous department chairs to engage, champion, scale, and sustain the work.

These cultural bending levers—a betterment impulse, the campaign orientation, and a collaborative ethos—are essential ingredients in the secret sauce of what makes IMPACT so successful. They are relatively easy to grasp conceptually but very difficult to enact consistently over time. Nevertheless, one major lesson from IMPACT is that these features can be intentionally cultivated for any major campus initiative to improve learning and teaching.

Last Word

Effective professional development programs do not just happen. Considerable planning and expertise are required to determine what instructional staff "need" (as distinguished from what they may "want") to improve their performance. But poor implementation can derail the best devised plans. The planning, implementation activities, and perceived benefits must be relevant and meaningful to sustain the interest and participation by university faculty who are highly autonomous skilled professionals. In these arenas, there is much to learn from IMPACT and this book about how to successfully deliver timely, substantive, high-quality professional development experiences to a particularly discerning audience.

George D. Kuh
Chancellor's
Professor Emeritus of Higher Education,
Indiana University

Note

1. My knowledge and understanding of IMPACT is informed by my work as an external evaluator of the initiative during 2018 (Kuh, 2018).

References

Collins, J. (2005). *Good to great and the social sectors: Why business thinking is not the answer*. HarperCollins.

Kuh, G. D. (2013). Culture bending to foster student success. In G. W. McLaughlin, R. Howard, J. S. McLaughlin, & W. Knight (Eds.), *Building bridges for student success: A sourcebook for colleges and universities* (pp. 1–15). University of Oklahoma Consortium for Student Retention Data Exchange.

Kuh, G. D. (2018, July). *The impact of IMPACT: Evaluation of the Purdue University Instruction Matters: Purdue Academic Transformation (IMPACT) initiative*. Purdue University Office of the Provost.

Kuh, G. D., & Whitt, E .J. (1988). *The invisible tapestry: Culture in American colleges and universities* [ASHE-ERIC Higher Education Report, no. 1]. Association for the Study of Higher Education.

Peters, T. J., & Waterman, R. H. (1982). *In search of excellence. Lessons from America's best run companies*. Harper & Row.

Purdue University. (2020). *Transformative education*. Purdue Moves. https://www.purdue.edu/purduemoves/initiatives/education/index.php

Schein, E. H., & Schein, P. (2017). *Organizational culture and leadership* (5th ed.). Wiley.

PREFACE

The purpose of this book is to not only describe and present Instruction Matters: Purdue Academic Course Transformation (IMPACT), the professional development, course transformation program at Purdue University, but also highlight the importance and implications of the underlying motivational theoretical framework guiding the initiative and draw out the implications and stimulate ideas for professional and faculty development for higher education.

This book is primarily intended for an audience of faculty developers. However, several chapters will also be of great interest to instructors and administrators.

Chapter 1 will situate the IMPACT program and the book in the context of previous course reform and course transformation programs and introduce the fundamental innovation of the program. In chapters 2 and 3, the book will introduce the fundamental motivational principles of self-determination theory (SDT) followed by the applications of these principles for transformative change in higher education. Chapter 2 is a deep dive into the theory. Faculty developers, practitioners, or people mostly interested in the application of the theory could skip chapter 2 and read chapter 3 instead. Alternatively, you could choose to read only the first section of chapter 2 focused on the description of the basic psychological needs of autonomy, competence, and relatedness to gain sufficient understanding of the core of the theory as it applies to the IMPACT program and culture change. In chapter 4, I will delve into the core and structure of the IMPACT program and describe in detail the faculty learning community (FLC). In doing so, I will discuss how the program evolved over the years and how the focus on SDT principles shaped that evolution, transforming our work with the IMPACT fellows and the program itself from a course redesign initiative to a professional faculty development program. This chapter will also introduce how the focus on SDT influenced the composition of the IMPACT teams and describe the process by which we formed them. This chapter may be of less interest to instructors who may not have a say in influencing the development of such a program on their campus. However, this chapter will be of great interest to faculty developers and administrators who can advocate for the creation and development of programs and initiatives like this at their institutions. Chapters 5 and 6 should be of particular interest to instructors and faculty developers. In these chapters, I focus on the applications of the SDT principles to a variety of active learning strategies and faculty development. In chapter 5, I explore the motivational mechanisms behind the effectiveness of various pedagogies often used to foster active learning in course redesigns (e.g., minute paper, flipped learning). In chapter 6, I discuss IMPACT as a faculty professional development program based in SDT and the broader application of SDT motivational principles to the creation of effective professional development opportunities. I touch on the implications for faculty developers as they work with instructors in their various programs, for directors of teaching and learning centers as they lead their staff of faculty developers, and for instructors as they mentor graduate students. Chapter 7 presents the IMPACT assessment plan used to document IMPACT's effectiveness. The assessment plan covers assessment of faculty change and professional development, student engagement, student course academic outcomes and retention, student learning outcomes, institutional change, culture change, and sustainability. The chapter focuses on how the IMPACT team has worked to document the evolution of the program and assessed and tracked its success from its inception, and it should particularly interest administrators and faculty developers. Chapter 8 presents a discussion of active learning and classroom spaces couched in terms of SDT and human motivation. The chapter will dive into the notion that spaces need to be conceptualized and designed with the instructor and learner in mind, taking into account both motivation principles and design principles. It highlights the importance of professional development in order to help instructors teach effectively in these new learning environments and presents the corresponding research evidence. In chapter 9, which was originally conceptualized as the final chapter before the COVID-19 pandemic, I engage with the reader in a discussion of how IMPACT and the collaboration among the units working on IMPACT have catalyzed a culture change at Purdue and beyond and suggest how other institutions can engage in a similar culture change. Other institutions can engage in their own broad culture change by adapting and integrating the theoretical principles and practical insights described in this book to their own contexts. Chapter 10, added after initially completing the manuscript, was written to describe IMPACT's emergency response to the changing conditions created by the COVID-19 pandemic and how we used and adapted the principles that led to the success and scale of IMPACT to pivot to meet the new circumstances we faced. It tells the story of how we as a team, using the research-based pedagogical principles and the SDT theoretical principles, worked together to help instructors successfully navigate the pivot to emergency remote teaching and beyond. While this story is not finished, what we have learned may offer lessons for future practice and for dealing with challenging and uncertain circumstances.

It has been a privilege to write about IMPACT and discuss how it was shaped by the focus on SDT and in turn how it influenced the institutional culture through this motivational lens. George D. Kuh in a review of the IMPACT program in 2018 wrote, "IMPACT is a textbook illustration of how to successfully deliver timely, substantive high quality professional development experiences over an extended period of time to a particularly discerning audience" (p. 8). It is my sincere hope that as you take the IMPACT journey through reading this book, you find that it lives up to this endorsement.

ACKNOWLEDGMENTS

This part of the book was the most difficult to write. How can I completely and truly acknowledge all who have in one way or another contributed to the conceptualization and writing of this book? This book was a long time coming. The ideas in this book have percolated in my mind since I began my career as a faculty developer, and most possibly before that, as I was dreaming of influencing in one way or another the world of higher education. I will not attempt to name here everyone who has influenced me in the writing of this book, because I would certainly miss many. Nonetheless, I will name a few and attempt to acknowledge the support I received and the contribution of certain people or groups of people who stand out in my mind at this time, as I'm writing these words.

The evening I received the email from John von Knorring inviting me to discuss this book idea, I sat with my colleague, Jason FitzSimmons ("Fitz"), in a little bar in Bergen, Norway, and brainstormed the concept for this book. Our conversation was inspirational and helped shape my vision.

I also would like to thank the IMPACT community of faculty fellows. The ideas in this book have been refined through the years of working with all of you, transforming higher education.

Over the years my colleagues on the IMPACT management team and the IMPACT evaluation team have been invaluable in shaping the FLC and the assessment of IMPACT and refining the ideas presented in this book. You have influenced the writing of this book in ways that I can't fully acknowledge.

Throughout the years, the opportunity to discuss and present IMPACT and course transformation based in SDT at many national and international conferences and at workshops in various institutions of higher education has significantly contributed to my desire to write this book. Many colleagues convinced me that I had something valuable to share. This endorsement, support, and encouragement greatly helped me stay focused throughout the process.

As I was putting the finishing touches on the book, during another research meeting I received some life-changing advice on formatting, and I would like to thank Emily Bonem, Heather Fedesco, Cong Wang (Vivi), and Erica Lott for this huge time saver!

I would also like to thank my research lab, who have read and commented on early versions of some of the chapters in this book. Thank you Emily, Erica, Dave, Dan, Fitz, Karen, Hyun Jin, Vivi, Horane, and Chorong for the exchange of ideas.

I also want to acknowledge my faithful canine writing companions, Bella and Alfred, who lay down at my feet or next to me every day as I worked on the book, either sitting on the front porch or at the kitchen table. Unfortunately, I had to say goodbye to Alfred part of the way through the writing of the book, but Bella held steady. She listened to me rattling off ideas for the book, looking somewhat interested, but always happy that I was home with her for an extra walk break over lunch as I was trying to clear my mind.

Finally, I would like to thank the staff of the Center for Instructional Excellence at Purdue, who have had to work extra hard in the last few months of the writing of this book, because I had to take time away from the office in order to focus on the book. It takes a village to write a book, truly, and I don't know if I will completely feel finished, but I have to stop at some point.

I

SITUATING IMPACT

What does higher education need to be transformed, disrupted, stay relevant? What is the next innovation that will significantly change higher education? Is the innovation a new tool, a new technique, or a particular redesign model? How can we be more focused on the students? How can we be innovative when we are not even meeting students' needs?

In his 2006 book, *Our Underachieving Colleges*, Derek Bok strongly argued that "colleges and universities, for all the benefits they bring, accomplish far less for their students than they should" (p. 8).

In their 2011 book *Academically Adrift*, Arum and Roska, using data from the Collegiate Learning Assessment (CLA), reported that almost half of undergraduate students assessed showed no significant improvement in critical thinking, complex reasoning, or writing during their first 2 years of college. Their study, conducted in partnership with the Council for Aid to Education, examined responses of students who took the CLA at 20 different 4-year colleges and universities during their first semester in fall 2005 and at the end of their sophomore year in spring 2007. The study aimed to understand how the college experience can influence students' general skills and broad competencies, such as critical thinking, rather than specific content knowledge gained in particular courses or majors. Sadly, and to the dismay of many, the anticipated gains were not observed. Although we arguably have one of the finest systems of higher education, filled with many opportunities for students, in recent decades the United States has fallen behind many other countries in terms of the percentage of students who graduate with a higher education degree (U.S. Department of Education, 2006). It is in fact why in 2014 the Department of Education, under President Obama's education agenda, released the First in the World (FITW) grant competition in order to foster innovations to improve quality and educational outcomes for our students and help accelerate our rate of discoveries in education.

It is during this critical era that Instruction Matters: Purdue Academic Course Transformation (IMPACT) was created, launched, and scaled (https://www.purdue.edu/impact/). It was an attempt by a research university (Purdue) to address the criticism leveraged by scholars at institutions of higher education. How could we do more for students? How could we help students learn? How could we help students succeed? How could we improve the institutional culture of teaching and learning, especially at large research universities, where teaching competes with research? How could we change the narrative? How could institutions of higher education fulfill their promise?

IMPACT, a cohort-based faculty development program that features a faculty learning community (FLC) to promote engagement and student-centered learning and teaching, was launched in summer 2011 by the Provost's Office. Dale Whittaker, vice provost for undergraduate academic affairs at Purdue at that time, brought together a group of representatives from the Provost's Office, the Center for Instructional Excellence (CIE), Teaching and Learning Technologies (TLT), Institutional Data Analytics and Assessment (IDA+A), Purdue Online (PO), and the Evaluation and Learning Research Center (ELRC) and asked them to collaborate in order to fulfill the vision of IMPACT. My office, CIE, was part of this group, although I had not yet arrived at Purdue. This original group constituted the IMPACT steering committee. On that day, and with a small amount of one-time seed money provided for a few years, the steering committee became the group responsible for general oversight and direction of the IMPACT program, reporting regularly to the Provost's Office. As a general rule, when I refer to "we" in this book, I typically mean the collaborative of the IMPACT team. Conceptualized from its inception as a comprehensive, campus-wide, collaborative effort, IMPACT aims to empower faculty to create student-centered learning environments by incorporating active and collaborative learning as well as other student-centered teaching and learning practices and technologies into their courses. The first cohort launched in fall 2011, comprising 12 faculty fellows redesigning 10 large gateway courses from eight different departments representing the humanities, social and physical sciences, engineering, and agriculture.

This campus-wide collaboration and the implementation of an FLC followed recommendations by the American Council on Education (Struthers et al., 2018) as well as the writings of Milton Cox (2004). Efforts to improve undergraduate education should include a focus on what transpires in classrooms across the entire institution, build on collaborations among many stakeholders, support the entire instructional community through faculty development built around FLCs, and value teaching and learning as a core mission of an institution of higher education. The American Council on

Education also highlights the need to examine the implementation of evidence-based practices that positively influence student learning and outcomes in the classroom (Struthers et al., 2018). IMPACT built on those principles to guide our overarching goals. These are as follows:

- Refocusing the campus culture on student-centered pedagogy and student success
- Increasing student engagement, competence, and learning gains
- Focusing course transformation on effective research-based pedagogies
- Reflecting, assessing, and sharing IMPACT results to benefit future courses, students, and institutional culture

In the beginning, IMPACT drew heavily from commonly accepted redesign practices and models, including backward design and the work of Carol Twigg at the National Center for Academic Transformation (NCAT). The FLC curriculum first emphasized the creation of learning outcomes and objectives and worked back from there to create the learning activities and assessment for the course (Wiggins & McTighe, 2005). As recommended by NCAT, faculty fellows had to select from a limited number of course redesign models offered to them (Twigg, 2003). The use of technology was emphasized as a way to improve student learning outcomes by fostering student-centered environments and to reduce cost. In short, in the beginning, IMPACT followed a fairly typical and accepted course transformation model. So where is the innovation? What is unique about IMPACT?

The Transition and the Innovation

In 2012, I joined Purdue as director of CIE and assumed an important role in the leadership of IMPACT. I was recruited based partly on my previous experience with course redesign and the NCAT model, conducted at my former institution. I am a social psychologist by training. My research area is in motivation. I brought with me to the IMPACT team and our work the principles of self-determination theory (SDT), a theory of human motivation focusing on the satisfaction of the three basic psychological needs (autonomy, competence, and relatedness) as a way to foster the creation of engaging and autonomy-supportive environments (Deci & Ryan, 1985; Ryan & Deci, 2017). My experience with NCAT and my background in motivation caused me to wonder whether the application of NCAT redesign principles was perceived as controlling by faculty fellows implementing the transformations. The IMPACT team was at first cautious, although curious, about my musing. Although SDT has been researched for more than 40 years by scholars from around the world, it was not a familiar concept in the realm of course redesign and transformation, and it was mostly foreign to the other members of the IMPACT team. This may actually be the first time you are hearing about SDT. However, examining the data from interviews conducted with the first few cohorts of IMPACT faculty fellows using the motivational lens of SDT confirmed my hypothesis.

Specifically, my hypothesis was that the close adherence to the NCAT redesign models was perceived as constraining and limiting and discouraged some faculty fellows who did not perceive the specific models as accommodating their disciplinary needs. In the data from the interviews, we were able to clearly hear that faculty fellows who participated in early iterations felt constrained by the lack of flexibility in the program imposed by the structure focused on a limited number of redesign models. One of our lofty aims with IMPACT was to shift the culture at the institution toward more student-centered practices, impacting instructors in all colleges at Purdue. Focusing on a particular technology or redesign model was not going to allow us to scale IMPACT to the entire institution. This approach was not going to be compelling to instructors from a variety of disciplines. Although each redesign focused on a commitment to greater active learning (Felder & Brent, 2009; Freeman et al., 2014; Prince, 2004), the strict adoption of the NCAT redesign models was not the answer to an attempt at scaling the program. The use of technology per se was not enough to make a redesign student centered. Although most of the early redesigns incorporated a substantial amount of technology, it became quickly apparent that technological tools were not driving the success of a redesign. Engaging faculty through a learning community model (Cox, 2004) was not enough. Backward design was not enough. Although the elements of a successful redesign model were present, the redesign needed something different to be scalable to the degree we were asked to scale the program.

The innovation was in the introduction of a motivational theory and a deep focus on the people doing the transformation, the "human factor" of course redesign. The focus on people and their needs is the innovation in IMPACT, and it is an innovation that is infinitely replicable because it focuses on people. The heavy focus on technologies, tools, and redesign models obscured an important factor in successful redesigns—the fact that at the center of a course redesign are the people teaching and learning. Often, "why" instructors would use a particular tool or technology was missed in the evaluation of successful redesigns. This human factor, it turns out, is usually left out of formal course redesign projects or programs. However, this human factor is often referenced by experts and scholars in the field of education, if you read between the lines.

For example, George Mehaffy (2018) argued that academic leaders must pay more attention to quality teaching—how to improve it, value it, foster it, and reward the improvement of it. To realize the needed culture change, classroom initiatives and course transformation projects in general must be engaging, relevant, and appealing to instructors and also be adaptable to a broad range of disciplines in order to influence the majority of students across the institution. It's about engagement and motivation. In order to positively impact student engagement, motivation, learning, performance, and retention, instructors must utilize pedagogies that are authentic, truly resonate with their practices and their fields, and go beyond institutional requirements to meet accrediting agencies' rules or simply "check a box" without the need for deep reflection and true transformative work (Brookfield, 2017; Haras et al., 2017; Kuh et al., 2017).

This speaks to the importance of the people doing the teaching. Faculty, instructors, and graduate teaching assistants—the entire instructional community—require support to effectively implement engaging pedagogical practices for all students and move institutions toward a deep culture change fostering the implementation and integration of student-centered practices. The instructional community is the most important asset in the transformation projects and needs to be valued and recognized. At a time where state funding is lower than prerecession levels (Mitchell et al., 2017), institutions must find ways to do more with fewer resources per student. Focusing on people and their needs has been our answer to this challenge.

The focus on SDT principles in particular and human motivation in general became the critical turning point, the thread that tied everything together. From that point on, the tenets of SDT were intentionally integrated and influenced everything we did, from how we structured course design and delivered the IMPACT program through the FLCs, to how we successfully scaled and assessed the program. It also led to a move away from a focus on course redesign per se and a move toward a focus on professional development. SDT provided us with the theoretical framework to inform the operationalization of active learning and student-centered learning using the basic psychological needs of autonomy, competence, and relatedness. Importantly, the focus on motivation also influenced how we interacted and engaged with each other as a collaborative team from diverse units.

The collaboration among the units in IMPACT is also crucial for the success of the program and contributes to its uniqueness and transformational nature. It took time for the IMPACT team to build this collaboration into a strong and genuine partnership working toward creating environments that are relevant for all instructors and engaging and motivating for students. This process was absolutely guided by the principles of SDT. It took time and many open and authentic conversations for us as an IMPACT team to figure out what truly catalyzes change, but I can say today that we have done this, and it has led to a culture change at Purdue. We have developed into a strong and growing community of faculty developers, focusing and supporting the needs of instructional staff, and through this process have developed meaningful connections with other stakeholders such as student success, enrollment management, and the registrar's office. As Adrianna Kezar (2017) noted, by partnering with stakeholders across the university and multiple units on campus, faculty developers have a crucial role to play in institutional cultural change. In the IMPACT model, faculty developers are not only the staff members of the teaching and learning center. They are the members of the teaching and learning technology unit, online learning, and the faculty of the libraries. To enact culture change, a broad group of stakeholders is needed at the table, and the partnership we built in IMPACT is a great way to be called to this institutional transformation mission. In these cross-campus collaborations, it is important to select the right partners to be present at the table. These would be the ones who have responsibility for providing teaching and learning opportunities on campus and people from these units who have budget and decisions authority.

Some of the important partners in a large initiative like IMPACT may not be obvious at first. For example, the Libraries and School of Information Studies (LSIS), who joined the team in 2012, turned out to be a significant partner fostering the growth of the IMPACT program as they worked to transform themselves. At that time, the libraries at Purdue had begun to experiment with and conceptualize space differently. To address the changing needs of the 21st-century student learner, many academic libraries in higher education were thinking about transitioning their formal and informal learning spaces, and Purdue libraries were leading the way in this area. Library space at Purdue was no longer considered a repository for books and microfiche, but rather a space to learn, think, create, grow, collaborate, discuss, and exchange ideas. The reconceptualization of library space into a collaborative student learning "place" changes the essence of the traditional library, moving from a book-centered to a learning-centered space. This newly available physical space could then be repurposed and converted into flexible, active learning spaces in order to enhance the teaching and learning mission. As the reputation of the program grew, and as we worked to scale IMPACT, the involvement of the Purdue libraries provided access to the needed space to accommodate IMPACT's ambitious transformation timetable.

Although the partnering units in IMPACT have unique missions and goals, we are united through our work with IMPACT by our focus on professional development, student learning, and engagement. We have built an

Figure 1.1. Institutional partners in the IMPACT university-wide collaboration.

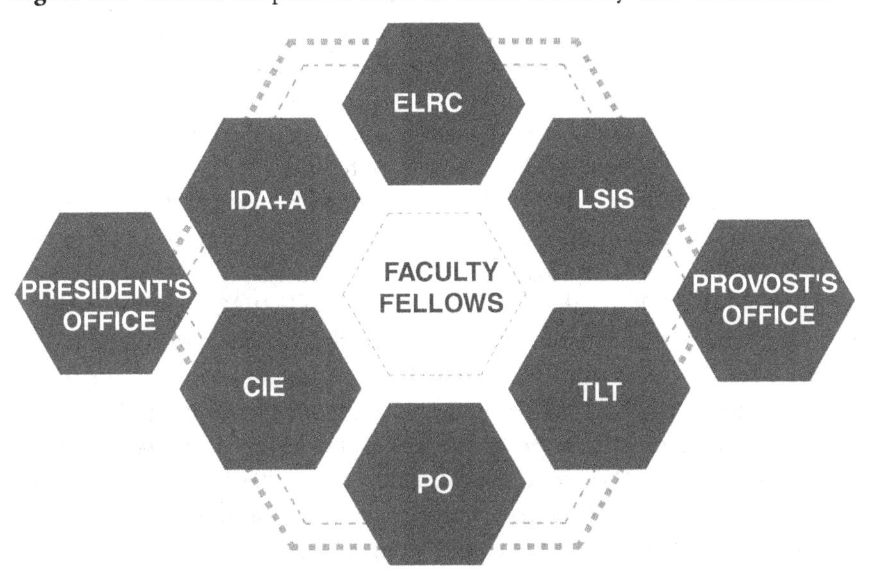

Note. Honeycomb unit collaboration model reprinted with permission of A. M. Allred.

authentic cross-campus collaboration in a research-intensive institution with a strong tradition of independence across units. Figure 1.1 depicts the units at the institution currently partnering on the university-wide collaboration.

While many institutions attempt to prioritize the teaching mission and active learning, few are able to do so at the broad campus-wide scale necessary to effect culture change through a sustained partnership between multiple campus units. Moreover, rarely do research-intensive universities attempt such large-scale efforts in order to systematically improve the quality of undergraduate education, especially where teaching may not be as emphasized as research, and for instructors who receive little or no support prior to their first teaching experience. This book is about one such successful attempt and how it was done through a focus on human potential and motivation. It's about the work of a research-intensive institution that chose to heavily invest in and commit to teaching and learning transformations. In spring 2013, Mitch Daniels, former governor of the state of Indiana, became the 12th president of Purdue. One of Daniels's first initiatives as president was the creation of the "Purdue Moves." The Purdue Moves are in essence Purdue's strategic plan and are four areas of focus and strategic growth in higher education, still in place at Purdue today. Affordability and accessibility, STEM leadership, world-changing research, and transformative education are the four strategic areas. The IMPACT program was recognized in

2013 as part of the transformative education area of focus. Incorporation into the strategic plan resulted in additional resources for instructional developers and faculty fellows, but also the strategic expectation to scale up and double the capacity of IMPACT. The focus on SDT was a crucial factor in our ability to successfully scale the program. A focus on human potential and motivation, professional development rather than course design, and the flexibility and ability to choose individual redesign elements from a multitude of course design options allowed us to successfully meet the challenge of scaling up the IMPACT program.

Part of this book tells the story and evolution of IMPACT and its implications for higher education but, more importantly, the thread throughout this book is about the innovation focused on humans and their natural propensity to learn and grow. It expands on the work presented in recent publications about the program in *Change* and *NILOA*, and featured in *The Chronicle of Higher Education* (Levesque-Bristol, Flierl, et al., 2019; Levesque-Bristol, Maybee, et al., 2019; McMurtrie, 2018). As I focus on the human innovation that made IMPACT unique and what it is today, I will describe how we, as a higher education community made up of faculty, instructional staff, faculty developers, students, and administrators, can build programs that are sustainable and that will lead to culture change. This culture change is one that will allow us to transform the experience of the instructors in our institutions of higher education and as a result the experience of the students in our classrooms, labs, and higher education community. As I will describe in this book and help you discover, the innovation is not about a tool, a technique, or a particular redesign model. It is about building a true collaboration and partnership between campus stakeholders and investing in people; the people who teach and the people who learn. It is about a deep commitment to students and professional development for our instructional community, which will transcend disciplines and content, and which can be easily adapted and implemented by other institutions. This is the innovation this book is about.

2

UNDERSTANDING SDT

SDT is a theory of human motivation (Deci & Ryan, 1985; Ryan & Deci, 2017) that approaches psychological growth, development, integrity, and wellness from an organismic integration perspective, which is typical in life sciences. SDT postulates that humans are naturally curious, active, social beings who strive to connect with people, their environment, and the world in general. In a healthy state, humans are naturally inclined toward proactive engagement, behavioral self-regulation, and actively internalizing information into a coherent and integrated whole. Under optimal and positive conditions, humans are equipped to deal with difficult environments and can remain oriented toward prosocial altruistic behaviors, kindness, growth, development, cooperation, and overall well-being. These inclinations manifest in behaviors of exploration and curiosity associated with intrinsic motivation; the development of mutually supportive relationships; and the internalization and integration of social norms, rules, and regulations. The latter is essential for critical processes associated with behaviors and activities that are necessary but not fun, pleasant, or interesting; this is often the case when we think about academic pursuits and, in general, behaviors that are necessary for the good functioning of society, or external valued goals, or pathways to some desired end. In contrast to a view where human beings are considered as inherently selfish, filled with poor intentions, lazy, and unmotivated, SDT postulates that humans are inherently benevolent and oriented toward growth, integration, and well-being. Ill-being or illness, under this framework, is often a reflection of deficient conditions in the environment rather than deficiencies in human beings.

SDT is functionally important because it empirically examines features of the environments and contexts that would foster or hinder motivation and satisfaction of the needs underlying effective growth, development, self-regulation, engagement, and well-being. It does so in a variety of life and social contexts, including education, but with relevance and applications to work and organizations, leadership, parenting, health care, sport and physical activity, leisure activities, and interpersonal relationships, to name a few of the most researched areas.

In this chapter, I will focus on describing the general principles of SDT by focusing on three of the mini theories associated with SDT: basic psychological needs theory; organismic integration theory and the internalization process; and cognitive evaluation theory (CET). The examples, empirical evidence, and the discussion specifically related to the application of the SDT principles to education, with a special emphasis on higher education, will be the topic of chapter 3.

Basic Psychological Needs Theory

According to SDT, basic psychological needs are nutrients essential for humans' growth, integrity, thriving, and well-being. Conditions that foster the satisfaction of the basic psychological needs will lead to growth, well-being, creativity, exploration, curiosity, proactive engagement, and optimal self-regulation. In SDT, positive or negative outcomes are predicted from the extent to which a person's basic psychological needs have been satisfied or frustrated or from the extent to which social conditions, environments, or contexts need supporting or need thwarting. The basic needs reflect our adaptive human design and are therefore universal. The needs are invariant across age and cultures, which means that although they can be expressed differently in different life stages or different cultures, the needs themselves remain the same. We will come back to this important notion later in this chapter with some specific examples.

Autonomy

Autonomy is the need to self-regulate and be the initiator of one's experiences and actions. When the need for autonomy is met, people feel volitional and experience their actions and behaviors as being in line with their values and beliefs and other parts of themselves. When acting with autonomy, behaviors are engaged in wholeheartedly with a sense of freedom; the person feels authentic and integrated. It is important to understand that autonomy does not mean independence, self-reliance, or doing only what one wants to do. Autonomy is about feeling volitional and choiceful. It is about ownership, a feeling of agency, and endorsement of one's actions. In different contexts, people can be autonomously dependent or independent. For example, someone could fully choose to do something for a friend and in doing so feel completely volitional and autonomous. In contrast, the same person could feel conflicted or forced to do something for a family member and in that moment feel constrained and forced and experience their behavior as not integrated or congruent with their values, interests, or other behaviors.

Relatedness

Relatedness is the need to feel connected; to care for, be responsive to, and be connected with others, as well as to be cared for and included by others. It is the need to experience mutually satisfying relationships. The need for relatedness is about belonging and feeling significant among others. It is characterized by a sense of closeness and trust. When a person's need for relatedness is met, they feel connected to close others and a part of social groups or organizations (Baumeister & Leary, 1995; Bowlby, 1979; Ryan, 1995). The need for relatedness, although central for human beings' growth, development, health, and well-being, is often neglected when discussing motivation and achievements in academic pursuits. I believe this is a fundamental gap in our understanding of what makes an academic learning environment engaging and autonomy supportive. We will come back to this issue in chapter 3.

Competence

Competence, according to SDT, is the need to feel effectance and mastery. People need to feel able and have the confidence to achieve their goals, have effective interactions with the environment, and master a variety of important life domains. In SDT, the need for competence is understood as effectance motivation (White, 1959) and as such includes the tendency to investigate and want to understand things that matter and are important to us, or to engage fully in the environment in general. The need for competence energizes numerous behaviors in the most diverse contexts from those engaged in during academic pursuits to those engaged in during leisure activities and relationships. Formal education is certainly an important area for many individuals at different times in their life, and the need for competence in higher education has been heavily discussed, from a variety of theoretical perspectives, as an important component of motivated action (Bandura, 1989; White, 1959).

Organismic Integration Theory and the Internalization Process

Organismic integration theory within SDT focuses on behaviors that are not intrinsically motivated or driven by curiosity or interest. Life is full of behaviors we engage in because we have to for the good of others and society, including chores, work, family duties, or goals we have set for ourselves.

We also refrain from engaging in behaviors that would be considered wrong or problematic. The internalization process allows these behaviors that are not fun but necessary to become more self-determined and valued by the individual (Wang, 2019; Wang & Levesque-Bristol, 2019). According to SDT, *internalization* is defined as the process of taking in values, beliefs, or behavioral regulations from external sources and transforming them into one's own (Ryan et al., 1985). But how are behaviors and activities that are often pushed, imposed, or expected by socializing agents integrated into the self and valued? According to SDT, this process of taking in and valuing behaviors that are not fun and extrinsically motivated is also innate in healthy humans. In other words, under optimal conditions, people are inherently motivated to integrate social norms and regulations. In general, the conditions in the environment that foster the satisfaction of the basic psychological needs of autonomy, competence, and relatedness will also foster self-determined motivation and the internalization of extrinsically motivated behavior. In this section, I present and discuss the different types of motivation proposed by SDT and the internalization process by which a behavior that is required becomes more self-determined. A schematic representation of the motivation continuum is presented in Figure 2.1.

Intrinsic Motivation

Intrinsic motivation is the prototype of self-determined motivation and is found on the right side of the continuum. It underlies behaviors that are engaged in purely for the enjoyment or interest derived from the activity. Intrinsically motivated behaviors are engaged in for their own sake. The primary reward when intrinsically motivated is the feeling of effectance and enjoyment.

Amotivation

At the other end of the continuum, we find behaviors that are not motivated or are considered impersonal. Amotivation represents lack of motivation and is associated with lack of engagement, perceived competence, and value. It is highly associated with drop-out rates, absenteeism, and lack of engagement.

Different Types of Extrinsic Motivation

SDT proposes the existence of different types of extrinsic motivation, which vary based on the underlying level of self-determination. Some forms of extrinsic motivation are considered to be self-determined, volitional, or autonomous, while other forms of extrinsic motivation are considered to be

Figure 2.1. Motivation continuum.

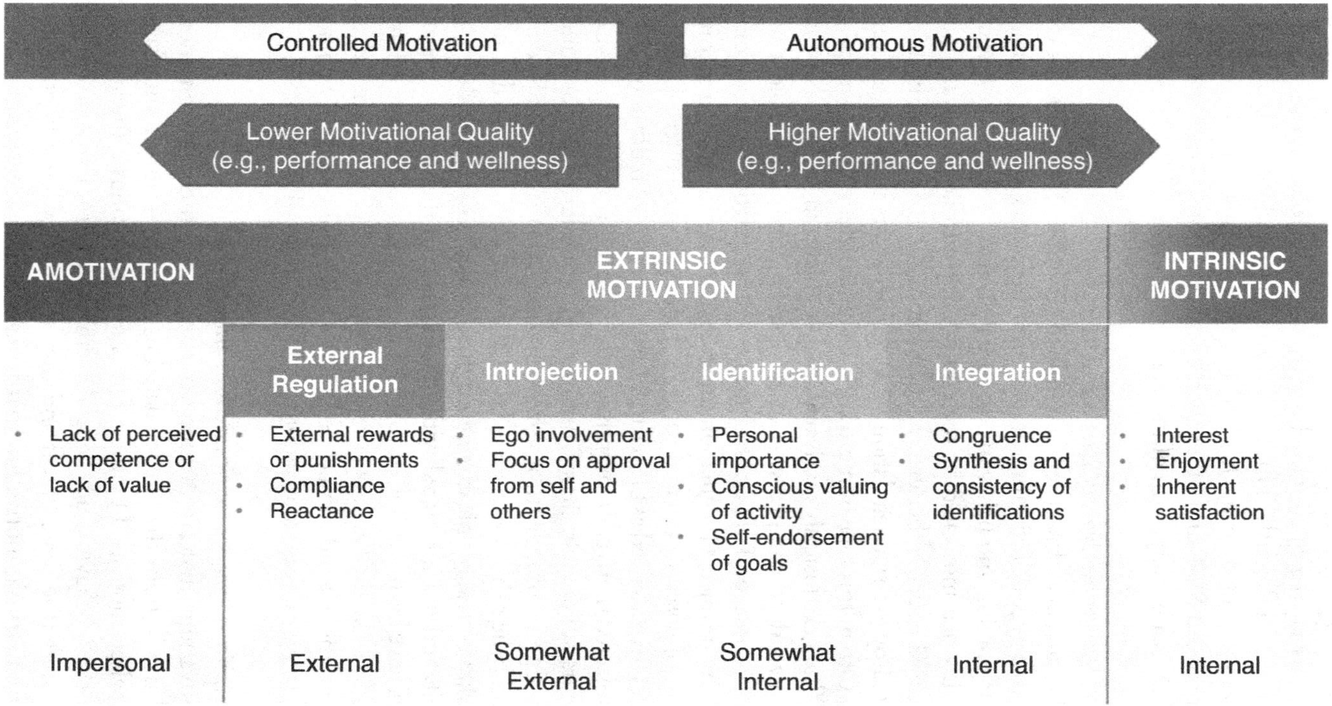

Controlled Motivation			Autonomous Motivation		
Lower Motivational Quality (e.g., performance and wellness)			Higher Motivational Quality (e.g., performance and wellness)		
AMOTIVATION	EXTRINSIC MOTIVATION				INTRINSIC MOTIVATION
	External Regulation	Introjection	Identification	Integration	
• Lack of perceived competence or lack of value	• External rewards or punishments • Compliance • Reactance	• Ego involvement • Focus on approval from self and others	• Personal importance • Conscious valuing of activity • Self-endorsement of goals	• Congruence • Synthesis and consistency of identifications	• Interest • Enjoyment • Inherent satisfaction
Impersonal	External	Somewhat External	Somewhat Internal	Internal	Internal

Note. Adapted from Ryan, R. M., & Deci, E. L. (2000). *American Psychologist*. ©2017 Center for Self-Determination Theory.

non-self-determined, coerced, or controlled. Although all forms of extrinsic motivation underlie behaviors that are instrumental or serve as a means to an end, some of them are more internalized or self-determined than others. This means that the quality of the extrinsic motivation can vary and affect outcomes very differently. This distinction between different types of extrinsic motivation and their quality and functional significance is a critical difference between SDT and other theoretical traditions, which view extrinsic motivation as a unitary form of motivation (Skinner, 1971, 1974).

Non-Self-Determined Types of Extrinsic Motivation

Under the category of non-self-determined (controlled) extrinsic motivation, we find two types of extrinsic motivation: behaviors that are regulated by external regulation and behaviors that are regulated by introjected regulation. In general, when motivated by these forms of controlled motivation, people feel pressured to act, either externally or internally. Extrinsic motivation that is regulated by external regulation underlies behaviors that are under external controls. Often, this type of motivation is simply referred to as extrinsic motivation. When extrinsically motivated, people engage in behaviors to obtain an external reward, to comply with an external demand, or to avoid a negative outcome or some kind of punishment. In contrast, extrinsic motivation that is regulated by introjected regulation underlies behaviors that are under internal controls as opposed to external controls. However, these internal controls are nonetheless experienced as pressuring. Often this type of motivation is referred to as introjected motivation or introjection. Under introjection, people engage in behaviors out of guilt, shame, or other forms of internal pressures and compulsions. Ego involvement, or contingent self-esteem, is a good example of values and beliefs that are taken in but that are not fully integrated or internalized. In these cases, people experience these values as foreign to them, as alien to the self, and not integrated with other aspects of themselves. It is as if the behaviors have been "swallowed whole" and not "digested." These behaviors or attitudes feel like they are not part of the true self, but they nonetheless exert pressure on the self and compel people to act in certain ways they do not fully endorse. It is why these motivations are labeled non-self-determined.

Self-Determined Types of Extrinsic Motivation

The motivations that are categorized as self-determined (autonomous) are extrinsic motivations that are regulated by identification and integration. In general, when motivated by these forms of autonomous motivation, people feel like their behaviors are generally emanating from true self-expression or from one's true sense of self and they feel fully willing to engage in the behaviors. Extrinsic motivation that is regulated by identification underlies behavior that is personally valued, relevant, and important. Often, this type of motivation is simply referred to as identified motivation or identification. Identification is a type of motivation that underlies behaviors that are consciously endorsed and valued. Therefore, people who mostly behave out of identified motivation perceive their behaviors as personally important to them and are able to clearly articulate the reasons why they engage in those behaviors. Having understood and personally accepted the value of a behavior allows people to feel volitional in carrying them. Extrinsic motivation that is regulated by integration underlies behavior that is integrated with other parts of the self or other behaviors. Often, this type of motivation is simply referred to as integrated motivation or integration. Integration is an active and transformational process that requires reflection. It is a difficult process of introspection and deep reflection that allows a person to bring a certain behavior or value that that could be introjected or simply identified into full congruence with the self and other values and identifications.

Another way to think about the differential qualities underlying the different types of extrinsic motivation is to bring in some useful concepts from mainstream psychology, such as attribution theory and the work of Heider (1958) and de Charms (1968). Specifically, Heider (1958) stated that behaviors and actions can be perceived as either intentional and personally caused or nonintentional and therefore impersonal. This notion in attribution theory is referred to as perceived locus of causality (PLOC). The intention for the behavior is essential for personal causation. De Charms (1968) further developed this work and argued that intentional or personally caused behaviors are not all created equal. That is, personally caused behaviors can be freely chosen or can be compelled. For example, some behaviors that are performed by an individual are engaged in because the person feels compelled or pressured to do so. The employee at work who stays late after regular work hours to complete a task out of fear of losing her job is not doing so freely. She is feeling pressured to engage in this behavior, although she is still personally or intentionally performing the behaviors. Therefore, the crucial contribution of de Charms (1968), which greatly influenced SDT, was to propose an important distinction between personally or intentionally caused actions that were freely performed and those that were externally induced. He coined the term *internal perceived locus of causality* (I-PLOC) to refer to behaviors or actions that are intentional or personally caused and experienced as freely chosen or endorsed. In contrast, he defined behaviors or actions that are personally caused but experienced as externally pressured or coerced as having an *external perceived locus of causality* (E-PLOC). Although the behaviors are carried out by the person, they are experienced as compelled or pressured and alien to the self. The person feels obligated to behave in a certain way and experiences the self as a pawn to external pressures or as highly influenceable by others. Only behaviors with an I-PLOC are truly experienced as intentional and volitional by people. Only in those situations do people feel like they are agents in their own life or at the origin of their actions. It is very important to understand that the term *internal* refers to the self and not the person performing the behavior. In terms of SDT, non-self-determined motivations have an E-PLOC whereas self-determined motivations have an I-PLOC. The concept of perceiving locus of causality as internal versus external is crucial in understanding the quality of the outcomes that will follow from the behaviors and the resultant effects on personal growth and well-being.

As discussed previously, according to SDT this is presented as a continuum from non-self-determined to more self-determined forms of motivation. For example, an employee may intentionally drive to work every weekday, but nonetheless feel forced to do so because he needs to pay the bills, or because this job looks good on his résumé and brings him prestige and external recognition and awards. In contrast, one of his colleagues may intentionally drive to work every day feeling grateful because she wants to go to work and is choosing this line of work and this life, even though she also needs money to pay the bills. She would experience her drive to work more as a choice rather than an imposition. In this example, the man would feel pressured and not self-determined or, in the words of de Charms (1968), experience himself as a pawn, and his PLOC would be experienced as external. His form of motivation is likely to be external motivation. In contrast, the woman would feel volitional, choiceful, and like an agent of her actions. In the words of de Charms, she would experience her PLOC as internal. Her form of motivation is likely to be identification. It is important to note that in both of these cases, the behavior is extrinsically motivated; both colleagues are working because they need money to live and pay the bills. However, the quality of their experiences going to work and being at work is very different because they experience their behaviors in a non-self-determined or self-determined way. Consequently, the outcomes will be very different, both in terms of vitality and well-being. In SDT, the terms *autonomy*, *self-determination*, and *I-PLOC* are used to describe the same concept, that is, that an activity or a behavior is either intrinsic or well-integrated within the self and that the behavior is performed out of choice and volition, that is, self-determined.

Conditions That Foster or Hinder the Satisfaction of Basic Psychological Needs and the Internalization Process

SDT offers a theoretical framework that allows clear a priori predictions to be made with regard to the social and environmental conditions and contexts that will foster or hinder the satisfaction of the basic psychological needs and in turn the internalization process, high-quality motivation and, as a result, success, health, and well-being. Although the three basic psychological needs can be theoretically separated and defined, they often work together, each one facilitating the other under autonomy-supportive conditions (Vansteenkiste & Ryan, 2013). Conditions that foster one need will tend to foster the other needs as well. Importantly, SDT proposes that all three needs are important and that human beings cannot truly thrive by satisfying only one need at the expense of or in the absence of the satisfaction of the other needs. All three needs are important, and SDT does not propose a hierarchy among the needs. However, each of the needs as supported will influence the internalization process differently. In certain life domains some of the needs will take the lead in predicting outcomes (Ryan & Deci, 2017). For example, in education, the need for competence may be more relevant and take the lead. A college student may study engineering because both her parents were engineers, and she may continue to do so under strong external controls and external regulation and mostly be motivated from extrinsic motivation. However, to continue to succeed, even under conditions fostering extrinsic motivation, she needs to feel minimally competent in order to pass all of her classes and continue in the engineering program. However, this type of motivation under these controlling conditions will not lead to positive psychological outcomes unless she can begin to internalize the reasons for studying engineering. Through social connection and a desire to please her parents (relatedness) the student could begin to internalize the reasons for studying engineering and feel some pull to introject the behaviors, because she cares about what her parents think and wants to impress them or show them she can become an engineer. However, it is only if the student can begin to value studying engineering or becoming an engineer and feel volitionally and autonomously engaged in the behaviors that the behavioral regulation can become identified and lead to self-determined behaviors. According to de Charms, the reason for the behavior would then shift mostly from an E-PLOC to an I-PLOC. At all levels of the continuum, a minimal level of competence is necessary whether the motivation is controlled or autonomous. However, at higher levels of the continuum, and to foster autonomous forms of motivation, all three needs will be engaged, fostered, and satisfied.

When engaging in leisure activities, the need for autonomy may be more salient and "take the lead" in determining the nature of the environment and the outcomes. For example, a boy playing with a basketball for fun and doing jump tricks as he makes baskets because he can will be feeling very autonomous while engaging in this activity. The behavior is performed mostly for fun and he feels very competent while doing it, although his skills may not be extremely sharpened or technical. He may be part of a family of basketball players, and that is his chosen activity to stay active. At that point he would be engaging in playing basketball mostly out of intrinsic motivation and integration. However, if a basketball coach walks by and sees that the boy has talent and potential that could be shaped and sharpened, the coach may try to recruit him on his team and then impose constraints on how the basketball skills will be used on the court as part of a team. The boy may become the highest scoring member of the team, leading to wins for the team. He would then become rewarded personally and as part of the team for his high performance and skills. However, this may lead to a shift in his perceived locus of causality from mostly internal (I-PLOC) to external (E-PLOC). He may begin to be less inclined to go to practice, and he may find himself not wanting to play or not enjoying basketball as much. He may start to feel guilty thinking about skipping practice or not putting in as much effort. He may have to pressure himself to work and try harder for the team after a loss. At that point, his motivation may be more experienced as externally regulated or introjected.

In personal relationships the need for relatedness may be the most salient. Often, however, relatedness is pitted against autonomy, especially in early developmental stages, contributing to environments that are controlling and not as autonomy supportive (Grolnick & Ryan, 1989). For example, if parents state, "If you love me or care for me or value me, you will do this for me," relatedness is put in direct competition against autonomy. The younger the child is, the more likely they will be pressured to forgo autonomy to maintain relatedness. This situation of pitting relatedness against autonomy will lead to long-lasting "ill"ness or adjustment problems, which can be associated with anxiety, depression, or other general illness. These forms of attachment can lead to problems in other interpersonal relationships. Situations where autonomy and relatedness are pitted against each other in workplace or leadership situations, or educational settings, can lead to other types of illnesses and compulsions and a lack of vitality, energy, and motivation to engage fully, passionately, and creatively in the work that one is doing. When one feels compelled or forced to do something for another for fear of losing respect, friendship, appreciation, or love, it can lead to disengagement and lack of focus, which translates to lack of creativity and productivity. Some of the implications of this concept will be discussed further in chapter 6 on professional development.

In education, great emphasis is often placed on the satisfaction of the need for competence. But as discussed previously, for optimal outcomes and for healthy functioning, the need for autonomy and relatedness will also be fostered. Basic psychological needs can be easily thwarted in environments that are not optimal. The need for competence is easily thwarted in environments that are too difficult or challenging, or where negative feedback is pervasive, or where there is persistent person-focused criticism and social comparison. Persistent social comparison or person-focused criticism will also thwart the need for autonomy and relatedness. These conditions, unfortunately, are often found in competitive environments such as higher education in STEM fields such as math and engineering. I will also expand on these concepts in chapter 3.

Research examining the social conditions that can foster or hinder basic psychological needs and internalization has often focused on autonomy support. This does not mean that satisfaction for the need of autonomy is more important than the need for competence and relatedness; rather, environments that are truly autonomy supportive have elements that tend to foster all three needs including competence and relatedness. Greater autonomy support is associated with the satisfaction of the three needs and subsequent positive outcomes, whereas controlling contexts hinder not only the satisfaction of the need for autonomy but also relatedness and competence fulfillment (Baard et al., 2004; Gagne, 2003; Kasser & Ryan, 1999; Sheldon & Krieger, 2007). Gagne (2003) conducted research examining the interrelationships and importance of the three basic psychological needs among animal shelter volunteers. Autonomy support was associated with stronger engagement and lower turnover in volunteers, and this relationship was fostered by the satisfaction of all three basic psychological needs. In a study by Kasser and Ryan (1999), the importance of the satisfaction of the three basic psychological needs was documented in nursing home residents as they reported their perceptions of care toward the nursing home staff, friends, and family members. Findings show that basic need satisfaction in the daily lives of the residents was associated with vitality and perceived health. The same pattern of results was replicated in the workplace, where the outcomes examined were satisfaction and enjoyment at work (Baard et al., 2004). A host of research also shows that these effects are present on a daily basis, which supports the idea that the basic needs are to be satisfied on a daily basis for optimal growth, development, and well-being (Reis et al., 2000; Sheldon et al., 1996). Daily variations in the satisfaction of autonomy, competence, and relatedness were associated with daily variations in well-being. In sum, autonomy-supportive environments are those that allow people to satisfy all three of their basic psychological needs, and they will be the focus when we discuss implications of SDT for professional development programs like IMPACT in chapters 4 through 6.

CET

CET, the last mini theory I will discuss in this chapter, is focused exclusively on intrinsic motivation. Intrinsic motivation is the natural and spontaneous propensity to develop through interesting activity, to play, explore, create, and in doing so become skilled and competent. There is a strong and pervasive belief that rewards in general are great motivators of intrinsically motivated behavior, mostly reinforced by the work and research inspired by the behaviorism and expectancy-valence theories of the 1970s and the 1980s (e.g., Porter & Lawler, 1968; Skinner, 1971, 1974). If you are good at something and engage in the behavior out of pure enjoyment, rewards should enhance and strengthen these effects, right? The hypothesis is that there should be an additive effect of intrinsic and extrinsic motivation. Well, not exactly. In fact, the bulk of the empirical evidence gathered on that topic since the first experiment conducted by Deci (1971) suggests that rewards and incentives in most cases tend to be perceived as controlling. Therefore, rewards and incentives have been consistently shown to hinder intrinsic motivation and internalization and to be a poor motivational strategy (for a review, see Deci et al., 1999). Leaders, managers, educators, and parents assume that rewards serve as an incentive that will direct behavior in a certain way toward certain outcomes. If you work harder, you get more of the reward, and if you work less, you get less of the reward. It's a simple concept. In fact, this is exactly why rewards tend to be perceived as controlling and reduce intrinsic motivation, self-determined motivation, and internalization (Deci et al., 1999; Ryan & Deci, 2017). Individuals start to focus on the rewards and incentives as the main reason to engage in the behaviors or actions. This focus emphasizes the controlling aspect and meaning of the reward or incentive and shifts the focus from an I-PLOC to an E-PLOC and deters people from wanting to do or engage in a certain behavior. The introduction of a reward for a behavior that is intrinsically motivated typically produces a change in PLOC from internal to external (Deci & Ryan, 1980, 1985). The first empirical study demonstrating the negative effects of rewards on intrinsic motivation was conducted by Deci (1971) using the free-choice paradigm, which has subsequently been used in most research examining these effects. Two groups of participants took part in the study, which had them work on interesting puzzles. One group received a reward of $1 for each puzzle they were able to solve. The second group did not receive any rewards for completing the puzzles. The first group of participants therefore had a strong desire to work to complete as many puzzles as possible because of the promise of the reward. The second group of participants did not have such a desire, since they did not expect a reward. After working on the puzzles during the experimental period, participants were left alone with additional puzzles they could choose to complete as well as other interesting activities they could engage in (e.g., reading some travel magazines). During this period, called the free-choice period, participants did not receive any incentives for working on the puzzles or completing them. What happened next is what behaviorists really struggled to interpret, because it ran counter to every prediction and hypothesis put forward by behaviorism principles. The participants who received the rewards for completing the puzzles during the experimental portion of the study spent much less time working on the puzzles and were more likely to choose to spend time on the other interesting activities compared to the participants who had not received the rewards. In other words, the people who had been rewarded for their work on the interesting puzzles showed a decrease in intrinsic motivation through their lack of persistence on the activity when they could choose to engage in other interesting activities. These findings were quickly and consistently replicated in several experiments by two independent groups of researchers (Deci, 1972a, 1972b; Lepper et al., 1973; see Deci et al., 1999 for a review).

The first empirical studies demonstrating the negative effect of rewards on intrinsic motivation were met with great resistance by behaviorists (e.g., Calder & Staw, 1975; Scott, 1976), since they were challenging the established behaviorist framework of the time. These were followed by much more experimental research attempting to understand the conditions under which rewards would be more or less detrimental. Most of them confirmed the deleterious effects of rewards (Deci et al., 1999). Knowing this, is there any way in which we can use rewards and not produce these detrimental effects? A summary of the large amount of evidence on the effects of rewards provides an answer to this question (Deci et al., 1999). Rewards carry two very specific and distinct functional meanings or significance; one is informational and the other one is controlling. The informational aspect of rewards provides competence-relevant feedback and, in that context, can foster improvements in performance through the provision of clear information and feedback on how to improve and grow one's performance. However, rewards are often perceived as controlling, because without the informational feedback, rewards provide information about one's standing in relation to others. They serve a strong social comparison purpose and often pressure people to do better than someone else, in order to obtain the reward or the incentive. Again, this contributes to shift the focus from an I-PLOC to an E-PLOC.

To be most likely to be perceived as controlling and therefore affect intrinsic motivation, rewards have to be salient, expected, and tied to a task, either through the level of performance on a task (performance-contingent), the task itself (task-contingent and completion-contingent), or obtained through a competition (competition-contingent) where there is a winner and a loser (Deci et al., 1999; Ryan et al., 1983; Vansteenkist & Deci, 2003). It is also the case that giving a reward for simply engaging in an interesting task for a certain period of time, without having to complete the task at all, is also likely to decrease intrinsic motivation (Deci et al., 1999). All of these effects can be explained by the shift in perceived locus of causality from internal to external. In other words, as soon as people engage in a task because they expect a reward, the more likely they are to experience their behaviors as controlled by the reward, and the more likely it is to affect intrinsic motivation.

So, the only way to safely provide a reward and emphasize the informational aspect of the reward, so as to not affect intrinsic motivation, is to provide it in a way that is not contingent to a specific task or is not expected, or is not made to be salient or the most important reason for engaging in the behavior. Providing a reward after a task has been completed, assuming the person did not expect the reward, has a less detrimental effect. Providing a relatively small reward and emphasizing that it is a token representing the level of competence or skill and providing informational feedback to the person could work (Deci et al., 1999). There is one more type of reward that I have not yet mentioned that actually fosters intrinsic motivation because of its informational nature, and this is the provision of positive verbal praise or feedback. The crucial notion here is to carefully pay attention to how you administer the reward and ensure that it carries informational feedback helping the person receiving the reward to grow and develop. It must not be used a way to control the person's behavior. Because the provision of rewards is so pervasive in higher education, we will return to this topic in chapter 3.

Universality of the Basic Psychological Needs

One of the tenets of SDT is that the basic psychological needs of autonomy, competence, and relatedness are innate, universal, and cross-culturally valid, and their satisfaction is fundamental to foster intrinsic motivation and the internalization process no matter who you are or where you are from, or whether you claim to need to meet these basic needs and feel autonomous, competent, and related. The ways in which psychological needs are expressed and satisfied will differ at different ages and in different cultures, but the needs remain the same. Research in SDT has supported this claim. The environmental contexts that foster the basic psychological needs of autonomy, competence, and relatedness apply to not only those proximal social contexts of parent–child, manager–employee, or student–teacher but also distal contexts of cultures. From the perspective of SDT, individuals and cultures are inseparable, in the sense that individuals develop being part of a culture and work to integrate the values, beliefs, norms, and regulations of that particular community in this particular cultural context. As discussed previously when presenting organismic theory, SDT argues that individuals are naturally inclined to integrate social values, beliefs, and practices.

One of the most controversial issues emanating from the claim that the basic psychological needs are universal is the one for autonomy. Some have strongly argued that autonomy is a construct only applicable to Western, male, and wealthy individuals and cultures (Iyengar & DeVoe, 2003) and in direct opposition to relatedness (Iyengar & Lepper, 1999; Markus et al., 1996; Markus & Kitayama, 2003). From a cultural relativistic perspective, these researchers argue that autonomy and relatedness are socially and culturally constructed rather than innate and universal. They claim that autonomy is more important and valued by people in Western individualistic cultures, whereas in Eastern collectivist cultures, autonomy is not considered that important and relatedness is conveyed and emphasized as important and valued. However, when we understand that according to SDT autonomy is about feeling choiceful, volitional, and agentic, and not about being independent, then we can more easily conceptualize and understand autonomy as a universal need. When we understand autonomy according to SDT as the experience of self-congruence and self-endorsement of one's actions and behaviors, the view that autonomy is only applicable to Western cultures does not appear accurate.

Research differentiating the concept of autonomy from the concept of independence has supported the universality of the need for autonomy (Chen et al., 2013; Chirkov et al., 2003, 2005; Downie et al., 2004; Sheldon et al., 2004). For example, Chirkov et al. (2003) examined the satisfaction of the need for autonomy in four different cultures, some individualistic and some collectivistic (Russia, Turkey, South Korea, and the United States). Participants rated the extent to which they would engage in different cultural practices for autonomous reasons (endorsing identified and intrinsic motivations for the practices). Despite the cultural differences, in all four cultures, and regardless of gender, and for all cultural practices, the extent to which individuals were endorsing the practices more autonomously was associated with higher levels of well-being. Similar findings were obtained by Sheldon et al. (2004), who examined the autonomous motivation for a variety of personal strivings for participants from China, South Korea, Taiwan, and the United States. Results demonstrated that although the mean level of autonomous motivation differed among the participants from the four cultures, the relationship between autonomous motivation and well-being was consistent across groups.

In contrast, the universality of the need for competence and relatedness has been more easily accepted. Regarding relatedness, Bowlby (1979) in his work on attachment proposed a need for secure emotional attachments that he conceptualized as basic and innate to all human beings. More recently, Baumeister and Leary (1995) proposed a fundamental need for belongingness that has been widely accepted. In fact, many theories have proposed and argued for the existence of a basic need for relatedness or belongingness (for a broad discussion, see Lieberman, 2013). With regard to competence, White (1959) proposed a basic need for effectance and competence that in fact became the origin of the concept of competence in SDT, which states that people engage in behaviors that promote competence because it satisfies an intrinsic need to interact with the environment. The same has been argued in the domain of achievement goal pursuit and goal theories (Elliott et al., 2002; Locke & Latham, 1990) as well as expectancy theory (e.g., Bandura, 1997) and flow (Csikszentmihalyi, 1975, 1990).

This notion of universality is very important when using a theoretical framework to conduct work in education with a broad and diverse group of students. The basic psychological needs are present in all human beings, whether they are instructors or students, and are satisfied under conditions or social environments that are autonomy supportive. In our application to education, this allows us to focus on the creation of learning environments that are engaging and autonomy supportive for all students. It becomes less about what we can do to make students better prepared and more about how we can create environments that are more autonomy supportive where all students can learn through the fulfillment of their basic psychological needs. Let's work together on improving the environment and not so much on fixing the students. Students are not dysfunctional; the learning environments are. In the remainder of this book, I will focus on applications of SDT to higher education as well as the structure and philosophy behind the creation and implementation of successful large course transformation initiatives such as IMPACT.

3

APPLICATION OF SDT IN EDUCATION

As discussed in chapter 2, people have a natural tendency to explore their environments and grow, learn, and develop. When applied to the education domain, an important goal of education is to create learning environments in order to cultivate this inherent interest and curiosity that exists within students as they work on their formal education. In his recent book, *How Humans Learn: The Science Behind Effective College Teaching*, Joshua Eyler (2018) dedicated an entire chapter to the science behind curiosity as an intellectual driving force and an essential part of the way human beings learn. When working with instructors in my role as a faculty developer, one of the common conversations I have with them relates to their concerns about how to motivate and engage students in their classrooms. Instructors will report that students lack motivation and enthusiasm for the subject they teach, are passive, or blatantly refuse to participate in classroom activities, and often do not even show up for class. Even worse, instructors may lament that when disengaged students do show up for class, they sometimes engage in disruptive behaviors, and classroom management becomes an issue. As a result, when I first present SDT to instructors, I am often met with some incredulous looks and suspicious laughs. The instructors are rarely seeing this natural tendency for growth, learning, curiosity, interest, and development in their students. When problems arise, it is hard for instructors to believe that students, when feeling cared for in an autonomy-supportive environment, would be able to engage in and fulfill their natural tendencies as self-directed and lifelong learners. It is hard to believe that students would become the engaged and self-directed students instructors want in their classrooms.

We have to remember that the environmental conditions students are placed in will either foster or hinder the satisfaction of the basic psychological needs and the internalization process. Students who have been repeatedly placed in controlling environments are living with impoverished basic needs satisfaction, a situation that leads to nonoptimal behaviors, lack of engagement, and lack of intrinsic and self-determined motivation. Once they get to college, students may have had years of controlling educational environments, which have sapped their desire and passion for learning. For illustration, think about a child who is about to enter kindergarten. Typically, the natural excitement and love for learning is clearly apparent. Children at that age are almost always highly intrinsically motivated for learning; they want to explore and understand their world, and they ask a million questions every day, often to the point of exhaustion for the overwhelmed adults around them! If you have a young child or nieces and nephews or a close friend with a young child, you are smiling now, because you know exactly what I'm talking about. Unfortunately, often by the 3rd grade, this excitement has greatly diminished, and children wish for a snow day or develop physical and mental health issues. The increase in the incidence of anxiety and depression in young children is alarming (Bitsko et al., 2018; Centers for Disease Control and Prevention, 2019), in addition to the many physical symptoms, such as chronic headaches and stomachaches, which accompany mental health challenges. In general, students' self-determined motivation, and in particular intrinsic motivation, significantly deteriorates with increasing age, and by the time students enter high school, many students have lost interest and excitement for school (Gillet et al., 2012; Harter, 1981; Lepper et al., 2005). Given the many benefits of intrinsic motivation, including deeper learning and cognitive growth, these decreases are also concerning (Danner & Lonky, 1981; Ryan et al., 1990). Recent longitudinal studies demonstrated the positive impact of intrinsic motivation on performance and achievement. In fact, in some of these studies, intrinsic motivation was the only type of motivation that was consistently associated with academic achievement over a 1-year period (Taylor et al., 2014). Even more recent studies in STEM that were conducted in our own research lab at Purdue, some of them not yet published, demonstrated the primary importance of intrinsic motivation on performance in college students (Wiles, 2020).

SDT offers a theoretical framework that can readily explain this deterioration in the quality of student motivation and then offers a critical perspective as to how we can modify educational policies and practices that are hindering rather than fostering student engagement and self-determined motivation. In the early school years, teachers reward good performance with gold stars and punish bad performance with isolation from other classmates or more work to do inside while other students go to recess. Very quickly, entire evenings are taken by a heavy homework load assigned by well-intentioned teachers. In high school and college, the list of controlling environmental factors continues to grow. As a learning community, we assign grades in ways that are often controlling, confusing, and lack transparency; we pit students against each other, fostering competition and emphasizing social comparisons, and only allow a certain percentage of them to earn an "A" through normative curved grading (more on this in chapters 5 and 10). We take off points for lack of attendance, and we structure our courses with a small number of high-stakes exams, which fosters anxiety. We don't value and foster collaboration and a sense of community, but instead choose to lecture to rows of hundreds of students with little opportunity for interaction. So why are we surprised that by the time they enter college, students' love for learning appears to have waned and been replaced with an extrinsic focus for learning and high levels of introjection and anxiety? Students quickly learn that to survive in college they need to be primarily concerned with doing what is necessary to pass a required course, worry about whether what is covered in class will be on the exam, perform better than the other students in their section, and succeed so they can secure a good-paying job. Furthermore, the school curriculum is rarely presented to students in a way that makes the content particularly interesting or relevant to students' lives and purposes. The content and class procedures often do not take the students' point of view or their backgrounds or lived experiences into consideration.

Learners' motivation is extremely important, and the role of instructors in fostering or hindering learners' motivation is paramount. Instructors thus face the challenges of changing the classroom culture to one which supports rather than thwarts basic psychological needs and creating environments that are autonomy supportive and provide structure without being controlling. Our challenge as instructors and developers is to foster the creation of learning environments that are warm and inviting as opposed to cold and impersonal. Fortunately, in many cases, there is a desire and willingness to create more autonomy-supportive learning environments through engagement and active learning. However, it is difficult to do. We almost intuitively understand what is needed in order to be autonomy supportive yet fail to consistently do so. As Freeman et al. (2014) and Prince (2004) pointed out when discussing the effect of active learning, we know that active learning works and is good for human development and learning, yet we have not found a way to consistently implement the research-based strategies fostering the development of student engagement.

There is an abundance of research evidence supporting and demonstrating the positive and negative impact teachers and instructors can have on student engagement, intrinsic motivation, the internalization process, and self-determined motivation by creating learning environments that are autonomy supportive and qualitatively different (Deci & Ryan, 2000; Ryan & Deci, 2017). Much of the SDT research in education has been conducted in K–12 schools and with elementary or secondary school students (for a review, see Ryan & Deci, 2017). These studies in general show that teachers who are more autonomy supportive are able to create environments that are perceived by students as being more supportive and in which students report greater satisfaction of the basic psychological needs of autonomy, competence, and relatedness, as well as a greater level of intrinsic motivation, self-determined motivation, and more positive learning outcomes (Deci, Nezlek, & Sheinman, 1981; Jang et al., 2010; Ryan & Connell, 1989; Ryan & Grolnick, 1986; Skinner & Belmont, 1993).

Through this research, clusters of behavioral markers have been associated with autonomy-supportive or controlling environments and students' autonomous motivation. In general, the behaviors of autonomy-supportive teachers were positively associated with students' autonomous motivation, whereas the behaviors of controlling teachers were all negatively correlated with students' autonomous motivation (Assor et al., 2005; Reeve et al., 1999). More specifically, this research suggests that autonomy-supportive teachers tend to acknowledge students' experiences and perspectives, listen to and are responsive to students' questions and comments, as well as give them an opportunity to talk and express themselves. They give them choices and options whenever possible, which could be as simple as letting the students choose their topic for a presentation or project or giving them the option of demonstrating their knowledge through a presentation or a project. It could be to let students have the option to take a final exam or count one of the regular semester exams for more points. Instructors who are autonomy supportive make time for students' independent work and encourage as well as acknowledge signs of effort, improvement, and mastery. They provide frequent and timely feedback and offer hints that foster progress when students are stuck, without overly directing their learning or immediately providing the answers. The feedback that they provide is informational, which means that it provides essential information to the student to guide the improvement of their performance, to help them master and develop skills, and to foster growth and a general sense of direction and competence. In contrast, educators who are more controlling tend to make more demands, give directives, use directed types of questions as a way to control the flow of the conversation, and make frequent use of controlling language such as "should" and "have to." They tend to monopolize the learning material, provide students too little time to work independently on solving problems, and tell students the answers without giving them an opportunity to formulate their own. The feedback that they provide tends to be vague and is not informational, which means it does not provide opportunities for improvement, development, mastery, or growth.

Out of the list of behavioral markers described previously, arguably some of the easiest and most meaningful to foster autonomy support are to provide choices and options to students and to understand, acknowledge, and take their perspective into consideration as they engage in a task. A meta-analysis reviewing 41 studies involving participants of different ages and for a variety of behaviors demonstrated that the provision of choice enhances intrinsic motivation and basic need of autonomy, as well as effort, task performance, and perceived competence (Patall et al., 2008, 2010). The provision of choice also led the students to perceive the course as more valuable, an important motivational construct in education (Patall et al., 2012). Even though the provision of choice in a variety of learning environments is associated with a host of positive outcomes, often instructors, especially in introductory required classes, feel compelled to teach certain content in a specific order to ensure that the students will be prepared to succeed in the following course in the sequence. In these cases, provision of choices and options may not be possible, and supporting students' autonomy has to focus on other factors such as listening to students' perspectives; giving students an opportunity to talk; being responsive to their comments and questions; encouraging students' efforts; and, very importantly, providing a meaningful rationale for the required and often difficult or boring academic work.

More recently, Haerens et al. (2013) extended this work by examining behaviors that would be associated with not only autonomy support but also relatedness support and competence support, operationalized as the provision of structure. In this work, the behaviors of being enthusiastic and eager and putting effort and energy into the class session were associated with relatedness support; the behaviors of giving clear instructions, offering the student a rationale for tasks, and providing positive feedback were found to be associated with competence support (structure). Overall, this work suggests that teachers and instructors who are autonomy supportive also tend to be relatedness and competence (structure) supportive. This provides further evidence that the three basic psychological needs work in tandem and that when instructors are autonomy supportive, they understand students' perspectives broadly, which allows them to notice when students are struggling or need extra support, which also supports students' need for relatedness and competence. Importantly, this work demonstrated that the provision of a strong and meaningful rationale not only supports the need for autonomy but also provides competence support through the provision of structure (Haerens et al., 2013). It is often necessary for students to follow requirements and work within a structure for attainment of optimal outcomes. Understanding why this is necessary through the provision of a rationale is very important for self-determined motivation.

On the further examination of the role of structure, Jang et al. (2010) also conducted work to demonstrate the importance of this construct. Although autonomy support has been consistently found to be the most important predictor of student engagement, provision of structure also predicts engagement over and above autonomy support (Jang et al., 2010), as well as positive learning strategies and positive affect (Mouratidis et al., 2008). When researchers examined the profile of high school teachers, two interesting patterns emerged: teachers who were (a) high in autonomy support and provided clear structure and teachers who were (b) low in autonomy support and provided vague structure. The teachers presenting the high autonomy/clear structure profile were more likely to have students in their classrooms who were autonomously motivated and who were more likely to use self-regulated learning strategies and exhibit deeper learning and persistence. In contrast, the teachers presenting the low autonomy/vague structure profile were more likely to have students who were less motivated, used more maladaptive learning strategies, and were more anxious (Vansteenkiste et al., 2012).

In elementary and high school education, parents also have a tremendous influence on the learning environment their children experience. The use of conditional regard, love withdrawal, psychological controls, and controlling and pressuring feedback to push students to achieve at high levels is prevalent and has been popularized in books such as *Battle Hymn of the Tiger Mother* by Amy Chua (2011). The book was taken by many as a justification for the use of high pressures and controls in order to obtain high levels of performance and achievement in children and adolescents, a level of performance often seen in the Chinese culture. However, although the book presents these pressures and controls on children as a way to help the students succeed by providing tough love, the research based in SDT suggests that such pressures, conditional regard, psychological controls, and pressuring feedback in general have the opposite effect. These strategies create environments that are perceived to be controlling, thus hindering growth, development, and well-being (Yu et al., 2016). Research strongly suggests that the best development and well-being outcomes are consistently found among children and students who have been nurtured and supported rather than pressured or controlled through contingent love and conditional regard. The use of these pressuring tactics can be even more damaging than the use of tangible rewards, such as grades and other incentives. This is the case because these tactics are designed to cause shame, guilt, and negative emotional experiences and force children to compare themselves to others or risk losing the love of a parent if they do not perform as desired or do not do what is asked or required of them (Roth et al., 2009; Yu et al., 2016). Although tangible rewards such as grades have been shown to decrease intrinsic motivation, the mechanism by which they do so does not engage the self in a way that creates shame, guilt, and self-loathing (Deci et al., 1999; Grolnick & Ryan, 1987; Ryan & Deci, 2017). What about the effects of verbal rewards, positive verbal feedback, or praise? Although in general verbal positive feedback tends to enhance intrinsic motivation, the effect is mostly noticeable for college students. This is probably because college students are able to focus on the informational aspect of the verbal praise or positive feedback, which fosters the satisfaction of the need for competence, whereas children mostly perceive the controlling aspect of the praise (Deci et al., 1999; Henderlong & Lepper, 2002). The praise for children serves as a way to control behavior, and this aspect is mostly salient for this age group.

Although the studies conducted during the precollege years are certainly important and relevant, in the remainder of this chapter I specifically focus on evidence gathered in higher education. It is important to note that there is still a lack of research using SDT motivation principles to understand learning environments in higher education. The work emanating from the research coming from our lab and the work of IMPACT is contributing to this body of knowledge and builds on the large amount of research conducted during the precollege years.

To begin, research with college students has also supported the importance of creating an autonomy-supportive learning environment. Black and Deci (2000) asked college students in an organic chemistry course to rate the extent to which they perceived their instructors as autonomy supportive. They then examined the relations between perceived instructors' autonomy support and the students' own self-reported, self-determined autonomous motivation, learning, perceived competence, well-being, and anxiety. Results showed that students who rated their instructors as more autonomy supportive also reported a greater level of autonomous or self-determined motivation to study chemistry over the course of the semester, greater well-being, increased perceived competence, and actual higher grades in the course, as assessed by a common final.

Reeve et al. (1999) categorized teachers based on their self-reported answers to the Problems in Schools Questionnaire (Deci, Schwartz, et al., 1981). The teachers were then observed teaching a small class. Teachers who were categorized as autonomy supportive were found to listen more, make fewer directives, resist giving students answers too quickly, respond more to students' questions, and attend more to students' interests. In our own research based on the data collected from the students taking IMPACT classes, we also find that autonomy-supportive learning environments, created by instructors and perceived by college students, are associated with greater satisfaction of basic psychological needs, self-determined motivation, and higher levels of achievement as measured by course grades (i.e., GPA) and higher levels of perceived learning as assessed by the Student Assessment of Learning Gains (SALG) (Seymour et al., 2000). In fact, the creation of an autonomy supportive environment, regardless of the course transformation implemented, is the most important and consistent predictor of the motivational and educational outcomes studied, including basic psychological needs, student motivation and engagement, perceived learning attainment and transfer, and actual performance as measured by grades (Bonem et al., 2016, 2019; Levesque-Bristol et al., in press; Wang et al., 2019, 2020; Yu & Levesque-Bristol, 2018, 2020; Yu et al., 2018). Some of the work we have conducted in the lab has focused on the replication and extension of the SDT model for teaching and learning in online learning environments and was based on previous study in online courses (Chen & Jang, 2010; Hsu et al., 2019). Recently, institutions of higher education have emphasized online learning as a way to reach students who would not otherwise benefit from higher education or to offer their programs to a wider group of students. At Purdue, a land-grant institution, online learning has been an important area of development and a priority of President Daniels. In addition, Purdue Online is a partner in IMPACT. Our work in this area suggests that the teaching and learning motivational model based in SDT (Deci & Ryan, 1985; Levesque-Bristol et al., 2006; Ryan & Deci, 2017) can be replicated in online learning environments and furthermore is consistent across online and face-to-face teaching learning environments (Hsu et al., 2019; Wang et al., 2019).

In some of the research we conducted, we noticed that certain variables in the model tend to take precedence over others in predicting the learning outcomes, such as perceived competence, intrinsic motivation, and identification (Wang et al., 2020; Wiles, 2020; Yu & Levesque-Bristol, 2020). We have been curious about the potential prevalence of certain basic psychological needs or types of motivation over others in certain situations. As mentioned in chapter 2, this issue has been recently raised in the SDT literature (Ryan & Deci, 2017).

In our research work in higher education, we have taken a special interest in exploring the relative importance of the various basic psychological needs and motivational constructs, and how the influence of those would manifest in the prediction of learning outcomes and academic performance in higher education (Levesque-Bristol et al., 2010). When introducing the importance of the basic psychological needs of autonomy, competence, and relatedness, instructors often wonder what it truly means to foster the basic psychological needs, especially the need for autonomy and relatedness. There are many answers for the satisfaction of the need for autonomy, as I have covered in this chapter. However, there is not much research to support the specific need for relatedness, as very little research has been conducted in this area. In addition, when we discuss the need for relatedness, is it more important to focus on the relatedness between the students themselves or the relatedness between the students and the instructor or a combination of both? To answer these questions, Fedesco et al. (2019) conducted work to formally differentiate the two components of relatedness. They created items to separately examine the connections students experience with their peers and their instructors. Results showed that considering the potential multidimensional nature of relatedness is important. The extent to which students reported feeling connected with their instructor was most predictive of student interest and enjoyment in the course as well as self-reported effort. In contrast, peer relatedness was not significantly associated with any of the outcome variables. In the current research work in IMPACT, we are continuing to use the multidimensional relatedness scale to further explore the implications of those differences.

Furthermore, in our recent work we have examined the structure of the basic psychological needs and differentiated between the construct of need satisfaction and need dissatisfaction, suggesting that the active satisfaction of the basic needs would be experienced differently and lead to different outcomes than the active dissatisfaction of the needs (Chen et al., 2015; Johnston & Finney, 2010; Sheldon & Hilpert, 2012). After examining and finding support for the structure of this balanced measure of psychological needs in both online and traditional learning environments, we examined the effect of the basic psychological needs on grades and perception of knowledge transfer. The differential effects we found on the academic outcomes examined were very interesting. Actual grades were predicted only by basic need dissatisfaction, such that need dissatisfaction predicted lower grades, while perceived knowledge transfer was positively predicted by only need satisfaction (Wang et al., 2019). Further work is needed in this area, but it is very interesting to consider the implications of need dissatisfaction on performance. Grades seem to be affected only when the basic needs are actively not met and dissatisfied. In contrast, perceived learning seems to be influenced only when the basic psychological needs are met and satisfied.

Although we are still trying to understand the meaning of some of these differential results, the research clearly and consistently shows that regardless of which motivational construct might take precedence in certain situations, the effect of the learning environment on learning outcomes and academic performance is mediated by the satisfaction of the basic psychological needs (Wang et al., 2019, 2020; Yu & Levesque-Bristol, 2020).

It seems appropriate at this time to take the opportunity to comment on the use of grades in models examining the effect of autonomy-supportive environments, as well as the general effect of grades, evaluation, and grading practices in higher education. A consistent variable included in our models testing the effect of autonomy-supportive environments on educational outcomes is grades in one form or another. Grades are considered a proxy of academic performance and often an outcome variable of interest. Research finds that the effect of autonomy-supportive environments and satisfaction of the basic psychological needs on a course or semester grade is often small, although positive and significant in the IMPACT samples. This is not surprising considering the very large sample sizes we are working with (Levesque-Bristol et al., in press; Wang et al., 2019). Grades, success, and retention rates are also common variables examined or required in studies funded by large federal grants, such as those from the Department of Education (DoE) or the National Science Foundation (NSF). Although grades and evaluations are ubiquitous in school and most certainly in postsecondary education, their effect on intrinsic motivation and engagement has been shown to be consistently deleterious when used as a motivator of behavior. In education, grades are perceived to be the ultimate reward and incentive and are a universal feature of classrooms around the country and in most of the industrialized world. In school, most everything is evaluated and graded, and normative comparisons are made with grades as a way to compare students against one another. This social comparison with grades is very pervasive, especially in normative grading practices. There is a strong and prevalent belief that grades and rewards in general are great motivators of behavior. In fact, nothing could be further from the truth. Grades and other rewards have been consistently shown to reduce intrinsic motivation and internalization and to be a poor motivational strategy (for a review, see Deci et al., 1999). Educators and school administrators assume that rewards and grades serve as an incentive that will direct behavior in a certain way toward certain outcomes. If you work harder, you get more of the reward or a higher grade, and if you work less, you get less of the reward or a poorer grade. In fact, this is exactly why grades tend to be perceived as controlling and reduce intrinsic motivation, self-determined motivation, and internalization (Deci et al., 1999; Ryan & Deci, 2017). Their main function tends to be perceived as a way to control behaviors. In fact, there is very little empirical evidence or theoretical support suggesting that grades and evaluations have any positive effect on motivation, engagement, and competence (Deci et al., 1999; Ryan & Deci, 2017).

Rewards in general and grades specifically carry two distinct functional meanings or significance; one is informational and the other one is controlling. The informational aspect of grades provides competence-relevant feedback to students and can foster improvements in performance through the provision of clear informational feedback. However, grades are often perceived as controlling and a way to rank students and place them in categories, with no information on how to improve. Without the informational feedback, grades simply provide information about one's standing in relation to other students. They serve a strong social comparison function and often pressure students to do better than someone else or to perform in a certain way under certain conditions. This focus emphasizes the controlling aspect and meaning of the grade and deters students from being interested in learning (Deci et al., 1999; Ryan & Deci, 2017). These effects are seen in longitudinal naturalistic settings examining the negative impact of grading on outcomes in subsequent years and in controlled laboratory environments (Benware & Deci, 1984; Klapp, 2015). In one of these laboratory experiments, college students were given 3 hours to study some neurophysiology course material. Half of the students were told that they would be tested on the material, and half were told they would have the opportunity to teach the material to other students. Then the students were all given an exam to assess their retention of the material, as well as a questionnaire asking about their level of interest toward the material. Results showed that the students who studied with the goal of taking a test reported lower levels of intrinsic motivation as well as worse performance on the actual test compared to the students who studied with the goal of teaching the material to other students. This can be explained because the students who studied in order to take a test mostly experienced the controlling aspect of the grading practice, focused on passing the test, and felt pressured and controlled by the experience. In contrast, the students who focused on teaching the material to others experienced more of the informational aspect of the activity and the opportunity to relate the material and actively use the material in an interaction with other students. This condition fostered an autonomy-supportive environment through the satisfaction of the need for autonomy, competence, and relatedness (Benware & Deci, 1984). Autonomy support is also associated with well-being markers such as lower levels of anxiety and higher levels of life satisfaction and well-being (Levesque et al., 2004).

The effect on well-being may be explained by how autonomy support affects biological markers. In a controlled experiment, students experienced either an autonomy-supportive or a controlling instructor. Samples of the stress hormone cortisol were collected during the experience (Reeve & Tseng, 2011). Students who experienced the controlling environment created by the controlling teacher had higher levels of cortisol than students who were taught by the autonomy-supportive instructor. It is interesting to note the implications of such research. Related research also demonstrates that emotional arousal and heart rate are positively affected when students are experiencing environments that are autonomy supportive and where social relatedness is emphasized.

College students spend a majority of their time in class, completing projects or studying for exams. As described previously, one controlling experience in a lab setting had a noticeable effect on physiological stress, not simply perceived stress. Now, imagine the cumulative effect of physiological stress experienced every day during an entire college semester, under environmental conditions created by instructors and institutional requirements that are controlling and not autonomy supportive. This helps explain the rise of mental illness on campuses across the country.

One academic discipline that is certainly recognized for being associated with a high level of pressure and demands is law. Law school is known to be a high-pressure, high-stakes, and controlling academic environment. Consequently, it is not surprising to find that law school students report high levels of stress and significant declines in their level of intrinsic motivation, basic psychological need satisfaction, and well-being over the course of their studies (Sheldon & Krieger, 2007). However, in Sheldon and Krieger's (2007) study, law school students who reported having instructors who were more autonomy supportive in some of their courses displayed less negative effect on their level of motivation and well-being compared to students who mostly had controlling instructors. In addition, the law school students in this generally high-pressure environment who reported experiencing some autonomy-supportive instructors also performed better in their courses and on the bar exam and reported being more self-determined in their first job after graduation (Sheldon & Krieger, 2007). Work by Yu et al. (2018) also reinforces the idea that some fields are more likely to support the satisfaction of basic psychological needs than others. In this research, students in the social sciences and humanities were more likely to be self-determined than students in business-related fields. Furthermore, this work suggests that it is both the students' individual differences in autonomous functioning and the learning environment fostered in different academic fields that can explain these differences (Yu & Levesque-Bristol, 2018). In addition, the process of choosing a major, when self-determined, is influenced by autonomy-supportive parenting and individual differences in autonomous functioning (Yu et al., 2018).

In higher education, choices are often limited because of accreditation requirements or course sequencing, which puts pressure on instructors to cover certain material in certain courses. Therefore, the power of a meaningful rationale to create environments that are autonomy supportive cannot be overstated in our work with faculty in higher education. When provision of choices and options for independent work is not possible, then the power of a meaningful and strong rationale is extremely important. Building on the work of Deci et al. (1994) on the effect of provision of a rationale for internalization and learning, Reeve et al. (2002) examined the effect of the provision of a rationale in a sample of college students studying conversational Chinese. The students were or were not provided an autonomy-supportive rationale for the importance of learning the language. College students who were provided the meaningful autonomy-supportive rationale were more likely to internalize the reasons for learning the language and subsequently put more effort into their learning.

The impact of positive feedback on creating environments that are perceived to be autonomy supportive is also critical for college students. In short, an autonomy-supportive environment that supports all three basic psychological needs fosters the engagement of the whole student's growth and development (Streb et al., 2015). In terms of the growth and development of the whole student, some new and emerging work in SDT is specifically examining how environments that are autonomy supportive can also be culturally responsive and inclusive and respect and foster the diversity of all the students in the classroom and their lived experiences (Holgate, 2016). This work builds on the research examining the psychosocial factors that influence the creation of positive learning environments, including but not limited to teacher support, student support, and autonomy support (Black & Deci, 2000; Reeve, 2002; Ryan & Deci, 2000). Holgate (2016) demonstrated and isolated the influence of four constructs fostering autonomy-supportive, culturally responsive learning environments: inclusiveness, cultural inclusion, diverse language, and diverse pedagogy. An autonomy-supportive learning environment that is also inclusive would fully include the students; allow them to communicate in their own language; be flexible; and adopt an open, warm, and curious attitude toward diversity and differences, which would allow instructors to gain a deep insight into the lived experiences and motives of their students. Although not speaking of culturally responsive and autonomy-supportive learning environments per se, the writings of bell hooks (1994) in *Teaching to Transgress: Education as the Practice of Freedom* are reminiscent of these ideas and constructs and very much in line with SDT. Based on SDT, I believe that any instructor can change, adapt, or tailor their instructions to the varying needs, interests, preferences, and backgrounds of their students as a way to create autonomy-supportive learning environments. In the words of hooks (1994),

> To educate as the practice of freedom is a way of teaching that anyone can learn. . . . Our work is not merely to share information but to share in the intellectual and spiritual growth of our students. To teach in a manner that respects and cares for the souls of our students is essential if we are to provide the necessary conditions where learning can most deeply and intimately begin. (p. 13)

Along the same lines, Parker Palmer (1998) in *The Courage to Teach* talks about bringing our whole and entire self to the act of teaching. Palmer also talks about the importance of relatedness or connectedness.

> Good teachers possess a capacity for connectedness. They are able to weave a complex web of connections among themselves, their subjects, and their students so that students can learn to weave a world for themselves. (p. 11)

4

THE CORE, CONTENT, STRUCTURE, AND EVOLUTION OF IMPACT

In this chapter, I will review how the focus on SDT and the satisfaction of the basic psychological needs guided and shaped the evolution of IMPACT from a course redesign to a faculty development program, emphasized the provision of autonomy in selecting redesign elements, and in turn allowed us to successfully scale the composition of the IMPACT support teams and the IMPACT program. This first part of this chapter will also describe the process by which the IMPACT management team forms the IMPACT support teams. In the second part of the chapter, I describe in some detail the FLC curriculum and the content of the FLC inspired by SDT. Throughout this chapter when I use the word "we," it is to refer to the IMPACT management team that meets weekly and makes decisions regarding the structure, content, and compositing of the IMPACT FLC and the support teams during the FLC. The IMPACT management team is composed of members from the CIE, which is the teaching and learning pedagogical center at Purdue; the TLT, which is the technology-focused teaching and learning unit at Purdue; and the Purdue University Libraries and School of Information Studies (PULSIS, now LSIS).

In the beginning, the IMPACT program closely followed the NCAT (Twigg, 2003) redesign program and models. Large gateway courses were targeted to be part of IMPACT, those lecture-based introductory courses with a high rate of D and F grades or student withdrawals (DFW). Faculty were required to choose a specific transformation model and identify specific technologies they planned to incorporate in their redesign. In early iterations of the IMPACT program, technology was emphasized as an important way to support the creation of student-centered environments, and faculty fellows were encouraged to incorporate technology, through the use of online quizzes, video lectures, or interactive students' response systems, to foster active learning in large courses. This was influenced by NCAT, which used technologies to foster student-centered learning and reduce cost. Three main course redesign models were presented as potential options to faculty—replacement, supplemental, and online only. In the replacement model, which includes the hybrid and flipped modalities, the amount of in-class time is reduced so students typically watch videos or complete interactive activities before coming to class, while the remaining in-class time is mostly used for working through problems, group work, and collaborative learning. The supplemental model retains all in-class time, but faculty change how this time is used. Faculty adopt more active and engaging learning activities, with many using technology to facilitate in-class and out-of-class activities. As the name implies, the online-only model moves all of the instruction and activities to an online environment.

When Mitch Daniels became president of Purdue in spring 2013, he envisioned IMPACT as a part of the Purdue Moves in the transformative education area of focus. As introduced in chapter 1, the IMPACT management team was presented with a huge challenge: Double the capacity of IMPACT by scaling the program from up to 30 faculty annually to 60. How were we going to do this? There was no model around the country to guide our efforts or provide us with a blueprint. Although course redesign programs certainly existed, they had not engaged instructors in course redesign or transformation on that scale or level!

This challenge provided us with an opportunity to reflect and think about the essence of IMPACT and course transformation more generally. It provided us with an opportunity to think about the philosophy, goals, and structure of the program and challenged us to think about the overall effectiveness of IMPACT. What is the common thread of successful redesigns? What is the innovation? The heavy focus on technologies, tools, and redesign models provided by NCAT obscured an important factor in successful redesigns: the human factor. The focus on SDT was the turning point. At the center of a course redesign are the *people* teaching and learning and using information and tools as they are doing so. "What" we were doing obscured "why" we were engaging in course redesigns and transformations. The feedback we obtained from the initial cohorts of IMPACT faculty fellows supported this notion. During the focus groups conducted by staff from the ELRC at the conclusion of the FLCs, instructors reported feeling restrained, constrained, and limited by the lack of flexibility and the imposition of certain redesign models for their transformation. Faculty fellows wished they could sample from the various redesign models and not have to make a choice for one over another. IMPACT faculty fellows reported frustrations and perceived the program as an imposition and a push toward certain redesign models and technologies. This was especially true for instructors in the social sciences who were making use of carefully crafted narratives and stories to engage students with their experiences as disciplinary experts. In these cases, faculty fellows were painfully aware that the value of their work on creative assignments and activities was being dismissed in favor of cookie-cutter redesign models. As discussed in chapters 2 and 3, faculty fellows were reporting a loss of in autonomy and agency as they were engaging in course redesign. The environment that we were creating by "forcing" the adoption of a certain redesign model was controlling and not perceived as autonomy supportive. By using SDT as a lens to understand and interpret the feedback provided by the IMPACT fellows, it became clear that in order to scale the IMPACT program, we were going to need to move away from the strict adherence to the NCAT models and move toward a more flexible approach to course redesign by focusing on the satisfaction of the basic psychological needs of autonomy, competence, and relatedness (Deci & Ryan, 1985; Ryan & Deci, 2017). After many lively and engaging discussions, the IMPACT team agreed that the real innovation and the real power behind the successful redesigns were the people and the focus on motivation. As part of IMPACT, we work to help instructors design classes in an intentional and transparent way so that students understand and value the importance of what they are learning, fostering the satisfaction of their basic psychological needs and the creation of autonomy-supportive environments.

How SDT Guided the Evolution of the IMPACT Program and Our Work With Faculty Fellows

The focus on a theoretical framework such as SDT and the satisfaction of the basic psychological needs guided and shaped the evolution of the program into a faculty development program, emphasizing the human factor and the satisfaction of basic psychological needs in successful redesigns. This focus on SDT clarified our design objectives and guided the successful scale-up of the program.

Providing Autonomy in Selecting Redesign Elements

Addressing the instructors' need for autonomy based in SDT, the FLC became a process of scholarly inquiry for fellows. In that process, the role of support team members is to guide faculty fellows, to come alongside them in their transformation journey. This approach, based on the satisfaction of the need for autonomy, determined the structure currently in place for the IMPACT FLC sessions and the strategies used to help faculty identify the best approach for them in working with their students. Through the FLC the fellows are able to explore a variety of redesign options in a scholarly way. It also models the integration of critical thinking skills, which many faculty fellows want their students to demonstrate. When done well, modeling the types of student engagement that accompany a collaborative classroom environment fosters greater reflection from the faculty fellows, support team members, and FLC facilitators. Everyone on the team is involved in a deep process of reflection, applying the principles presented in the sessions to their experiences in the classroom, outside of the classroom, and facilitating the FLC. It also provides a renewed emphasis on student engagement and student-centered learning. Throughout our discussions, we strive to bring focus back to the student and the student experience. How will what you want to do in your class influence the satisfaction of the basic psychological needs of students? How does it foster the success and sense of belongingness of all students? This emphasis on student engagement and student learning as a primary goal also enhances the focus on mastery and competency and deprioritizes grades and DFW rates as the only or most important measure of student success.

To further foster autonomy, the IMPACT program does not push faculty toward a certain type of redesign model or a specific technology, but rather encourages faculty, in collaboration with their support team, to clarify their redesign goals and appropriate student learning outcomes. The selection of technologies for the redesign is not a primary goal of the redesign decision but instead is viewed as one tool among many to foster student engagement and support the attainment of learning outcomes. De-emphasizing the need to select a certain type of redesign model represents a move away from more commonly accepted redesign practices, which tend to focus on a certain strategy (e.g., flipping), a certain pedagogy (e.g., team-based learning), or a certain educational technology (e.g., clickers). This approach is much more autonomy supportive and allows the positive engagement of a diverse group of instructors. It respects and engages the disciplinary expertise of the faculty fellows as they are guided to reflect on their courses and the nature of their learning outcomes, objectives, activities, and classroom assessments—the building blocks of their courses. Obviously, some of the commonly used redesign strategies work well and produce great redesigns, which have been shown to enhance student learning outcomes. Flipping works well if done well. But if there is a disconnect between what is presented out of class and the in-class activities, students' need for competence will be hindered. An instructor who has been lecturing for years should not be pushed to flip their class. We need to take into consideration the person's development and what they are comfortable doing as we work on fostering greater student engagement. Why and how a pedagogy is implemented are important considerations. I will further explore this question in chapter 5 and describe, using the

SDT framework, how and why different active learning strategies, tools, and pedagogies produce enhanced learning outcomes.

Even though many of these evidence-based redesign models and practices can be successful, our surveys, interviews, and focus groups with faculty fellows suggested that enabling faculty to create student-centered and engaging learning environments mattered more than adopting a particular course structure or redesign model. Being less prescriptive allowed fellows to define their own transformation goals while also allowing the support teams to be more flexible and draw from their particular expertise to foster successful transformations. Offering choices and options in selecting redesign elements fostered fellows' autonomy, volitional engagement, and agency and encouraged a broad group of instructors from all colleges at Purdue to engage in the inquiry-based course transformation process. IMPACT's emphasis on meeting the basic psychological needs of both instructors and students encourages faculty members to think critically and act intentionally in order to enhance student engagement and learning aligned with the intended goals and outcomes of the course. This allowed us to effectively scale the IMPACT program to all colleges at Purdue. I will discuss this further later in this chapter.

IMPACT as a Professional Development Program

The focus on SDT changed the emphasis and philosophy of the program from a course redesign program and a focus on redesign models to a faculty or professional development program. This flows very naturally from the previous discussion on providing choice and autonomy in the selection of the redesign elements. Through professional development, faculty fellows apply teaching and learning principles in new contexts and situations and to other courses they are teaching, not only to the course they brought to the program with the intent to redesign. This shift toward professional development has led instructors to apply and transfer the skills and insights they acquire during the FLC to hundreds of other courses they are also teaching. This professional development process generates transformations in a large number of what we refer to as influenced courses. This growth will be discussed more specifically in chapter 7 on assessment. In the early years of the program, administrators and colleagues would often ask me, "Is IMPACT a course transformation program or a faculty development program?" Very early on, based in SDT principles, my sense was that we were doing much more than course transformation and that the magic of IMPACT was in our ability, as a support team, to work with instructors to transform and change how they thought about and considered their own teaching and their work with students. Our work was about supporting basic psychological needs as they explored their teaching practices. For some instructors, especially in STEM disciplines, this shift led to a fundamental philosophical transformation about their role in higher education. One faculty member in mechanical engineering described this transformation very well. He stated that in his field, instructors used to tell students in their class, "Look to your right, look to your left; one of you will not be there at the end of the semester." This used to be worn as a badge of honor. However, our work with IMPACT faculty fellows is changing this culture. Our work is about helping faculty understand the importance of creating an autonomy-supportive, student-centered learning environment for all students. This is the nature of our work as educators and the right thing to do. We need to aim to support all the students entering our classrooms and come along on their learning journey. This does not mean or imply that we become less rigorous, make the curriculum easier, or foster grade inflation. It is about nurturing the talent of all students, supporting their motivation for learning by fostering the satisfaction of their basic psychological needs, and in the process fostering the attainment of related motivational and educational outcomes. These ideas regarding the role of professional development for a broad range of instructors, and the ways in which instructors support students in their growth and development, are reminiscent of the writings of Ken Bain (2004) in *What the Best College Teachers Do*. Although Bain (2004) does not specifically refer to SDT, he does cite work by Deci and Ryan (1985) and does feature in his book instructors who would by all means be considered autonomy supportive. The best college teachers described in Bain's book, which he identified following a 15-year investigation, are those who support the basic psychological needs of autonomy, competence, and relatedness and use many of the active learning strategies I will describe in chapter 5 to create learning environments that are autonomy supportive.

Students in our classes most often are novice learners and as such do not have the frame of reference to think about and unpack the discipline in the same ways as disciplinary experts. As instructors, thinking and conceptualizing our field and the disciplinary content is second nature to us; we are experts in our field. However, it is not the case for students, and as we work with faculty fellows, we emphasize these differences and help instructors think through ways they can be more intentional about unpacking the content of the discipline. Not doing so could be perceived as controlling to students. In contrast, making an intentional decision to begin with the students in mind and think like a novice or less experienced learner allows instructors to craft environments that are autonomy supportive for a diverse group of students. It allows instructors to create environments that meet the needs of autonomy, competence, and relatedness. This process, informed by

SDT, shares similarities with the process described by Joan Middendorf and Leah Shopkow (2018) in their recent book on *Overcoming Student Learning Bottlenecks: Decode the Critical Thinking of Your Discipline.* Our work with faculty fellows helps them uncover and discover ways experts think about a discipline and understand why and where students, as novice learners, would struggle or experience a bottleneck to learning or understanding important concepts. The way disciplinary experts think about the field is not obvious to students; often the only thing they see is the ease with which instructors solve problems, talk about the discipline, and manipulate disciplinary concepts. Students need to explicitly see instructors' thinking processes as they approach a problem, understand strategies they use to get unstuck when they face difficulties, and through practice and repetition develop expertise in their field. Students need to understand how to decode implicit expert knowledge and turn it into explicit learning tasks (Middendorf & Shopkow, 2018; Pace & Middendorf, 2004). Doing so fosters the satisfaction of all three basic psychological needs of autonomy, competence, and relatedness. When this process is implemented well, students can begin to see themselves developing the competencies in order to master the discipline, while becoming closer to their instructor by realizing that their instructors can also struggle with concepts. It ultimately helps students work toward developing their own sets of strategies to be successful in the class and discipline. This is hard work and it requires professional development for instructors to do so effectively. Thus, IMPACT fosters faculty and course "transformation" rather than course "redesign," and this is how culture change can occur. These ideas will be further developed in chapter 6 on professional development and chapter 9 on culture change.

The members of the support teams all function as faculty developers when they work with IMPACT faculty fellows. In many ways this actually modified the goals and focus of the partnering units representing a diverse group of staff members with different expertise. As IMPACT grew, the philosophy of the units involved morphed and adapted (Flierl et al., 2019). While this approach may seem counterintuitive to the goals of the respective units partnering on IMPACT, creating engaging learning environments necessarily involves considering how students engage appropriately with information (Flierl et al., 2018; Maybee, 2018; Maybee & Flierl, 2017), how technology and social media tools facilitate teaching and learning (Gundlach, Maybee, & O'Shea 2015), and how pedagogical learning activities and assessments support learning outcomes and objectives (Fedesco et al., 2017; Gundlach, Richards, et al., 2015; Levesque-Bristol, Flierl, et al., 2019; Levesque-Bristol, Maybee, et al., 2019). The common goal of the units involved is to work with faculty to help them create environments that are autonomy supportive and student centered. This common goal unifies the various units working on IMPACT. The commonalities among our goals and practices while working on IMPACT draw the different units closer together. Much like the different circles of a Venn diagram, the common shared space has grown larger over the years of collaboration on the IMPACT program. While the unique goals of the different units are still present, when working on IMPACT student-centered pedagogy is the unifying theme, and all are oriented toward supporting faculty fellows with their own particular expertise.

Scaling Up the Program and the Support Team Composition

As mentioned in chapter 1, the first cohort in fall 2011 was composed of 12 faculty fellows redesigning 10 courses from 8 different departments representing the humanities, social and physical sciences, engineering, and agriculture. In the first few iterations of IMPACT, each faculty fellow worked with a dedicated support team of two to three support members from the partnering units (CIE, TLT, PULSIS). This model was resource intensive and not sustainable or scalable as we worked toward our goal of up to 60 courses annually. In addition, this structure generated little sense of community and was isolating, as each fellow only worked with their support team with almost no opportunity to share their experiences with other fellow instructors (Cox, 2004). In order to scale the program and increase the number of faculty fellows who could participate, we turned to the SDT principles to look for a sustainable way to scale the program.

A focus on the satisfaction of the need for relatedness from SDT provided an answer. To foster a greater sense of community, belongingness, and relatedness, we focused on forming teams of faculty fellows working with teams of support members from the different units involved in a larger collaboration. In the current structure of the IMPACT program, up to 30 staff members from CIE and TLT and faculty from the libraries collaborate to form the support teams and facilitate the FLC. IMPACT faculty fellows now work in teams with two to three other fellows and three to four support team members, ideally one from each unit, creating groups of six to eight members. The process by which we form the teams is very intentional. We colloquially refer to this process as draft day. The teams we create are permanent for the duration of the FLC and even beyond as the instructors implement their transformation. The faculty fellows often work with their support teams during their implementation semester. The instructors are grouped based on a common teaching and learning challenge (e.g., all large classes), a course topic (e.g., aviation technology), a stated redesign goal (e.g., desire to enhance student engagement), or curriculum redesign work (e.g., all calculus instructors to transform the calculus sequence). The support team members are assigned to the group of instructors based on expertise, skills, or past or ongoing working relationships with the faculty fellows. In fact, the support team members are asked to express their desire or preference to work with certain faculty fellows and, whenever appropriate, these preferences are honored. In forming the teams, we also pay attention to the diversity in the teams, aiming to create teams that are diverse with respect to gender, personality, and skills. The groups also meet on average once every other week on their own as necessary in order to work on the IMPACT weekly curriculum assignments and the course transformation. The support team members are assigned the role of primary or secondary. All groups meet during the 75-minute working FLC sessions for 14 weeks during a semester. The only important difference between the primary and secondary support team members is that the primary members are responsible for keeping the faculty fellows on track with the completion of deliverables as well as scheduling the additional outside FLC meetings.

The emphasis on autonomy while selecting redesign elements and professional development, discussed previously, flows nicely into the process by which we were able to scale the IMPACT program. To provide the needed space and time to engage in deep conversation, inquiry, and reflective practices, the IMPACT management team loosely adopted a flipped approach, moving some of the presentation content and exercises outside of the FLCs into an online learning management system (LMS). Each week, the IMPACT faculty fellows are asked to prepare for the face-to-face FLC sessions by reading selected literature and completing prework while considering the potential influence on their particular discipline and class. They do so by visiting the LMS site to view short videos, read articles, and complete prework before the face-to-face FLC sessions. During the FLC sessions, as topics such as student characteristics, redesign goals, student learning outcomes, and evidence of learning through assessment are discussed, instructors are encouraged and guided to think about their redesign through the perspective of a reflective practitioner keeping in mind their own motivation and their students' motivation (Brookfield, 2017; Deci & Ryan, 1985; Ryan & Deci, 2017). Given dedicated time to reflect on course goals and desired student attitudes, skills, and competencies, many fellows identify misalignment between their stated outcomes and in-class activities and assessments. In some cases, this course realignment with a student-centered perspective is the core of a transformation.

By focusing on motivational principles of human engagement and providing a positive professional development experience to faculty fellows, we gained advocates of the program. As we were called to scale the IMPACT program and broaden recruitment, many of the early adopters became strong allies for the program, encouraging their peers to participate. The early adopters made a strong case for the administration to expand the resources assigned to sustain and grow these transformation efforts for faculty development. The support of department heads and deans and the endorsement of senior institutional leaders were also crucial in this scaling up effort. Whereas early recruitment targeted instructors teaching courses with high DFW rates in large enrollment foundational courses, the expansion of IMPACT no longer required courses to meet these criteria. The new recruitment philosophy opened IMPACT to any interested full-time faculty, including clinical faculty, as well as part-time faculty with responsibility for a lower- or upper-level undergraduate course that they could teach for three semesters. This change in practice resulted in a more diverse set of lower- and upper-level division courses, all of which helped broaden and cultivate the desired culture change valuing teaching and learning. To fully engage deans and department heads in the process, they sign a service-level agreement (SLA), which is a sort of contract for participation in the IMPACT program between the deans and department heads, the faculty fellows, and the IMPACT team. We ask that the faculty fellow and the department head sign this document as a way to signify and accept the level of deep commitment necessary to engage in this transformation process. This SLA also specifies that the faculty fellows will receive $10,000 for each course transformation. These funds are disbursed to the fellow's department, in three installments, based on a sequence of deliverables. The first installment of $2,500 is given once the faculty fellows attend the first FLC session and sign the SLA. The second installment of $2,500 is given after the faculty fellows have completed all the FLCs activities and provided all deliverables. The last installment of $5,000 is provided once the faculty fellows begin teaching their transformed course, typically the semester following participation in the IMPACT FLC (see Appendix B for the presentation of the SLA). As we discussed in chapters 2 and 3, incentives and rewards are likely to be perceived as controlling unless the informational functional significance of the reward can be highlighted. In this case, the incentive is not too large, meaning that it can only partly fund a teaching assistant, which is an important marker at Purdue and a resource that is often needed for the implementation of a successful transformation. This means that the faculty fellows' departments need to commit additional resources if this is what is needed for the transformation. In addition, this incentive is typically perceived as signifying that the Provost's Office is valuing the effort instructors are putting into their teaching. Therefore, the way in which we administered the incentive is less likely to be detrimental for the motivation of faculty fellows. As you think about implementing and incentivizing course transformation on your campus, the size and the functional significance of the incentive is an important consideration.

Structure of the IMPACT FLC Curriculum

The IMPACT curriculum is based in an FLC, which spans an entire semester (Levesque-Bristol, Flierl, et al., 2019; Levesque-Bristol, Maybee, et al., 2019). This basic structure emerged from recommendations from the work of Milton Cox (2004). The curriculum is divided into 14 weekly sessions of 75 minutes each. The general structure and syllabus for the program is presented in Table 4.1.

The 14 weeks are organized into five broad units ranging from 1 to 5 weeks in length, drawing from principles of backward design (Wiggins & McTighe, 2005). The five broad units are as follows: (a) Welcome and Meet Your Team, (b) Learners' Motivation, (c) Learning Outcomes and Objectives, (d) Assessments and Learning Activities, and (e) Drawing It All Together.

TABLE 4.1
IMPACT FLC Curriculum With Units, Topics, and Major Deliverables

Session	*Unit*	*Topic*	*Major Deliverables*
Session 1	Welcome and Meet Your Team	Welcome to the IMPACT program: Meet your redesign team	None
Session 2	Learners' Motivation	SDT as the motivation framework for student engagement and learning Guests: Students	Initial redesign goal
Session 3	Learners' Motivation	Student characteristics: We are all different Guests: Students	None
Session 4	Learning Outcomes and Objectives	Learning outcomes	Initial learning outcomes

(*Continues*)

TABLE 4.1 ***(Continued)***

Session	*Unit*	*Topic*	*Major Deliverables*
Session 5	Learning Outcomes and Objectives	Informed and inclusive learning objectives	None
Session 6	Assessments and Learning Activities	Assessing student performance, part 1	None
Session 7	Assessments and Learning Activities	Assessing student performance, part 2	Revised learning outcomes and objectives
Session 8	Assessments and Learning Activities	Learning activities, part 1	None
Session 9	Assessments and Learning Activities	Learning activities, part 2	Initial course design plan (CDP) (including revised learning outcomes and objectives)
Session 10	Assessments and Learning Activities	Connecting the dots Guests: Students	None
Session 11	Drawing It All Together	Redesign decisions	Revised CDP (including revised redesign goal and revised learning outcomes and objectives)
Session 12	Drawing It All Together	Redesign presentations Guests: Students	None
Session 13	Drawing It All Together	Scholarly Practitioner	None
Session 14	Drawing It All Together	Closing the loop and focus group with IMPACT faculty fellows	Final CDP (including final redesign goal and final learning outcomes and objectives)

Welcome and Meet Your Team

The first unit is one session and is designed to give a chance to the faculty fellows and the support team members to meet each other and begin the process of creating connections to build the FLC. From the first session, we set the stage by emphasizing the connections that will be made throughout the semester. This is reinforced by past IMPACT fellows who are asked to come back and share with the current cohort of fellows their experiences with the IMPACT program and how it transformed their teaching and their course and impacted their students. In terms of SDT, this immediately emphasizes the creation of an autonomy-supportive environment by fostering the need for relatedness in this learning community.

As described previously, the teams are built in a very intentional way, and the members of the teams will begin to discover these connections during this welcoming session. The welcoming session is also a time for the FLC facilitators, who are members of the IMPACT management team, to introduce the members of the IMPACT management team and facilitators and also present the program expectations, the LMS in which the FLC curriculum is set up, and some of the scope and results regarding the effectiveness of the IMPACT program. The program expectations are also described in the IMPACT syllabus as well as the SLA, which both the faculty fellow and the department head sign. For your information and convenience, these documents are presented in Appendix A and Appendix B. Everything that we do in IMPACT is based in the spirit of sharing. Therefore, any of the materials presented in this book can be used and adapted freely. Feel free to use some or all of the materials, and modify and adapt them to meet your needs, the needs of your individual professional development programs, and workshops at your institution. During the welcoming session, faculty fellows who have not yet turned in their completed SLA have a chance to ask questions about the purpose and philosophy behind the SLA, as well as the deliverables that are tied to the program incentives.

Learners' Motivation

IMPACT highlights student (human) motivation and student characteristics as the two topics in the unit on learners' motivation to immediately orient instructors to think about their classes through the experience of their students, focusing on student learning rather than faculty teaching or course content. In this unit we emphasize to instructors the importance of thinking about their students before their own teaching; that is, we invite the faculty fellows to begin with the student in mind; to reflect on the importance and need to place the students first; and to think about the course, the material, and their teaching in relation to the students and their needs.

Session 2 focuses on SDT as the motivation framework that will guide the entire IMPACT program and the experience of the instructors as they work with their support teams to redesign their course. The basic psychological needs of autonomy, competence, and relatedness (see chapters 2 and 3) are presented as the way in which we operationalize student engagement and student-centered learning and teaching. The basic psychological needs are discussed and connected to the redesign work throughout the entire FLC. The course transformation that faculty are about to engage in is framed as the creation of learning environments that are autonomy supportive and that enable students to feel autonomous, connected, and competent. Accordingly, many of the discussions, reflections, and questions in the IMPACT teams revolve around how a proposed change to the course may foster or hinder the satisfaction of students' basic psychological needs. In recent iterations of the FLC, undergraduate students have joined this session in order to provide their views and opinions on the elements of a course and pedagogical practices that tend to foster basic psychological needs. Students are actually invited to four of the 14 FLC sessions (see Table 4.1). During this motivation session, one of the key activities is to think about how students' skills and competencies (need for competence) can be developed by supporting the other two basic psychological needs of autonomy and relatedness. A think-pair-share activity is used for this exercise, in which the instructors first reflect on their own, then discuss their ideas with their IMPACT team, and then share their team reflections on whiteboards and then with the larger group of 30 faculty fellows. The students' group completes the same exercise in the same manner. The results of the exchanges among instructors, support team members, and students during the sharing time are eye-opening and begin this process of deep nonjudgmental sharing built in trust of each other and the larger group. This activity immediately models for instructors the positive influence of an autonomy-supportive environment.

Throughout the FLC, faculty fellows have to provide deliverables at key points during the semester. As faculty fellows first begin to think about their course and their students and their basic needs, as well as engage in conversations with their redesign team, they are asked to upload to the LMS their initial redesign goal for their course. This redesign goal is an initial intention for the redesign, a starting point, a discussion starter, but it rarely remains unchanged. This redesign goal will be revisited throughout the semester, as you can see from the list of deliverables in Table 4.1. For many of the sessions, supplemental material will be made available to faculty fellows as a way to reinforce or expand a concept. In session 2, the seven principles of good practice in undergraduate education by Chickering and Gamson (1987) are provided. This is mostly done because Chickering and Gamson provide a familiar frame of reference in education, but the parallels with SDT are striking enough that important connections can be made for instructors unfamiliar with the motivational principles from SDT.

Session 3 asks instructors to reflect on the characteristics of students in their classes and recognize and appreciate the differences in their students. During this session, instructors begin to think about ways in which they can satisfy the needs of all students, not just the ones who look and think like them. As discussed in chapter 2, the basic needs of autonomy, competence, and relatedness have been found to be universal and cross-culturally valid, which means that all humans, regardless of their cultural background, possess and are naturally inclined to satisfy these basic human needs. What can differ across groups of students is how the satisfaction of these needs is manifested and achieved.

In this session, faculty discuss and participate in exercises focusing on adopting the student perspective and how different factors like pre- and post- requisites, being multilingual, being from an underrepresented minority group, or being a first-generation student can have an impact on how the learning environment is perceived, which therefore influences how students learn in their course. In the FLC, faculty fellows discuss with their support teams how a particular learning environment would contribute to support the basic human psychological needs for various groups of students. Most recently, we have invited the vice provost for diversity and inclusion, John Gates, to come and share his perspective with the faculty fellows. During his presentation, he highlights the diversity and inclusion context at Purdue, speaking about the data on achievement gaps and the experiences of underrepresented minorities in an institution of higher education like Purdue. He then invites instructors to reframe the achievement gaps as opportunities to maximize students' potential. He makes the point that it is all of our responsibility to do so, as humans, fostering the development and the growth of other humans. He asks us to consider how we can create environments in which all students can feel like they belong while we work to maximize students' potential. In terms of SDT, belongingness is akin to satisfying the need for relatedness. Recently, we have also invited students to participate in this session. As you can expect, the conversations are sometimes difficult, but necessary. Discussing the challenges and opportunities associated with diversity and inclusivity is often messy. The conversations that occur during the debrief within the support teams following the presentation by Gates are emotional and sometimes raw. The more the teams are able to unpack these emotions and their underlying thread, in an environment that is autonomy supportive and where trust is fostered, the more progress is made toward deep course transformation.

Learning Outcomes and Objectives

This unit begins the process of faculty fellows more intentionally investigating the learning outcomes and objectives for their course, thinking deliberately about what they want their students to be able to know, do, and appreciate. The learning outcomes are course level and broad and delineate concepts that are critical for students in order for them to master the course content. The learning objectives represent the more specific actionable processes; that is, building blocks or stepping-stones by which the students will be able to attain the broader learning outcomes. Outcomes and objectives need to be simple, clear, and easily understandable when communicated to students. The work around the learning outcomes and objectives is guided by Bloom's (1956) taxonomy and informed learning. Bloom's work is highly recognizable, and the verb lists that have been developed for the different levels of the taxonomy are very useful as faculty fellows revise existing learning outcomes or develop new ones. However, Bloom's taxonomy readily focuses on the cognitive domain, or what students are able to know. This is appropriate for most course transformations. Recently, the work of Claudia Stanny (2016) has been influential in our presentation of the potential verbs associated with the cognitive domains when working with faculty fellows on the creation of learning outcomes. Her work summarizes how often certain verbs are associated with the different levels of Bloom's taxonomy, providing a meaningful compilation of the most commonly used verbs for the cognitive domain. However, when instructors want to create outcomes that are more in line with the affective, interpersonal, or psychomotor domains (what the students are able to value, appreciate, or do), which is becoming more and more frequent, other resources are offered to faculty fellows. A few that we commonly discuss within our teams for the interpersonal and affective domain is related to the work of Lynch et al. (2009) and Bolin et al. (2005). In building the learning outcomes and objectives session around Bloom as the framework, but then offering additional resources depending on the needs of the faculty fellows and the goals for their course, we are following SDT principles. We are creating autonomy-supportive environments for the faculty fellows by providing them choices and options within a structure.

Learning outcomes rarely remain unchanged throughout the 14 weeks. Through critical reflections and discussions with their support teams, faculty fellows consider how detailed they need or want their outcomes to be and what would be most helpful to foster the success of all students in the class. Although they will most likely change, at the end of session 4, faculty fellows are asked to input their initial learning outcomes and objectives into their course design plan (CDP) on the LMS site. The CDP is a formative tool used to guide the redesign process and the decisions made throughout the semester. The CDP is used throughout the rest of the FLC sessions and is presented in Figure 4.1.

The purpose of the CDP is to help faculty fellows visualize the decisions they are making in their course redesign and to ensure alignment among the learning outcomes, assessment strategies, and learning activities (Carriveau, 2010). It also is a place for faculty fellows to reflect on how the learning activities foster the satisfaction of the basic psychological needs of autonomy, competence, and relatedness.

By putting their learning outcomes on paper, faculty fellows have to justify and prioritize their decisions regarding their learning outcomes and connect them to the taxonomic dimensions. Faculty fellows actually go through a very difficult exercise in this unit, in which they are asked to reduce the number of their learning outcomes to the three most essential ones, and then add a few more only if necessary to capture their course goals and objectives. Learning outcomes continue to be modified through their work in the following sessions on assessments and learning activities, in which faculty and support team members refine and align the language used to depict specific learning outcomes and objectives. The learning outcomes and objectives are also revised, refined, and adapted in the context of SDT. The faculty fellows are invited to reflect on the appropriateness of their learning outcomes and objectives for a broad range of students with various backgrounds and experiences. They are asked to think about which learning outcomes would be best for their course content and objectives and would simultaneously guide and orient learning for all students. Can the learning objectives selected for each learning outcome be framed in a way that would contribute to the creation of an autonomy-supportive environment for all students? This type of inquiry is carried very intentionally into the next session in this unit on informed and inclusive learning objectives.

Session 5 on informed and inclusive learning objectives emphasizes ways in which students will need to use information to achieve a learning outcome as well as the creation of learning objectives that will also highlight the ways in which students will use information in the course. This session is built around informed learning design (Maybee, 2018; Maybee et al., 2019), emphasizing information literacy, which is essentially about teaching learners to use information within the context of disciplinary content (Bruce, 2008). Informed learning design was inspired by the research of Maybee et al. following his work on information literacy and IMPACT (Maybee et al., 2016, 2017, 2019; Maybee & Flierl, 2017). Drawing from SDT, library faculty members involved in IMPACT and other IMPACT support team members are able to guide faculty in the design of informed learning activities that address students' perceptions of autonomy, competence, and relatedness (Maybee, 2018; Maybee & Flierl, 2017).

Informed learning design follows a series of stages similar to the ones in backward design (Wiggins & McTighe, 2005). First, it involves identifying critical aspects of learning and goals for learning, which include using

Figure 4.1. CDP.

CDP

Name: Course Name: Course #

Learning Outcomes	Learning Objectives	Assessment					Active Learning Activities, Pedagogies, and/or Educational Practices					SDT		
		A1	A2	A3	A4	A5	S1	S2	S3	S4	S5	Autonomy	Competence	Relatedness
Learning Outcome (Enter Learning Outcome 1 here.)	LO 1.1 LO 1.2 LO 1.3 LO 1.4 LO 1.5													
Learning Outcome 2	LO 2.1 LO 2.2 LO 2.3 LO 2.4 LO 2.5													
Learning Outcome 3	LO 3.1 LO 3.2 LO 3.3 LO 3.4 LO 3.5													
Learning Outcome 4	LO 4.1 LO 4.2 LO 4.3 LO 4.4 LO 4.5													
Learning Outcome 5	LO 5.1 LO 5.2 LO 5.3 LO 5.4 LO 5.5													

Redesign Goal:

REDESIGNING EDUCATION

IMPACT

FLC Semester:

Reflections on educational technologies as a way support student engagement.					Reflections on informed learning as a way to support student engagement.	Reflections on diversity and inclusivity as a way to support engagement.
T1	T2	T3	T4	T5		

*These columns are an open space for you to reflect and jot down notes on how you will use technology, informed learning, and inclusive teaching to support student engagement in your classroom.

https://www.purdue.edu/impact/

information and course content. Second it requires the design of assessments for evaluating students' increased awareness of critical aspects associated with using information and course content. Third, it involves creating activities that enable students to learn about critical aspects associated with course content by intentionally using information (Maybee et al., 2019). Importantly, during the first part of the process, instructors critically examine their past teaching experiences as well as students' current experiences. In the subsequent parts, instructors connect these experiences to an assessment plan as well as learning activities, enabling students to become more aware of and intentional about how they interact with the particular information used to meet the goals and learning outcomes established in phase 1 of IMPACT. Writing learning outcomes and objectives following this process helps faculty fellows communicate course expectations to students so they have a better understanding of why they are expected to know, do, and appreciate certain things. Essentially, the support teams are providing a meaningful rationale to faculty fellows so they can communicate it to their students as they are going through the course and mastering course content. By doing so we are fostering transparency, which contributes to the creation of an autonomy-supportive environment through the enhancement of perceived value and relevance. This framework follows SDT principles and is especially suited to discuss how various learning outcomes and objectives can foster or hinder inclusivity and gather information from students as they develop their awareness and abilities of how they use information in the course. Drawing attention to how different students think about and use information in authentic ways, and contrasting this to how the instructor or disciplinary experts use information, can open up conversations about inclusion and diversity of thoughts and actions. In doing so, it puts an emphasis on the satisfaction of basic psychological needs for all students and the creation of autonomy-supportive environments. Openly and intentionally discussing ways in which different students and instructors consume and use information as they learn a discipline fosters this process. As students become more aware of and understand the importance of the disciplinary content they are learning, it fosters the need for relatedness (relevance), which allows them to do more and perform well on learning tasks and activities (competence) and then feel more empowered to voice their opinions and engage the material presented in a more agentic and volitional way (autonomy). This also fosters complex learning outcomes such as critical thinking and problem-solving, which are important and valuable to most instructors we work with. This work has led to the creation of an informed learning self-report scale (Flierl et al., in press), completed by students and used as part of the overall assessment of IMPACT. Further research has supported the previous points by finding that the frequency with which faculty ask students to synthesize and communicate information does correlate with student motivation and academic performance in the course (Flierl et al., in press). This work will be further described in chapter 7 on assessment.

Assessments and Learning Activities

The process of examining learning outcomes and objectives, which begins in session 4, continues in this 5-week unit, which globally encompasses assessments and learning activities. Faculty fellows continue to consider Bloom's taxonomy in relation to their learning outcomes and objectives, aligning the assessments students take and learning activities students engage in with the specific language chosen for their learning outcomes. They do so by continuing to intentionally consider SDT principles, informed learning, and inclusivity.

As organized and presented in Table 4.1, the sequence of topics for sessions 6 through 9 follows the typical phases of backward design, introducing assessments then learning activities. Even though the sessions in this unit are presented in a linear fashion in Table 4.1, they could be interchanged and interwoven in a flexible course transformation program with 10 being the final topic. I will come back to this later in this section. The five sessions in this unit lead to many deep discussions among the faculty fellows and the support team members, and plenty of time needs to be set aside for discussions during the FLC. Consequently, most of the sessions in this unit serve as working sessions. For example, during sessions 6 and 7, faculty fellows in collaboration with their support team members work to align a major assessment with the course learning activities and learning outcomes. If you follow a traditional backward design model, these sessions are used to map a summative assessment (usually a final exam or project) onto learning outcomes and objectives. For instance, for a final exam the faculty fellow would go through each question and determine which learning outcome the question is measuring. This allows the fellows to identify areas of pedagogical misalignment and determine whether all of their learning outcomes are being adequately assessed. This is also an opportunity to think about the course assessments as a whole (e.g., final exam) and how the other assessments (formative and summative) in the course support and align with the final summative assessment. It's an opportunity to think about the balance between the formative and summative assessments in the course. At the end of session 7, faculty fellows typically would have revised learning outcomes and learning objectives and a mapped summative assessment before they are even introduced to crafting a variety of learning activities.

However, in practice, that is not often the case, and in reality the process of engaging with assessments and learning activities and mapping one onto the other and back to learning outcomes is not that linear. In fact, this may be where the backward design process does not fit neatly the structure followed in IMPACT. In IMPACT, because students as humans are at the center of the learning process, and because faculty as humans are at the center of the transformation process, the considerations of what learning activities will meet the various learning outcomes and objectives, how these learning activities will be assessed, and what assessments will be used in the course form a dynamic and fluid process. Therefore, I want to argue that in many cases, it is desirable to approach the five sessions in this unit as a whole, and in many cases, this will reflect the way in which the support team members actually work with faculty fellows during this unit.

In a course redesign that is guided by the motivational principles of SDT, it is very difficult to think about assessments independently of learning activities and vice versa. Assessments and learning activities are ideally representative of the growth and development of the human beings both doing the teaching and the learning. The way in which students performed on a learning activity may prompt an instructor to modify or adjust their assessment rubric. Alternatively, the results of an assessment may prompt the instructor to add a learning activity or modify an upcoming one. In that sense, even though in the IMPACT FLC we ask faculty fellows to consider the balance of formative and summative assessment, any assessment can be considered as formative, and the results of these formative assessments can be summed into an overall performance score or grade at the end of the semester. In terms of SDT, formative assessments are more informational and carry meaningful feedback that can be used to learn how to adjust one's performance. In addition, formative assessments tend to be lower-stakes assessments, which help create environments that are autonomy supportive by reducing anxiety and increasing competence. These also tend to foster growth and development in a broad range of students, not only those with prior course experience or relevant knowledge. In short, creating meaningful assessments and learning activities is not always as linear and straightforward as figuring out whether assessments were successful in assessing the intended learning outcomes (Barkley & Major, 2016). It often makes sense to begin with learning activities and map those onto the learning outcomes and objectives and then engage in discussions regarding how these activities can best be evaluated and assessed. In thinking about how to represent this fluid concept, I came up with a sort of double helix representation, which is depicted in Figure 4.2.

Often, IMPACT fellows find discrepancies or misalignment between what they want their students to be able to know, do, and appreciate, and how or what they assess. For example, a fellow may want students to achieve greater development of higher-order thinking skills, like create an appropriate safety plan for constructing a building, but they realize that they are only assessing student learning via lower-order assessments—like basic multiple choice questions where students classify or compare information relating to a safety plan.

Figure 4.2. Learning activities and assessments helix.

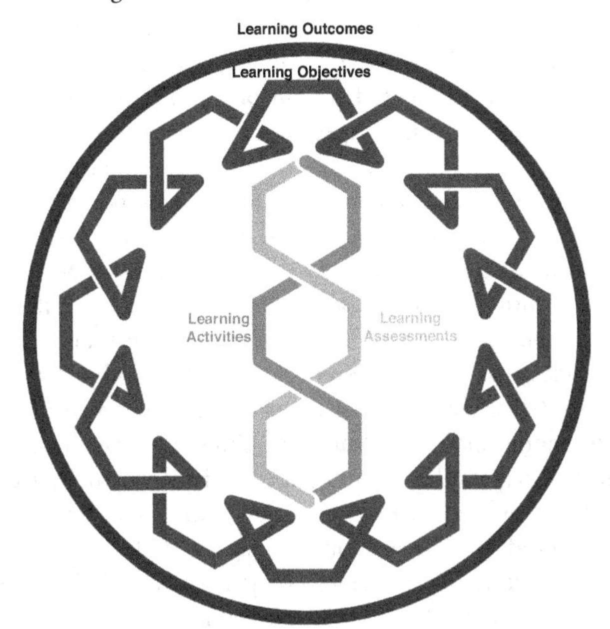

Note. Thanks to Alyse Marie Allread for creating this visual. Reprinted with permission of A. M. Allred.

IMPACT also provides the fellows with opportunities to review their overall assessment strategies in light of SDT principles. For example, a fellow may realize that they do not have enough formative assessments to help students build competence in their course and may only have one or a few high-stakes summative assessments, which increases students' anxiety, especially for certain groups of students (e.g., women in the sciences). The identification of these misalignments leads to a reevaluation and revision of the assessments or a revision of the learning outcomes and objectives or both. In some cases this realization, and the subsequent realignment, is the most important piece of the transformation.

In sessions 8 and 9, as currently outlined in Table 4.1, faculty fellows explore the literature on learning activities. This is an opportunity to present what we have done in the FLC as learning activities drawn from the literature. In addition, particular emphasis is placed on fellows exploring different learning activities they may not have experienced or heard of before. Learning activities are evaluated in relation to SDT and informed learning. In exploring the literature and looking for learning activities to implement in their courses, we use the FLC to model intentional engagements with information. In addition, we encourage fellows to consider ways in which these learning activities enable the creation of autonomy-supportive learning environments by supporting the satisfaction of the basic psychological needs. In doing so, we emphasize the satisfaction of the needs for all students considering issues of diversity, equity, and inclusion in the selection, implementation, and assessment of learning activities. Scaffolding activities over time to build student competence is of particular importance, as students may not be familiar or comfortable with new learning activities when they expected a more lecture-style of classroom environment. Ultimately, fellows document and justify their proposed learning activities for their redesigned course, acknowledging potential difficulties and mapping activities to learning outcomes, objectives, and assessments.

Rather than focus on often vaguely defined notions of active learning, fellows work on identifying how chosen learning activities meet the needs for autonomy, competence, and relatedness. They develop the tools to implement and assess new ideas and techniques effectively, which will support student learning for all students. We emphasize the need for faculty to critically engage with implementation of particular learning techniques through SDT because our own research suggests that it is not the particular learning activity that influences student learning. Instead, it is how you implement the learning activities while considering satisfaction of basic psychological needs that do significantly impact learning outcomes (Bonem et al., 2019). In addition, internal data suggest that faculty who adopt active learning techniques without this critical reflection or who are uncomfortable teaching with these methods tend to receive lower student evaluations than they would when using traditional lectures. Accordingly, our emphasis on instructor autonomy in choosing class structure and activities results in greater comfort, sustainability, and adaptability while refining future course iterations with new learning activities.

At the end of session 9, fellows submit an initial full draft of their CDP. This initial draft of their CDP documents alignment between the course learning outcomes and objectives, assessments, and learning activities. In this submission of the CDP, faculty fellows also document how their students' basic psychological needs will be met and identify potential educational technology tools and ways that information will be used in their transformed course.

Session 10 on connecting the dots, the last session in this unit, provides one last opportunity to put it all together and connect the dots between the learning outcomes, the learning activities, and the assessments of those learning activities as they tie in to the learning outcomes (Carriveau, 2010). Students are also invited to this session and provide feedback on the structure of the course transformation and the choices that have been made on these key alignment pieces. Another general resource that is very useful for the conceptualization of learning outcomes and objectives is the work of Dee Fink (2013) on creating significant learning experiences. Some of the support team members make great use of these additional resources, and I will come back to these in chapter 5.

Drawing It All Together

Taken together, the next four FLC sessions aim to help fellows revise, refine, and prepare to implement their intended transformation. This involves considerations of pace—how quickly they can realistically implement their intended changes; scholarly practice—how they will gather and analyze data to tell the story of their redesign; and sustainability—how to continually revise and refine one's course over time. In effect, this involves helping faculty develop practices and habits that cultivate a reflective attitude in their teaching, which will continue well beyond the conclusion of the IMPACT FLC. During sessions 11 and 12, faculty fellows have the opportunity to prepare and give a short presentation on their course transformation and receive feedback from other faculty fellows in the cohort. Students are invited to this presentation session, which gives the opportunity to faculty fellows to receive feedback from students, which provides a very interesting perspective at this point in the process. Faculty fellows also have the opportunity to hear from previous faculty fellows who have gone through the program and are at different stages of their redesign implementation in session 13. The faculty fellows, through careful and respectful discussions, challenge each other on the nature of their redesign decisions. They reflect on how such decisions support the students' basic psychological needs of autonomy, competence, and relatedness and contribute to the creation of learning environments that are autonomy supportive and student centered. Issues of diversity, equity, and inclusion are considered and discussed through the presentations; these relate to learning objectives and outcomes, assessment strategies, and learning activities. All these are considered so that student success is possible for all students.

The last session provides an opportunity for faculty fellows to reflect and close the loop on what has been covered during the semester. The support team members engage in discussions about ongoing support with the faculty as they move toward implementation of their redesign. During this session, the ELRC conducts focus groups with the faculty fellows. This is an important piece of the overall program evaluation plan, and the results of these focus groups inform future revisions and iterations of the IMPACT program and the FLCs. Some of this data will be presented in chapter 7. At the conclusion of the FLC, the faculty fellows submit their final CDP, including their final redesign goal and final learning outcomes and objectives. Although the final CDP is only due at the end of the FLC following session 14, as discussed previously, the CDP is drawn on heavily during the sessions leading up to the redesign decisions and presentation sessions. This is where faculty and the support team members work on drawing all that has been discussed and covered during the FLC.

5

ACTIVE LEARNING STRATEGIES

It has been known for quite some time that active learning works (Freeman et al., 2014; Prince, 2004). In higher education, there is an emphasis on moving away from a teacher-centered learning environment or a focus on lecturing to a student-centered learning environment or a focus on active learning. But from examining the research, it appears that not all active learning is created equal. In some instances, what would be considered active learning does not lead to improved student perceptions, improved learning outcomes attainment, or performance. In other cases, large lectures delivered with a focus on student engagement have been shown to produce change in student attitudes and learning outcomes comparable or even superior to a "flipped" redesign model (Gundlach, Richards, et al., 2015). Research conducted in collaboration with faculty fellows on some of the IMPACT transformed courses support this idea. In one particular study, course sections offered as traditional lectures were augmented by online material, taught fully online, or offered as flipped sections. They were all taught by the same instructor and were compared with regard to student attitudes and statistical reasoning as well as performance on common exams, homework, and a project. Increases in positive affect, cognitive competence, and perceived easiness with regard to statistics were observed for all sections. In addition, increases in statistical reasoning skills and decreases in misconceptions were also equally noted for all sections. With regard to performance on the three common exams, students in the traditional sections of this transformed course scored higher on average, although no significant differences were observed between the sections on homework or the project. In addition, all of the teaching modalities were associated with similar levels of engagement and autonomy support.

How could a large lecture be perceived as autonomy supportive? Why are flipped modalities not always associated with better learning outcomes? How can we explain the effectiveness of various active learning strategies? Are some strategies better than others? Using SDT as our framework, we have postulated that active learning works when it fosters the creation of autonomy-supportive environments. In the IMPACT work, we have defined environments that are student centered as those that meet the basic psychological needs of autonomy, competence, and relatedness (see chapters 2 and 3). Recent research based on the IMPACT program has demonstrated that autonomy-supportive learning environments are consistently associated with increased motivational and academic outcomes. The results clearly suggest that what is most important for students is not the specific techniques used by instructors but the quality of the interactions students have with instructors and the learning environment that is created. In short, what you do is less important than how you do it (Bonem et al., 2019). This same idea is conveyed in the writings of Parker Palmer (1998) in *The Courage to Teach*. He strongly argues that teaching cannot be reduced to the use of techniques. Teaching is not about "how to do it," but it is about discussing our deep experiences as teachers. It is about teaching with our hearts, from a true sense of self, identity, and integrity.

An important implication from the previous findings is that these autonomy-supportive learning environments can be created with a range of pedagogical strategies, from simple techniques or small teaching interventions to larger broad-scale course transformations. In this chapter I will examine a variety of these strategies from the SDT perspective and propose that their effectiveness comes from the way in which they are used by instructors to support the creation of environments that are autonomy supportive (i.e., meet the basic psychological needs of autonomy, competence, and relatedness). These strategies are effective and lead to increased engagement and achievement of student learning outcomes as long as they foster the satisfaction of basic psychological needs. In short, throughout this chapter I will argue that the effectiveness of these strategies resides in how the learning activities or strategies are implemented and not in what types of learning activities, strategies, or by extension course redesigns are actually used (Bonem et al., 2019). Many of the strategies described in this chapter are ones that the college teachers featured in Ken Bain's (2004) book, *What the Best College Teachers Do*, implement naturally. In SDT terms, I would say that the teachers featured in Bain's book are autonomy supportive.

Small Teaching Strategies

Some small teaching strategies have been popularized by Angelo and Cross (1993) in their book on classroom assessment techniques (CATs). Two of these CATs, which are widely used in a variety of contexts and situations, are the minute paper and the think-pair-share. Adaptations of these small teaching strategies are also discussed in a recent book by James Lang (2016).

Minute Paper

The minute paper is very simple in its conception, practice, and application, but can be very effective at fostering engagement and active learning. Typically, a few minutes before the end of the class, the instructor asks students to take a piece of paper or a note card and answer two simple general questions. On one side of the note card, students could answer the following question: What about the class today was clear, or what did you learn? On the other side of the note card, students could answer the other question: What about this class could be further clarified, or what remains unclear? The instructor then collects the note cards and sorts through them and looks for common themes. This helps the instructor pinpoint common areas of misunderstanding or knowledge gaps as well as identify what is well understood by students.

One very effective variation of the minute paper is to ask students to complete this exercise after they have just attempted a task they may not have all the knowledge to successfully complete. This may be a difficult task or a problem that students will learn how to solve with the knowledge acquired in class. However, in this variation of the minute paper, they are asked to attempt it before they are fully skilled to be successful. This strategy helps students draw on any and all available knowledge they already have, and in that process they realize they do have important knowledge and experience to bring to the class. As they learn how to complete the task throughout the semester and build on previous knowledge, they will come to appreciate their ability to learn and grow. This helps spark learning for students. As they retrieve and work with that knowledge, they are creating what the authors of *Make It Stick: The Science of Successful Learning* call fertile grounds for new knowledge and skill acquisition (Brown et al., 2014). Furthermore, the students' partial or unsuccessful attempts to complete the task will give the instructor great insights into the current state of their understanding, knowledge they can use to shape the rest of the course or semester.

Conducting minute papers throughout this learning process can be very informative for the students and the instructor. The crucial piece of the minute paper is the provision of feedback. For students to feel that the insights they are providing regarding their learning process through the minute paper are valued and integrated into the structure of the course, the instructor needs to provide timely feedback to the students. The instructor needs to do so in a transparent way, sharing with the students, ideally at the beginning of the next class period, what insights have been extracted from the minute paper responses. These insights may include how the instructor will integrate that information in subsequent class periods, what changes may be made to the class or the learning activities presented, or how knowledge gaps or learning challenges will be addressed.

The minute paper pedagogy has also been described by James Lang (2016) as an example of a successful retrieving technique. In this variation, students are asked, a few minutes before the end of class, to answer a question related to a concept that has been covered in class that day. Instructors who have tried this have often been surprised by the proportion of students who can't remember enough of the material to answer the question correctly. Nonetheless, the informational feedback provided by the minute paper, both to the students and the instructor, is enough to lead to significant improvements in performance. In sections where the technique was implemented compared to sections in which it was not, the difference observed in failure rate was almost 20%! Another powerful variation is to present a problem at the beginning of class or a question and ask students to predict what will happen next or how the class period will unfold (Lang, 2016).

From the SDT perspective, regardless of which variation is used, the minute paper is successful because it helps foster an environment that is autonomy supportive, primarily by supporting the satisfaction of the needs for competence and autonomy. The informational feedback provided by the results of the minute paper fosters the need for competence. In addition, the opportunity to provide feedback to the instructor with this simple technique, especially if the instructor is diligent at summarizing what has been noted from the minute paper responses during the next class session, fosters the sense of autonomy. The act of seeking feedback from students fosters the need for autonomy since the students are able to express their opinions and provide insights on the course, the class, or a specific learning activity. The minute paper provides a way for students to give meaningful feedback to the instructor, which, when heard and acted on, provides a voice to the students. This fosters a greater sense of agency and autonomy, therefore supporting the basic psychological needs. In the most successful applications, when the feedback is integrated into the class and the instructor is responsive to the students' areas of understanding and misunderstanding, the students become participants, shaping the structure and content of the class. This is a key element of an environment that is perceived to be autonomy supportive through a sense of competence and belongingness. When students can see the effect of their participation in class it contributes to a feeling of community or belongingness, which helps foster the satisfaction of the need for relatedness.

Think-Pair-Share

In think-pair-share, students are asked to respond to a prompt or a question and spend some time trying to answer the question on their own. This amount of time can focus homework to complete before coming to class or a few minutes spent in class reflecting or working on the prompt. This part is the "think" portion of the strategy. During the "pair" portion of the strategy, students turn to another student in class or a group they are part of and discuss what they thought about, what they found, the answers to the problems, or how they arrived at the solution. Finally, in the "share" portion of the strategy, some students are asked to share the outcomes of the discussions with the whole class. The sharing portion could be framed in terms of things that were discovered that were unexpected, challenges encountered during the completion of the exercise, or elements that remain unclear and need to be further addressed. This technique can be implemented whether the students are typically working individually or in groups during the class period.

The think-pair-share strategy resembles another small teaching strategy discussed in Lang (2016)—the pause-predict-ponder teaching strategy. In this particular example, a professor teaching introductory French partnered with two experts in computer-assisted learning to develop the technique in order to help students improve their intercultural competence skills (Ogan et al., 2009). At various points while watching a short film, the film "paused," and a probe asked students to make a "prediction" about what would happen next. Possible outcomes were then presented to students, who had to select one and explain in writing why they chose this particular prediction. At the end of the short film, students would "ponder" the actual outcome of the film. Students would be asked to think and reflect on whether they had seen anything unexpected. If they made a mistake, they would be asked to reflect on why they made a mistake in their prediction and whether they could now explain what had happened even though their prediction was originally incorrect. Students then posted the results of their reflections in an online discussion board so they could read and review what others had discussed. As reported by the authors of the study, the use of this small strategy resulted in improved scores on exams.

From the SDT perspective, we can explain why the think-pair-share strategy is effective by examining the extent to which it fosters an environment that is autonomy supportive. In the think-pair-share, instructors are allowing students to reflect on their own as they try to answer a question or solve a problem and then write something down regarding the results of their reflection or their work. This act fosters the need for autonomy in students. The act of pairing and discussing with other students allows students to test their knowledge, insights, and ideas with other students in the class. This fosters the need for competence. The simple acts of asking students to think about the material and then giving them an opportunity to discuss with others foster both the need for autonomy and competence, because students are able to express their opinions and provide and receive feedback. If the think-pair-share is done in the context of an established group in class that remains stable over the course of the semester, then the act of pairing and discussing also contributes to foster the need for relatedness. In the last portion, the act of sharing with the larger class fosters the satisfaction of all three needs: competence, because the students are sharing the results of their reflections, which at this point have led to a better understanding of the concepts discussed; autonomy, because the students are given a voice that is heard in class; and relatedness, because the students have brainstormed and discussed their ideas in a smaller pair or group and are now sharing with the larger class, which fosters a sense of belongingness. In this process, students will realize that other groups of students in the class are having similar insights or challenges. During the share portion the instructor can encourage groups of students to ask each other questions either to clarify a point or ask for more details on the thought shared. I have reviewed here only a few small strategies with some of their common variations. Many other small teaching strategies (Angelo & Cross, 1993; Lang, 2016) are effective for very similar reasons and based on the same mechanisms.

Technology-Focused Pedagogical Tools

As I open this section on the use of technology to foster active learning, I would like to emphasize that although most of the instructors who participated in IMPACT used some kind of technological tool in their course transformations, these tools did not produce the autonomy-supportive learning environment or student learning. The tools are simply that—tools. They are really helpful in many cases at leveraging our ability to create student-centered learning environments, but the introduction of the tools does not produce the learning or make the learning environment student centered. Once again, it is far less what we do or what types of pedagogical tools or strategies we use, but it is how we implement these strategies that is most important and crucial at creating autonomy-supportive, student-centered learning environments. Again, the human factor needs to remain front and center in our work with instructors and the implementation of the transformations.

For example, the Classroom Students Response System (SRS), commonly referred to as "clickers," is a technology commonly used to foster active learning. When used well, the tool fosters peer-to-peer connections (Bruff, 2009) and helps create autonomy-supportive student-centered learning environments. It allows students to answer questions in class, in real time, and allows the instructor to uncover areas of misunderstanding or confusion. Typically, a problem is presented to students with a set of possible multiple-choice answers. The students use their clickers to enter their responses, and instructors can see in real time the percentage of students selecting each of the possible answer choices. If most of the students get the correct answer, then the instructor knows that the concept has been mastered and can move on. However, if the responses to the questions are diverse and show misunderstanding from students, then the range of responses can be used to spark discussions among students. The instructor can ask students to find someone in class who did not have the same answer to the question and discuss why they selected a particular answer. The instructor could ask the students to attempt to convince the other student that their answer is the correct one. In this example, it is not so much getting to the correct answer that is important, although it is certainly desirable, but it is the process of understanding and trying to defend and explain their position that leads to greater and deeper understanding of the concepts. After a short period of time, perhaps 5 to 10 minutes, students are asked to "vote" again with their clickers on their answers. Typically, the result is that a much greater percentage of students obtain the correct answer. Importantly, most of them are then able to explain why they changed their answer if they did, as well as why the correct answer is the right one. The students who initially had the correct answer but had to explain their position to a student who had a different answer now have a deeper understanding of the correct answer and why other students may get confused, because they had to go through the process of explaining their rationale to another student.

By this point in the chapter, you may have a good sense of how and why the use of technology tools might foster the satisfaction of the basic psychological needs. Can you make a prediction? What do you think?

From the SDT perspective, the use of clickers in the way described here allows the need for competence to be fostered in students by providing them an opportunity to test their knowledge and receive immediate feedback. The discussions that follow serve to deepen the students' understanding and help them strengthen their skills, which further fosters the need for competence. Student reflection on why they selected a particular answer in order to attempt to convince another student that their answer is the correct one, fosters the need for autonomy. It does so because it allows students to clarify their choices and own them. Doing this exercise with another student or a group of students fosters the need for relatedness and, when the answers are displayed in a graph to the entire classroom, helps the students feel they are an integral part of a community of learners and not the only one with a different answer. Instructors can also implement this technique using a low-tech alternative. Voting cards that are premade either by the instructor or the students work very well. These cards can be colored, one for each of the possible answers, A, B, C, D, and so on. The cards are then assembled on a metal ring. When the students come up with their answer, they select it from the ring of cards and display the chosen card by holding it in the air. What if you don't have any ready-made cards and you want to use the technique? You can also ask students to use their fingers to vote; one finger for A, 2 fingers for B, 3 fingers for C, and so forth. The important point here is that the particular technique used does not create the learning or the engaging environment; it is how and why you use the technique that does (Bonem et al., 2019).

Hotseat is another form of classroom response system, this one developed at Purdue. It provides all students a way to quickly and easily participate and engage in a productive backchannel discussion during class, providing a voice to students who may otherwise remain silent in class. It gives students an opportunity to engage with class content on their own terms and to think about what they want to communicate before they post a question or comment. In a large lecture class with hundreds of students, it's impossible to hear from everyone in class. In this situation as an instructor, you can call on different students in the class, some in different areas of the classroom, but it's still difficult to make everyone feel engaged and feel belonging in the classroom community. Using a technology like Hotseat or the clickers described previously allows you to do so. Hotseat lets the students post questions and comments using whatever technology they have at their disposal, such as texting directly with their phones, using an app, or using a desktop or laptop to access the Hotseat website. Students can post comments and questions anonymously, which encourages and empowers some students to participate and contribute. This fosters the need for autonomy. One advantage of using a high-tech way of gathering students' feedback such as Hotseat over the minute paper, for example, is that the students' comments and questions can be stored and viewed by the instructor online long after the class is over. Hotseat is a versatile technology and can be used in ways that are similar to the minute paper or the think-pair-share and therefore foster the creation of very similar autonomy-supportive environments by satisfying the basic psychological needs. Again, the technique or technology you choose to use (e.g., index cards versus Hotseat) is not as important as what you are trying to foster by using the tool. When you think about it, even your voice, as an instructor, is a tool! It is how you use your tools to engage students and create an environment that is autonomy supportive that is most important to consider and keep in mind.

Large Course Transformations

In this section I present a few examples of the types of course transformations that were completed as part of IMPACT and, by doing so, illustrate how student-centered, autonomy-supportive environments can be created in a variety of ways. These examples are by no means exhaustive, but they will help you get a sense of the breadth and scope of the transformations implemented and how they contribute to the creation of an autonomy-supportive environment.

Team-Based Learning

The team-based learning (TBL) strategy (Michaelsen et al., 2002, 2004; Sibley & Ostafichuk, 2014; Sweet & Michaelsen, 2012) has been the topic of many books and publications where the strategy is presented and its effectiveness at fostering critical thinking and engagement is discussed. It is based in four essential elements: (a) the effective use of teams, (b) the readiness assurance process (RAP), (c) the use of application activities, and (d) the importance of accountability. The implementation of TBL requires a commitment to examine beliefs about what good teaching is and how it impacts learning. It requires a shift in beliefs and thinking from a teacher-centered to a student-centered perspective. It requires the instructor to ask the question from the student perspective: What do I want my students to be able to do, know, or appreciate? TBL challenges the instructor to shift their role as teacher from a "sage on the stage" to a designer of high-quality, significant learning experiences, as well as a coach, facilitator, mentor, and guide (Fink, 2013). This philosophy is closely aligned with the overarching principles of SDT and the philosophy behind IMPACT. You can consult chapter 4 for more on this topic.

TBL is based on the concept of learning communities, which is also the structure we follow in IMPACT. It harnesses the power of teams and social learning combined with accountability structures. From the perspective of SDT, this concept is akin to the use of autonomy with structure, which is an important consideration when creating effective environments that are student centered. We need both the elements of autonomy in student choices and volition combined with the structure to lead to results (see chapter 3).

TBL provides a reliable and coherent framework to navigate the learning-centered class and fosters powerful results (Michaelsen et al., 2002, 2004; Sibley & Ostafichuk, 2014).

Autonomy without structure would not lead to productive results in the classroom context, as there are goals to achieve and milestones to reach. Autonomy without structure is akin to chaos and a free-for-all, which is not motivational! In contrast, too much structure would be perceived as controlling and would not provide the opportunity for students to identify with the activities and tasks to do and integrate with their overall learning. Just as our IMPACT transformations are very intentional and require deep reflection on the part of the faculty fellows, TBL requires intentionality and preparation. TBL is not a strategy that you can implement at the last minute and expect good results. It is a deep and risky transformation. But when done well, it can lead to powerful transformation and deeper student learning. For students, being part of a class in which a deep transformation like TBL is implemented may be unsettling if they are used to the large lecture format. At the beginning of any course in which a transformation such as TBL has been implemented, it is very important to explain to students what they are going to experience and why these design choices have been made. The provision of a rationale for the implementation and the use of such a strategy is very important. In order to feel self-determined, and for the environment to be experienced as autonomy supportive, students need to understand why the learning environment looks and feels so much different from the traditional classroom they are most familiar with. The students need to understand why they are asked to learn in a way that may challenge their preconceived notions regarding college classes. In SDT terms, the provision of a meaningful rationale for students is extremely important.

In this section, I will briefly review the core principles of TBL and in doing so apply the lens of SDT to understand why this pedagogy is so effective. Some of the IMPACT fellows have implemented TBL in their transformation. Notably, Marie Allsopp, clinical assistant professor of nutrition science, transformed her entire course following the TBL strategy.

The constitution of the teams in TBL is important and, when done well, creates an effective learning community. The teams need to be diverse, large, and permanent. When the teams are created following these principles, the members of the team are able to negotiate, following a give-and-take process, through productive disagreements, reflections, and defending their answers; this is where the deep learning occurs. The constant dialogue and peer teaching that occurs in the teams generate deeper understanding. If we apply the SDT framework, we could say that when the teams are effective and created well, the teams will foster the need for relatedness through the development of the learning community. The group dynamic that forms throughout the semester leads to a certain way in which the team members negotiate and discuss. Similar principles are applied when we form the teams in the IMPACT program (see chapter 4).

The RAP in TBL, at first glance, resembles what we traditionally think of as the assessment process or testing. However, in TBL, assessment is not about testing. It is about preparing the students and helping them get ready for the activities that will follow. It helps the students come to class prepared, being aware of what they know and don't know. Therefore, to be effective the RAP needs to be carefully aligned and integrated with the class learning activities. In the SDT framework, the RAP provides rich feedback to the students and highlights the functional significance of the assessment. It fosters the satisfaction of the need for competence by providing immediate informational feedback on one's understanding as well as knowledge gaps. TBL refers to the purpose of the RAP as providing immediate corrective feedback to the students as they prepare and get ready for the in-class application activities that will follow. In addition, when the purpose of the RAP is clearly explained to the student, and when a clear rationale is provided for this part of TBL, the RAP is not likely to be perceived as controlling like a traditional test would. As mentioned in chapter 3, providing a strong rationale for tasks that are necessary or perceived as difficult, boring, or tedious is a powerful way to create autonomy-supportive learning environments, even in situations where choice is not possible (Wang, 2019; Wang & Levesque-Bristol, 2019). In order to feel self-determined, students need to understand why and how they need to prepare for the RAP and see it as a way to gather feedback and prepare them to engage in the learning activities that follow. In the TBL literature, authors emphasize the need to "sell the technique" by emphasizing how "fun," "interesting," and "useful" it will be to solve complex real-world problems. The use of these qualifiers immediately reminds me of an autonomy-supportive environment through the provision of a meaningful rationale.

In TBL, there are two components to the RAP: an individual RAP, which is referred to as the iRAT (individual readiness assurance test), and a team RAP, which is referred to as the tRAT (teams readiness assurance test). In terms of the SDT framework, the individual accountability of the iRAT fosters autonomy as skills are being developed, because it allows students to figure out for themselves whether they know something or not. High-quality iRATs are not based on rote memorization and instead focus on important major concepts. In terms of SDT, the tRAT fosters the need for relatedness as students develop skills and deepen their knowledge as a team. Furthermore, each RAP session is followed by a debrief, which includes an appeal process and a mini lecture to clarify areas of misunderstanding. This process leads to even richer feedback, which informs and strengthens the learning and increases the perceived functional significance of the feedback. According to SDT, timely feedback is also an essential part of an autonomy-supportive environment, which fosters the need for competence and autonomy. This is something essential that we highlight in the IMPACT FLC.

The application activities are at the heart of a successful TBL implementation. The RAP without good application activities is useless, because the RAP serves as preparation for the application activities. When creating and developing the learning activities, the instructor needs to begin from the student perspective, start with the end in mind, and think about what they want their students to be able to do at the end of class. In terms of IMPACT, we follow a very similar approach during the FLC when we work with the instructors in creating learning outcomes. The learning outcomes need to be specific and measurable and focus on what the instructors want the students to be able to know, do, and appreciate by the end of the class (see chapter 4). TBL and IMPACT are informed by backward design principles (Wiggins & McTighe, 2005). In TBL, the learning activities are hands-on, conducted in class, and need to present a significant problem to students; that is, they need to be optimally challenging. A significant learning activity is one that is complex and meaningful and that can engage the entire team and draw in the different skills and perspectives on the team (Fink, 2013). Again, in terms of SDT, these types of problems foster the satisfaction of the need for competence. From the SDT perspective, I would add that these problems need to be appropriately complex and provide an optimal level of challenge. If they are too complex, they will be perceived as demotivating. If they are too simple, they will be perceived as irrelevant. Both situations will damage student self-determined motivation and lead to poor learning outcomes. In addition to being significant, TBL specifies that the same problems need to be used for the entire class, the teams need to decide on one specific answer, and the teams all need to simultaneously report their choice. In TBL, this is called the 4S framework: (a) significant problem, (b) same problem, (c) specific choice, and (d) simultaneous reporting. When the entire class works on the same problem, it fosters cohesion and enhances community building and relatedness. Specifying that each team needs to come up with one specific choice shifts the conversation from finding the correct answer to identifying the reasons for selecting a particular answer (Sweet & Michaelsen, 2012). This shift in conversation occurs because students need to feel comfortable with and understand why they are selecting a particular answer as they seek team consensus. In terms of SDT, this leads to a greater sense of relatedness and competence. Having to justify the reasons for selecting a certain answer also fosters the need for autonomy. Finally, requiring that teams reveal their agreed-on answer simultaneously enhances accountability and teaches cohesion through community building (relatedness). This process also motivates the team members to really take the activity seriously, because they will have to openly take responsibility for that answer.

In terms of SDT, this fosters the creation of a student-centered, autonomy-supportive environment by meeting all three basic psychological needs of autonomy, competence, and relatedness. There are various ways in which the instructor can conduct the simultaneous reporting. The standard approach often discussed in the TBL literature is the use of voting cards, which I have described previously. Alternatively, a more high-tech solution, such as the clickers, could be used. When the teams agree on their answers, they display their response simultaneously by holding up the card or placing the card in a highly visible place or submitting answers via clickers. Alternatively, sticky notes can be used, which can be displayed on the walls. Location here could be used to reinforce the different answers, one location per answer choice, making the disparity in the answers from the different teams immediately obvious. Otherwise, the answers could be written on huddle boards if those are available, one per team, or on a common whiteboard in the classroom, one color marker per team. How the answers are reported is not as crucial as the fact that a common answer per team is reported simultaneously.

It is important here to again note how critical it is that the problems presented to the class are significant, complex, and meaningful. If the problems are too easy, the answer is obvious, or the distractors are not plausible, then all teams are likely to get the same answer. Nothing kills class discussion like all teams revealing the same answer! From the SDT perspective, the lack of optimal challenge and the lack of follow-up discussions do not contribute to the satisfaction of the need for competence. To avoid this, the instructor needs to take the creation of the learning activities extremely seriously. This is also a point that we reinforce in the IMPACT FLC (see chapter 4).

The Concept Point Recovery Technique

This technique was created by an IMPACT faculty fellow, Mike Melloch, and implemented in an electrical engineering junior-level undergraduate course on electric and magnetic fields (Cho et al., 2019). This technique, however, could be easily applied to other courses in any discipline where exams are a large portion of the assessment mechanisms and concepts are important building blocks of the course.

As mentioned previously in this chapter and in previous chapters on SDT, exams tend to be primarily viewed by teachers and students as assessment exercises and are often perceived to be extrinsic motivators and therefore controlling. However, an exam can also be perceived as a learning activity or, in other words, a demonstration or celebration of knowledge (I have heard instructors refer to exams in this way!). Working a problem on an exam can be an elaboration exercise if it is structured in such a way to connect a course concept with something students already know. It can also be a great source of informational feedback if the exam is set up to provide the student with an opportunity to test their knowledge, receive feedback on their understanding, and try again. Typically, when exams are returned to students, most students spend minimal time examining the solutions and their responses, thereby missing a learning opportunity. Concept point recovery (CPR) fosters student learning by shifting students' focus from perceiving the exam as a way to evaluate them and control their behavior to an opportunity to learn and show their understanding; in SDT language, it shifts the E-PLOC to an I-PLOC (see chapter 2) (de Charms, 1968).

After each exam, provided that the students attended at least 80% of the class sessions where content was covered, they have an opportunity to recover all of the points on one problem. Each student has 15 minutes to explain to the instructor a problem of their choice that they missed on the exam. The incentive for the students is the possibility of recovering points lost on the exam. This is why this technique is called "concept point recovery." Very clever! If an exam consists of 10 problems, the possible point recovery is small enough to not influence the amount of effort students dedicate to preparing for the exam. However, an opportunity to recover up to 10% of the exam points is significant in many ways and leads to several important outcomes, such as deep learning, improved learning from exams, reduced exam anxiety, increased class attendance, and utilization of office hours. Let me discuss the advantages further.

In the current example, this junior-level course on electric and magnetic fields is a mathematically intensive course that relies heavily on using vector calculus. In this case, equations can quickly become meaningless mathematical abstractions for students who have little or no understanding of a concept. It takes considerable effort on the part of students to develop mental models of what these equations actually represent, which is essential to do well in the course. For the students to be able to teach the concept behind a problem, they must develop such mental models, and this fosters a focus on deep learning as opposed to surface learning. Knowing that they will have the opportunity to recover points lost by teaching a concept on a problem of their choice helps the students engage in studying in a deeper way and immediately start creating and building these mental models. This fosters the satisfaction for the need for autonomy and competence. To teach the material, the students cannot simply memorize a procedure or solution to a particular problem; rather, they must understand the concepts behind the equations, which fosters deep rather than surface learning. With the CPR teaching strategy, the student receives no points for only reworking the problem. The student must be able to explain the concept behind the problem to recover lost points. Therefore, most students will put in considerably more effort and understand the material more deeply as they learn the material to recover lost points on an exam. In addition, the act of teaching others contributes to the satisfaction of the three basic psychological needs of autonomy, competence, and relatedness and fosters the creation of an autonomy-supportive learning environment.

Most students do not spend much time reviewing a past exam. However, the CPR technique encourages students to do so in order to recover lost points. Students who experienced difficulty on several problems on their exam tend to spend time reviewing the concepts behind most of the problems they missed to determine which problem they should choose for their CPR teaching session. Through the process of selecting the right problem to present and how to best present the problem to the instructor, both the needs for autonomy and competence are fostered. In addition, because the problem is presented in person, one on one, to the instructor, it also contributes to meeting the need for relatedness, especially in students who would not have otherwise visited the instructor. As discussed in chapter 3, the relatedness to the instructor is the most important relatedness component predicting learning outcomes (Bonem et al., 2019). The CPR technique greatly benefits students who would not have otherwise come to office hours. The opportunity to recover lost points is a sufficient incentive to schedule their 15-minute session with the instructor. In addition, after their first successful experience with the CPR session following the first exam, students are likely to take the opportunity again following subsequent exams and approach studying differently. An autonomy-supportive instructor, through this one-on-one experience connecting with a student, will build and foster the need for relatedness in the students as they build greater experience. This first positive experience helps the students become more comfortable seeking the help of the instructor; builds relatedness with the instructor, which fosters future office hours visits; and in turn contributes to student learning and the satisfaction of the need for competence. Especially if you give an exam early in the semester, students who have not prepared well enough can then be advised on effective strategies to learn the material and better prepare for the next exam and their next CPR teaching opportunity. It provides a built-in opportunity for the instructor to meet one on one with the students and advise them, satisfying the need for competence through relatedness.

Many students experience anxiety preparing for and taking an exam, which affects their performance and thereby reinforces their anxiety. Knowing ahead of time and during the exam that they will have the opportunity to recover all lost points from one problem alleviates some of the anxiety students normally feel. If during the exam students have difficulty with a problem, they can move on to tackle other problems without becoming paralyzed by anxiety during the exam.

The CPR technique fosters class attendance in a positive and autonomy-supportive way. Unless a student has attended at least 80% of the lectures, they are not eligible to recover lost points on an exam. Therefore, instead of punishing students for not attending class, the opportunity to recover lost points provides a positive incentive for class attendance. In this particular redesign example, the implementation of the CPR teaching strategy resulted in attendance greater than 95% for all lectures.

The "Flipped" or Hybrid Transformation

If you have read anything lately on active learning pedagogies, chances are you read about the benefits of the flipped classroom. As James Lang (2016) noted in his recent book, active learning has become a sort of catch-all phrase used to describe situations in which students are first exposed to course content outside of the classroom and then spend time in class doing things like problem-solving and critical thinking. This model has been common practice in many of the humanities but has recently gained popularity over the traditional model in STEM disciplines. It is important to recognize, as others have done, that the flipped model often taught in active learning classrooms (ALCs) is not what produces enhanced learning experiences per se. As frequent contributor to *The Chronicle of Higher Education* Robert Talbert (2014) noted,

> The flipped classroom does not automatically provide . . . outstanding learning experiences. What it provides is *space* and *time* for instructors to design learning activities and then carry them out . . . But then the instructor has the responsibility of using that space and time effectively. And sometimes that does not work. (para. 8, italics in original)

The likelihood of successfully implementing a complex active learning pedagogy such as the flipped model or TBL is greatly enhanced by the professional development available to support instructors as they develop and implement the strategy. I will further elaborate on the importance of professional development and support for instructors as they implement complex active learning pedagogies in ALCs in chapter 8. The transformation that occurred in the mathematics department at Purdue was comprehensive, involved the many pathways through the applied calculus and calculus sequence, and followed the flipped model. In part based on recommendations from the Mathematical Association of America (MAA) national study (Bressoud et al., 2015), a team of instructors in the math department engaged in their reform/transformation as part of their participation in IMPACT in fall 2015. The recommendations of the MAA were very much in line with the work and philosophy of IMPACT and included goals such as the construction of challenging and engaging courses; the use of student-centered pedagogies and active learning strategies; and the coordination of instruction, including the building of communities of practice.

The Calculus Sequence

The transformation to a collaborative, problem-based learning environment in Calculus I and Calculus II featured learning activities that created an environment fostering the satisfaction of the basic psychological needs of autonomy, competence, and relatedness. Table 5.1 presents an overview of the features of the collaborative problem-based learning environment compared to the traditional learning environment.

TABLE 5.1
Course Features

Collaborative, Problem-Based Learning Environment	*Lecture-Based Traditional Learning Environment*
Programmatic interaction with peers, peer mentors, and faculty	Systematic direct instruction of mathematics content by worked examples
Routine formative assessment and feedback	No opportunity for interaction with others
Collaborative work and goals	No engagement or attendance expectations
Open-ended and conceptual problem types	No feedback except on quizzes and exams
Required attendance and expected engagement	Little to no student control over how class time is spent
Student control over how class time is spent	

The traditional, lecture-based learning environment follows a structure common to many math programs in institutions of higher education all around the country. It consists of three 50-minute lectures (Monday, Wednesday, and Friday) and two 50-minute recitations (Tuesday and Thursday) per week for the entire semester. New material is presented in a large lecture classroom with up to 500 students, with little to no interaction between the instructor and the students or among the students. Attendance is not tracked. Recitations are hosted by first-year graduate students in mathematics. Recitations are convened in small classrooms with fewer than 50 students per classroom and are used for answering questions on homework problems and taking quizzes. The graduate students are selected by a panel of faculty mathematicians based on their ability to teach. They receive a short training on how to conduct the recitations, which essentially amounts to going through as many homework problems as time allows. The amount of interaction in recitation will vary, but the structure is rigid and no other activities other than going over homework and taking quizzes are allowed during this time.

In contrast, the collaborative mode consists of one 75-minute large problem session (Tuesday) and two 50-minute small problem sessions/ collaborative learn recitations (Wednesday and Friday). The large problem session meets in a classroom with round tables with no more than 120 students per classroom placed into groups of three or four per table. The small collaborative sessions, which serve as recitations, are capped at 40 students. No new material is presented during the large problem session or the small collaborative sessions. The lectures are recorded, and students watch the lectures online before they come to the class to work on problems. However, attendance is tracked and mandatory for all students to facilitate continual engagement within student groups. This continual engagement fosters consistency and helps build the sense of community, which fosters the sense of relatedness.

The large problem sessions are used to introduce and work on new problem sets with procedural, open-ended, and conceptual items. One faculty instructor, three graduate teaching assistants, and three undergraduate teaching assistants facilitate these sessions. Each of the instructional staff is given extensive training in how to facilitate and lead a problem-based class session like this. In general, students have control over how class time is spent and are able to get on-demand assistance from their peers, peer mentors, graduate students, and the instructor. This allows students to get real-time help with problems or concepts they do not understand, fostering the satisfaction of the need for autonomy as students develop skills and competencies. Comments from students emphasize the advantage of being able to get access to help and answer questions in real time when issues arise, whether from the instructor or the teaching assistants. The students also appreciate the learning communities created by having the opportunity to work alongside other students in class, take notes, and compare their notes with peers as they work on real problems connected to what will be covered in the exams. These learning communities foster and satisfy the need for relatedness as students build skills and competencies.

The small collaborative sessions replace the traditional recitation. Like a traditional recitation, they are used for presenting problem solutions, reviewing homework, and taking quizzes. Unlike a traditional recitation, these small collaborative sessions involve extensive interactions among students, peer mentors, and graduate students, as students work on problems in small groups, which are permanent for the duration of the semester. This structure fosters a deep sense of community, satisfying the need for relatedness and competence, as students learn to work the problems. The small collaborative sessions are facilitated by a graduate teaching assistant and an undergraduate teaching assistant. Importantly, the student groups (and associated teaching assistant) from the large problem sessions are preserved within the small collaborative sessions, fostering a deep bond and partnership between students and teaching assistants. In these circumstances, autonomy-supportive environments are created through the satisfaction of autonomy, competence, and relatedness. The ability to work on the problems in class with other students, while help is available, is crucial in fostering competence and building this learning community, which fosters relatedness. Asking questions and watching lectures covering the new material on their own time foster students' autonomy. Overall, the transformation contributes to the satisfaction of the basic needs of autonomy, competence, and relatedness in a way that is not possible in the traditional section.

In both cases calculus students have access to recorded online lectures, but it is not required to view them. In the transformed collaborative "flipped" redesign, these are the only lectures available to students, and students can watch them on their own time either in preparation for the large problem sessions and the small collaborative sessions or afterward. In the traditional classroom design, the recorded lectures are optional, but the students are registered in a large lecture section that meets three times a week.

Whether based in the traditional design or the collaborative design, one of the significant common features of the calculus sequence is that the assessments are graded on a normative curve, which fosters a more controlling environment. As is the case with many calculus courses at institutions of higher education, in addition to the norm-based graded practices, the curve is set in a way that is not transparent. The grade curving process is typically determined by departmental and course policy. For example, in the math department at Purdue, the grade curving process and the distribution of the grades for the course are based on three common, multiple-choice midterm exams and a common, comprehensive, multiple-choice final exam. Homework, quizzes, and activities do not change the overall section grade distribution or average but can affect who in each section receives which grades from that distribution. Homework and quizzes help the students prepare for the exams but will not have a large influence on the student's grade in the course. The final grades are mostly based on the sum of the common exams and the cutoffs established from these exam scores. The goal to make the grade distribution uniform for the entire course, regardless of sections, makes a lot of sense if you are only concerned about uniformity across multiple sections of a course. It is also very advantageous when it is time to compare scores across sections that did or did not implement an IMPACT transformation. However, this uniformity and standardization can be very disadvantageous to students, especially in a semester in which a larger proportion of students are doing well or are coming in with previous experiences such as advanced placement (AP) courses from high school. Depending on the totality of the scores for every student in the class, grades cutoffs are established, which are then applied to each of the sections. Although approximate cutoff scores can be given to students at the start of the semester based on historical data, these are not likely to be the exact grade cutoffs for a particular semester. The cutoffs are all dependent on how well the entire body of students is performing, therefore fostering competition among students and heightening the level of anxiety in students who are not the strongest students in the class or are close to the next letter grade. Students can be bumped up or down in certain sections depending on their homework scores and the strength of the constitution of each section. However, the process by which this is done is not clear to the students and not known ahead of time as they are preparing for the exams. These practices and policies lead to the creation of environments that are perceived as controlling. It is not autonomy supportive to only allow a certain percentage of students, such as the top 10% based on a normal distribution, to obtain a grade of A, even if more students have done enough or learned enough to merit an A. These policies and practices diminish the potential influence of the autonomy-supportive IMPACT transformation.

This norm-based, nontransparent way of determining grades, in combination with the high-stakes multiple-choice assessments, fosters a competitive environment that is perceived as controlling. Research supports this assertion (Grolnick & Ryan, 1987; for reviews, see also Deci et al., 1999; Ryan & Deci, 2017). Grades and performance assessments can have two functional meanings (see also chapters 2 and 3). They can convey information or control. The informational aspect of the grade provides input about competence, which can affirm success and achievement, or ways in which one's performance could be improved if informational feedback is provided along with the grade. For example, the ways in which performance assessments are done as part of TBL and the CPR technique highlight the informational aspect of the grading process. The controlling aspect of the grade generally provides information about inadequacies and pressures the student to perform better or in a certain way toward specific outcomes that are imposed by external stakeholders (instructors, curriculum, administration). It is such because the feedback is not a reflection of the student's ability or learning, and thus the feedback is not informational. As discussed in chapters 2 and 3, informational feedback fosters an autonomy-supportive environment, whereas controlling or noninformational feedback fosters competition and controlling environments. This is especially real for students in calculus who have earned enough points to receive a letter grade of A in the class and have in principle learned and mastered the material, but they can be dropped to a lower letter grade because they are located in a strong section with more than 10% of students above the "A" grade cutoff. The norm-based practices in general emphasize the controlling aspect and meaning of the grades and not its informational meaning. The transformed course, using a collaborative, problem-based learning environment, fosters the satisfaction of the basic psychological needs of autonomy, competence, and relatedness and has been associated with significant gains in learning, improved course performance, and significant decrease in DFW rates; however, the assessments and grading practices mitigate those effects by adding a layer of controlling, nontransparent, and non-autonomy-supportive elements. These policies and practices reduce the influence of the course transformation. Unfortunately, these situations are common across many educational settings and most of the gateway STEM courses and should be part of a larger discussion around grading practices and the alignment of pedagogical transformations and assessments in higher education.

The applied calculus course sequence was also part of this overarching transformation, and it was designed in a very similar way except for one major difference. The main difference between the transformation in Applied Calculus I and Applied Calculus II, which is extremely significant in terms of student motivation and the creation of an autonomy-supportive environment that fosters learning, is the grading process. In applied calculus, the grading process is not normed. Therefore, the students clearly know on day 1 how many points are associated with each possible letter grade. Each student obtains the grade that reflects their own performance in the class, independent of the performance of other students in the class or their section. The process is completely transparent. In addition, the quizzes/worksheets that are completed in the collaborative problem sessions, which are worth almost the same as one midterm exam, fully count in the student final grade and not simply as a factor in bumping up or down the letter grade of students. Because all of the work students do, whether it is on quizzes, homework, or exams, counts toward the final grade, students have a greater sense of agency and autonomy as they grow in their understanding of the concepts and master the math skills. The transformation of the applied calculus course sequence also led to significant improvements in academic performance in the forms of increased course GPA and a decrease in failure rates, as expressed in DFW rates. These effects are in line with an increase in perceptions of autonomy supportiveness and satisfaction of basic psychological needs.

The Supplemental Transformation

The supplemental model is one in which the large lecture format is retained, but it is supplemented by active learning strategies that foster the creation of an autonomy-supportive environment. As described in Gundlach, Richards, et al. (2015), it can be a superior model for fostering the performance on certain learning outcomes. Another IMPACT fellow, Larry DeBoer, professor of agriculture economics, implemented the supplemental transformation successfully. When he tells the story of his transformation journey, he relates a moment in which he had an epiphany: Don't ask what you want your students to know; ask what you want your students to be able to do. This moment in IMPACT was transformational for him and allowed him to intentionally focus on the improvement of the ability of students to apply their knowledge, critically think, and solve problems. He used most of the teaching strategies presented in this chapter to transform his large lecture into a more active and engaging learning environment. He recorded lecture content into short videos, which he made available to students on demand. Some of the videos were short summaries of the lectures. Some of the videos were "how-to" videos, demonstrating the application of an important concept. Examining the data on the videos, he noticed that the videos that were most watched were the demonstration videos. As a result, he increased the number of "how-to" videos he created. He engaged the students in group projects and used regular, low-stress quizzes. He also made use of the Hotseat technology as a way to foster student engagement and create an autonomy-supportive environment. Because he wanted students to be able to become better at problem-solving and critical thinking, he organized most of the class time to emphasize interaction and collaborative learning and focused on application learning activities that fostered the development of these higher-order thinking skills. Results showed that performance on critical thinking and problem-solving significantly improved following the IMPACT transformation. The students greatly improved their performance on the analytical questions on the quizzes and exams. However, the students showed a decrease in the performance on the memorization questions. Because DeBoer wanted his students to become better able to perform well on analysis and problem-solving, and because he intentionally focused on those learning outcomes and associated learning activities in his transformation, these results made sense to him. As a result of his experience in IMPACT and the transformation, the nature of his exams and assessments shifted substantially. He modified his assessments so that none of the quiz or exam questions could be answered simply based on rote memorization. In his transformation, he focused almost exclusively on applications and analysis of concepts, which resulted in increased performance for those concepts. In addition, the learning environment was perceived by students to be autonomy supportive.

In sum, when we look closely and we apply the lens of SDT, the effectiveness of all the strategies described in this chapter can be explained by the principles of SDT: the creation of an autonomy-supportive environment through the satisfaction of the needs for autonomy, competence, and relatedness. Now when you examine other pedagogies, you may be able to conduct this analysis in your work with instructors, if you are a developer, or in your own teaching, if you are an instructor.

6

PROFESSIONAL DEVELOPMENT

As discussed in chapter 4, the application of SDT principles allowed us to take the IMPACT program in a different direction, from a mostly prescriptive course redesign model to a more flexible, autonomy-supportive model of professional development. The focus on SDT changed not only what we did and how we did it but also the emphasis and philosophy of the program. Through professional development, we prepare instructors to not only transform the course they are bringing to the IMPACT program but also examine their philosophy, attitude, and teaching practices so they can apply teaching and learning principles in new contexts and situations. This shift also encourages faculty to apply the skills they acquire during the FLC to other courses they are teaching, generating transformations in courses not directly impacted by the program. The number of "influenced courses" instructors have been able to transform has now reached the number of courses faculty fellows have directly transformed through their work with IMPACT. By aiming to satisfy the three basic psychological needs of autonomy, competence, and relatedness, we are engaging the faculty fellows and creating an environment in which they can safely and deeply explore and question their teaching practices and their teaching philosophy. The environment created allows them to discuss with other fellows their challenges and successes and find ways to integrate pedagogical practices in order to create learning environments that will foster the same engagement in their students. Our work is about helping instructors understand the importance of creating autonomy-supportive, student-centered learning environments that will meet the basic psychological needs for autonomy, competence, and relatedness for all students. Through supporting faculty fellows' basic psychological needs, the support teams engage a broad group of instructors in discussing teaching and learning, modifying their practices, and preparing instructors to transfer their knowledge and insights to new situations. These changes in faculty fellows from across the institution can spark the beginning of a broader teaching and learning culture change. Thus, IMPACT fosters instructors and course transformation rather than course redesign, and this is how culture change can occur, through professional development and instructor support. We empower faculty and instructors as catalysts for culture change through professional development. It is a sort of metacognitive and "meta-affective" exercise, engaging faculty fellows in thinking about what will engage their students by reflecting on the types of environments that contribute to motivate and engage them. When faculty fellows realize and deeply understand that students are humans just like them and therefore guided by the same motivation principles that contribute to engagement, well-being, and growth, they start to think, feel, and act differently in regard to their teaching. In IMPACT we foster this through the FLC by supporting the instructors' basic psychological needs of autonomy, competence, and relatedness. These lessons can be expanded and applied more broadly to professional development and our work as faculty developers, professional coaches, advisers, mentors, managers, and supervisors. In the following pages, I will explore some of these lessons learned and concepts in more detail.

Fostering Autonomy

Providing support for the need for autonomy during the FLC means that faculty fellows are provided choices with regard to their redesign strategy and goals. The IMPACT support team members do not prescribe a certain redesign model or a specific technology, but rather encourage faculty to clarify their redesign goals and desired student learning outcomes. The innovation of IMPACT is in part achieved through the realization that focusing on human potential and human needs, and therefore de-emphasizing the importance of a certain redesign model, technology, or classroom space as the most important factor in meeting learning outcomes, is the way to foster greater student engagement, growth, and success. We must consider the satisfaction of the need for autonomy in our interactions with the people we work with, and as a result we find ourselves spending less time focusing on the benefits of a certain type of redesign model or a certain pedagogical practice (e.g., team based, problem based), the benefits of a certain educational technology (e.g., clickers or Hotseat), or the advantages of putting a class online, and we spend more time listening to the expressed challenges of the instructors as well as their expressed interests and desired outcomes. We focus on the people we work with, their needs, their strengths, their skills, their goals, their desired outcomes. We listen. Then we propose appropriate solutions that will work for the instructors and help them meet their goals and tackle challenges. In our role as faculty developer, we support the instructors in their pedagogical development by coming alongside them and taking part in their journey, but it's nonetheless their journey. We can't force it or direct it. We can only create an autonomy-supportive environment in which instructors will choose to make changes to their pedagogical practices that will work for them; foster their own development; and in turn allow them to foster the growth, development, and success of their students.

How can the principles used to foster autonomy be applied more broadly to professional development activities in our roles with students (as advisers or mentors) and in our roles with our colleagues or staff (as professional coaches, mentors, managers, and supervisors)?

We gain trust by providing autonomy to people we work with, whether they are students, employees, or other team members. For example, in my work with students, when I'm mentoring or advising a student, I seek to support their need for autonomy by first understanding the student I'm working with. What are their goals, including not only professional goals but also personal goals? What do they want to accomplish in their program of study? What truly interests them? Why did they choose to study in the United States if they are international students? Do they plan to go back to their country of origin once they graduate? Only after understanding where the students are coming from and where they are wanting to go can I truly work with them to advise and mentor them in the best way possible. My goal when I advise or mentor a student is not to force them to become a mini version of me by following the path I followed. My goal is not to impose my values and my vision of what an appropriate career, a professional goal, or even a personal goal should be. My goal is to provide them with the environmental conditions and the resources they need in order to help them grow and develop in a way that meets their needs and their goals. This concept is simple but very hard to implement well. It requires practice and dedication. It requires an acceptance of failure when our attempts at mentoring in an autonomy-supportive way do not work immediately. It necessitates seeking feedback and asking questions from the people we work with. I have mentored students over the course of my career who have chosen very different paths based on their own interests. I'm fortunate to serve multiple roles at the university and function as a faculty member, director, and professional developer. But even early on in my career, as a tenured faculty member, my graduate students did not all become faculty members in research-intensive institutions. I did not push a certain path, nor did I emphasize a certain trajectory. I aimed to ask them "What is it that interests you the most? What questions do you have about different career paths?" When I did not have the answers, I sought to put them into contact with people who could inform them on their chosen trajectory or answer their questions. This approach also applies to the research they choose to engage in. The students I mentor are not forced to work on the research projects that I am currently working on. They are encouraged to pursue their own interests and research questions. In my current position, the work that I do with IMPACT provides me with access to large data sets useful in exploring research questions around motivation, instructional design, and pedagogies in higher education. The students are invited to work with these data sets and explore relevant research questions if that is what truly interests them. I provide them with the structure within my area of expertise around motivation and student engagement. But within that general structure, the students are provided choices and options to research what they want and what interests them. If the IMPACT work does not truly interest them, then they are encouraged to explore and pursue other research paths broadly related to motivation.

Similarly, in my work as director of a teaching and learning center, I also provide opportunities for my staff to follow their interests and engage in work that is meaningful and valuable to them. Of course, certain things in the center have to be done; we have to "keep the trains running," so to speak. Even though a majority of the staff time is dedicated to certain tasks that have to be done, about 30% of the staff time can be directed toward projects that truly meet their development goals and needs. For this portion of their work, staff members get to express themselves and pursue their interests, as long as these fit within the overall mission of the Teaching and Learning Center. Every member of the staff is provided with the opportunity to suggest new projects or programs to develop and new ways of doing things. Very importantly, I aim to carefully listen to the staff members when they suggest new programs or new ways of engaging the faculty and instructors they work with. The team members know and trust that their ideas will be listened to with respect. They know and trust that their ideas will not be dismissed immediately without consideration. They know that open dialogue is encouraged and welcomed. In my work with my staff, who are really more team members than employees, I strive to create an environment that is open and autonomy supportive, and where opinions can be freely expressed, even though they may, at times, challenge me personally.

Again, this is very difficult to do well. When you begin implementing autonomy-supportive strategies, you have to allow yourself to make mistakes. You have to be patient with yourself. You have to bring your entire self and being to the act of teaching, mentoring, leading, and it's difficult to do. It's a courageous act. As Parker Palmer (1998) wrote in *The Courage to Teach*, teaching, and I would say mentoring and leading, is about opening up, love, heartbreak, and courage.

> The courage to teach is the courage to keep one's heart open in those very moments when the heart is asked to hold more than it is able so that teacher and students and subject can be woven into the fabric of community that learning, and living, require. (Palmer, 1998, p. 11)

We must strive to value everyone's presence and recognize that everyone influences the dynamic of the work or learning environment.

> Seeing the classroom always as a communal place enhances the likelihood of collective effort in creating and sustaining a learning community. (hooks, 1994, p. 8)

In hooks's quote, the word "classroom" could be replaced by any environment in which learning occurs, be it the workplace, a partnership, a mentoring relationship, or a school. I'm bringing forward the ideas from these quotes, because they are useful in humanizing our work with people, whether it is our teaching or by extension our mentoring and leadership work. It is useful to understand that because we are humans, effective interactions with others need to draw on human principles, and this is where SDT and the construct of basic psychological needs become very useful in operationalizing effectiveness.

Importantly, however, this autonomy is not without necessary boundaries. As discussed in chapter 3, it is about providing autonomy with structure (Jang et al., 2010). The structure may be the 70% of the work that has to be done to "keep the trains running." It may be about certain metrics of performance that need to be met. It may be about the budgetary constraints that are imposed on the institution or the unit. It may have to do with the leadership philosophy of the top administrators at the institution. There is a structure that can't be ignored, but within that structure, there are many opportunities for personal interests and values to be expressed and acted on. Regardless of the reasons for the structure or constraints, as a leader it is imperative to work within these constraints and explain to the team members the reasons behind these boundaries. Clearly here, the provision of a meaningful rationale for the structure in place is very important, especially if the structure is likely to be experienced as a constraint or provided for tasks that are required, imposed, or uninteresting (Reeve et al., 2002). Then, when the reasons for the structure are understood and when the parameters are clearly established, providing choices and options within this structure is crucial in order to be successful at creating an environment that will be motivating, empowering, and engaging. Team members can then propose solutions, new ideas, and ways to meet their goals and follow their interests and passions within this structure. In doing so, people are afforded agency, which gives them a sense of ownership over their life and their behaviors and gives them the opportunity to integrate what they do at work with their overall personal life, vision, and goals. This fosters the satisfaction of the basic psychological needs and moves the level of motivation toward greater internalization and greater levels of self-determination and toward forms of motivation such as identification and integration (see chapter 2, Figure 2.1).

Why is this a good way to manage and lead? Because people are our most important asset and investing in people is our most important responsibility. SDT predicts that a greater level of autonomy support is associated with higher quality engagement and wellness in the workplace. In turn, greater levels of autonomous motivation reported by staff members are less likely to be associated with the experience of physical and emotional exhaustion, burnout, and ill-being (Richards et al., 2018). Staff who perceive their work environment to be autonomy supportive are more likely to exhibit high levels of performance, remain committed to their work, and feel happier and more satisfied at work. This is even more important if the work performed requires a great investment of energy, care, thought, or creativity (Moran et al., 2012; Otis & Pelletier, 2005).

Fostering Relatedness

Providing support for the need for relatedness during the FLC means that we, as an IMPACT team, are aiming to create an environment in which connections between faculty fellows and between faculty fellows and support team members are facilitated and encouraged. In the focus groups conducted at the end of the FLC, faculty fellows report that the opportunity to create meaningful connections with other faculty fellows and the support team members is one of the most important and beneficial aspects of the IMPACT program. The FLC provides a space to regularly exchange ideas and observations and to share challenges and successes with other instructors, educators, instructional designers, and developers who are experiencing very similar things in their classrooms or as part of their professional consulting and development work. The aim of the support team members in regard to supporting the need for relatedness is to create an environment in which belonging and trust are cultivated and fostered. It begins with an intentional focus on the instructor going through the IMPACT program, sharing their design goals, challenges, concerns, and hopes for their students and their class. The support team members have to commit to the practice of active listening and take the perspective of the faculty fellows when working with them on the course transformation. As mentioned previously, the great innovation of IMPACT is to focus on human potential and human needs and therefore de-emphasize a prescriptive model focused on the importance of a certain redesign model, technology, or classroom space.

How can the principles used to foster relatedness be applied more broadly to professional development activities in our roles with students (as advisers or mentors) and in our roles with our colleagues or staff (as professional coaches, mentors, managers, and supervisors)?

It is important to invest in our relationship with people. In that process, we aim to truly listen to and become deeply interested in the people we work with. It is tiring work to really get to know people and build thoughtful connections with them, but it is undoubtedly the only way we can create lasting transformations in people, which would lead to meaningful change. When we are engaged with people in a work relationship, be it through mentoring, advising, managing, or supervising, we need to respect and acknowledge what the other person is bringing to the interaction and where they are coming from. We need to start where they are and come alongside them on their journey. We need to be present to the person we are working with and actively listen. It is very difficult to do this well, especially if we are tired or feel pressured. Self-care is therefore very important if we are going to be called to supervise, mentor, or lead others. The mentoring or professional relationship we have with others is about leading with compassion and heart. We can do so by taking and understanding others' perspectives, listening to others' concerns and hopes, and creating environments where it is safe to explore, experiment, fail, receive feedback, and try again. This is the way to create autonomy-supportive environments. The people we supervise, especially if we had the opportunity to be part of their selection and hiring process, were chosen because we valued their expertise and what they brought to the table. We saw something in them that we appreciated, valued, or wanted to foster; therefore, we need to continue to nurture them and value their lived experience once they join the team. We have not selected everyone we work with; nevertheless, we need to seek and be open to seeing the unique value, talents, and potential they bring to the table and the work to be done.

What I am sharing in this section may sound too soft and fuzzy, but it is so important in our work with human beings. Our work as mentors, facilitators, and developers is less about the tools and techniques we provide to people we work with and more about how we care and treat them as part of the team. Hopefully, by this point in the book, you have come to expect that this is what I'll emphasize and recommend. Focus more on the people you work with, their needs, their entire person, their emotions and feelings, and how and why you engage in the work that you do and less on the techniques and nuts and bolts of the work itself. In her recent book, *The Spark of Learning: Energizing the College Classroom With the Science of Emotion*, Sarah Rose Cavanagh (2016) demonstrated the science behind the importance of various affective states such as interest, curiosity, and flow (Csikszentmihalyi, 1990) to energize motivation and learning. It's not just about fluffy, fuzzy feelings. Importantly, watch your tone. We can convey so much in the tone of our voice and how we choose to speak to people. A tone that is belittling or demeaning is more than enough to create a controlling environment, even if the words spoken are with good intentions. These concepts, guided by SDT, are incredibly simple but very difficult to implement well, but it is essential to try to do so—every day. I fail at it many times a day, but I am always committed to learning from my failures, treating them as learning opportunities, seeking and welcoming feedback, and trying again.

Fostering Competence

Providing support for the need for competence during the FLC means that faculty fellows are guided to succeed in working through the transformation. Each week, they are provided with meaningful tasks and activities, either through prework or during the FLCs, in order to make progress toward the creation of meaningful and clear learning outcomes as well as learning activities and assessments in alignment with these learning outcomes. Each week, faculty fellows are also guided to reflect on the ways in which the basic structure of the course (e.g., content, learning activities, assessment tasks) can be presented in a way that is engaging for the student, in a way that is student centered and autonomy supportive. As IMPACT support team members, we constantly encourage the faculty fellows to think about how the skills and competencies they aim to foster in their students can be developed in an environment that is autonomy supportive. Our own research supports this assertion. Although the need for competence is often a proximal predictor and a most important factor in predicting learning outcomes and student success including grade, the satisfaction of the needs for autonomy and relatedness are essential contextual motivational factors supporting the effect of the need for competence (Levesque-Bristol et al., in press; Wang et al., 2020; Yu & Levesque-Bristol, 2020). There is significant overlap among the satisfaction of the three basic psychological needs of autonomy, competence, and relatedness (Vansteenkiste & Ryan, 2013). This overlap is often difficult to disentangle in conceptual and theoretical models aiming to understand the relationship among the three basic psychological needs and how they each affect the attainment of perceived and actual learning outcomes. Some of the research conducted in our own lab has highlighted these complexities in the interrelationships among the three basic psychological needs (Levesque-Bristol et al., in press; Yu & Levesque-Bristol, 2020). Nonetheless, it is clear from drawing on the theoretical models, the results of the research based on those models, and our own observations that the three basic psychological needs are crucial in fostering engagement and in turn well-being and success for instructors and students. Helping faculty fellows build competence toward their transformation in an environment that is fostering autonomy and relatedness is crucial for the growth of a program like IMPACT at scale. In turn, faculty fellows learn how to foster students' competence in an environment in which autonomy and relatedness is also fostered. This is paramount to cultivating growth, health, happiness, and success in students and instructors. Our role as developers, instructors, and mentors should be to not merely foster the development of skills but foster the development of those skills in environments that are autonomy supportive, engaging, and positive, promoting and fostering the growth and development of the entire person.

How can the principles used to foster competence be applied more broadly to professional development activities in our roles with students (as advisers or mentors) and in our roles with our colleagues or staff (as professional coaches, mentors, managers, and supervisors)?

Here once again, the importance of structure and autonomy must be emphasized (Jang et al., 2010). One of the many important roles of an educator is to foster the development of skills and competencies. There is no doubt about that. But how can we most optimally foster the development of these skills and competencies? It is important, according to SDT, that we do so in an environment that is autonomy supportive. One important way to do so is through scaffolding and the provisions of optimal challenges. I do so in a very similar way whether I am working with my students or with the members of my team. I begin by considering student or staff interests. From there, we discuss together how their interests can be shaped in ways that can meet the assigned goals of a program of study or the performance metrics of the unit. We collaboratively negotiate those parameters, and then we structure the activities and tasks to complete so they build on each other, each one being a stepping-stone for the successful accomplishment of the other. The tasks selected need to be optimally challenging. That is, they need to be challenging but within reach. The difficulty or complexity of the task or activity must be right outside or right on the edge of the person's current level of skills or competencies. In other words, the jump in skills needs to be difficult but within reach with the proper support and resources. If the task is too easy, it leads to boredom; in contrast, if the task is too challenging, then it leads to frustration, because success is not attainable at the time, given the person's current level of skills (Csikszentmihalyi, 1975, 1990). The work of Dee Fink (2013) on the creation of significant learning experiences is also relevant here. Also, crucially important to supporting the need for competence with the students we mentor and the staff we supervise is providing plentiful, appropriate, constructive, timely, and relevant feedback. As discussed in chapters 2 and 3, the feedback needs to be informational in order to support the need for competence. Although we provide some examples in chapter 2 and chapter 3, it is useful to go over this concept here in the context of professional development. What does it mean exactly for professional development? What does it look like in practice to provide informational feedback as a way to support the need for competence?

Informational feedback is quality feedback that provides information to the person as to how to improve on their future performance (Ryan & Deci, 2017). Informational feedback is supportive, positive, and constructive. Informational feedback provides clear guidance on the elements of the tasks that were performed well and the elements of the tasks that are in need of improvement. In addition, it provides information on the factors determining why it was done well, in addition to the reasons why improvements are needed or necessary and the parameters for an improved performance in the future. Being able to try at a task, receive informational feedback, and then be given an opportunity to try again is most important to support the need for competence and create environments that are engaging, person centered, and autonomy supportive. In addition, an important component of informational feedback from the other person's perspective is that the manager or supervisor needs to be able to hear the feedback they receive from those they guide, supervise, or mentor. In contrast, feedback that is not informational is negative, critical, and controlling. Here again, the importance of tone should be mentioned. When feedback is provided, ensure that the messages match the tone in which you convey the message. A supportive message delivered with a demeaning tone will not have positive effects on the recipient and will not be experienced as autonomy supportive.

For example, going back to something discussed earlier in the section on autonomy, in my work with students and the staff members on my team, I aim to provide a clear structure with goals to achieve but then also provide the opportunity and the space for them to negotiate those boundaries and that structure and come to a common understanding regarding aims and goals. It is important to emphasize again that autonomy and choice are not without boundaries. Autonomy with competence is autonomy with structure. It's not a free-for-all. The structure is often necessary and put in place by a program of study, a supervisor, the need of the department or college, or the larger institution in order to achieve important aims and goals. As mentioned earlier, the structure may be about the work that has to be done, the elements of the work or the program of study that are nonnegotiable, or certain metrics of performance that we need to meet in order to show proficiency, such as for program or institutional accreditation. Contingencies can be perceived as constraining. However, in an autonomy-supportive environment, these constraints are reframed as structure and the need for the structure is explained to the students, the staff, or the people on the team, the people we are entrusted to lead, manage, or advise. Under these circumstances, motivation that is instrumental or performed as a means to an end can still be self-determined, as in the case with the forms of motivation associated with identification and integration. Autonomy-supportive leaders are able to explain the reasons behind the required structure and listen to people as they express concerns or frustrations with the structure. As mentioned previously, the provision of a clear and meaningful rationale for the structure in place is very important for team motivation and morale (Reeve et al., 2002). Then, when concerns have been heard, ways to provide options and choices within that structure have been considered and identified, and parameters have been established, people are more likely to understand and come to value the importance of the structure and endorse the reason for its necessity. At that moment, the perceived imposed constraint becomes more of an understood and valued structure, which actually contributes to the creation of an autonomy-supportive, engaging, and productive learning or working environment. In doing so, people are afforded agency and competencies, which gives them a sense of empowerment and ownership over behaviors; it provides meaning to their lives and fosters a sense of integration between the different aspects of their lives, as well as a way to meet challenges and reach valued goals.

But Wait! Will I Not Lose Control of My Classroom or My Team?

Amid all this discussion of basic psychological needs satisfaction, is there not a risk that providing too much autonomy support will lead to chaos? Is there a chance I will lose control of the students in my classroom, my graduate students, or the people on my team by providing them with so much autonomy? People need to be told what to do, right? What about classroom management issues? That's important, right? What is the risk of implementing all these autonomy-supportive strategies?

Although it is common for instructors to fear change as they shift their paradigms (hooks, 1994), the only thing you risk losing by implementing the autonomy-supportive strategies presented in this chapter and throughout the book is unhappy and unproductive staff, employees, colleagues, and students. Research and our own experience working on the IMPACT program support this statement. You can only gain by consistently using the strategies presented in this book and trusting in the process of healthy growth and human development. You will gain not only productivity but also growth and wellness for yourself and your team. This is the case because it is also much more beneficial for you as a supervisor, manager, developer, or leader to lead with autonomy support and aim to create engaging and autonomy-supportive working and learning environments. If I could summarize what we have been discussing in this chapter by extracting a handful of main concepts for supporting autonomy, I would emphasize the importance of the following:

- Supporting others' initiative, choice, and agency
- Understanding others' perspectives
- Providing informational feedback
- Providing autonomy within a structure
- Providing a sound rationale for the structure

It will take time to build autonomy-supportive learning or work environments. Especially if the environments have been controlling for quite some time, changing the culture to a more autonomy-supportive environment will take patience, consistency, and a true change in attitude. However, over time, as autonomy support from leaders, managers, and supervisors grows, the employees or students supervised will become more trusting of the relationship, which will then lead to higher levels of autonomous motivation, engagement, well-being, and satisfaction in not only their program of study or the workplace but also the larger organization and upper-level administrators, which are often many layers removed from the person directly supervised (Deci et al., 1989; Harde & Reeve, 2009). These effects also translate into substantial economic savings for the organization (Forest et al., 2014), which is meaningful in the long run. Working and supporting human potential is not a quick or easy fix, but it's a long-lasting one that will lead to transformation and culture change. Every other week, the support team members meet with the members of the IMPACT management team and debrief the weekly FLCs. What is going well? What is challenging? We also provide each other support and seek to continuously develop as we continue to work toward creating these autonomy-supportive learning environments with the faculty fellows. Each semester is different and brings new challenges that we face using the lens of SDT.

Investing in humans and human growth and potential is the critical innovation I have been discussing throughout this book. It is simple and does not cost much to implement, unlike a fancy technology solution or software program to track student engagement, for example. However, it takes deep commitment from the people engaging and supporting the transformation; it is "heart" work, and, in this sense, it is extremely difficult work, which calls on us to be vulnerable. To reduce our vulnerability, we disconnect from people and ourselves. Especially in an era in which we are bombarded by social media gadgets and inundated by things to read and things to do, it almost seems that as humans we have forgotten how to be humans—the power of slowing down, sitting down, connecting, and engaging in a deep conversation and exploration with other human beings. Once again, I am reminded of the writings of hooks (1994) and Palmer (1998). Teaching is a human endeavor; it's not about tips and tricks, and it cannot be reduced to teaching techniques. It is about creating powerful learning environments in which people can grow and develop, teachers and students together.

> If we want to develop and deepen the capacity for connectedness at the heart of good teaching, we must understand—and resist—the perverse but powerful draw of the "disconnected" life. How, and why, does academic culture discourage us from living connected lives? How, and why, does it encourage us to distance ourselves from our students and our subjects, to teach and learn at some remove from our own hearts? (Palmer, 1998, p. 35)

> More than ever before in the recent history of this nation, educators are compelled to confront the biases that have shaped teaching practices in our society and to create new ways of knowing, different strategies for the sharing of knowledge. (hooks, 1994, p. 12)

7

ASSESSMENT

Documenting IMPACT's Effectiveness

From the onset, the IMPACT partners collaborated to evaluate the effectiveness and outcomes of the IMPACT program. Although over the years adjustments have been made based on prior results, feedback from the administration, or changing emphases and needs, the assessment of the program generally focuses on the following areas:

- Faculty change and professional development
- Student engagement
- Student academic outcomes and retention
- Student learning outcomes
- Institutional change, culture change, and sustainability

Staff from the partnering units facilitate the monitoring and evaluation activities for IMPACT in all five areas, which include comprehensive data collection, analyses, and reporting. Because IMPACT is part of Purdue Moves, monthly short reports on various aspects of the program outcomes are sent to the president's office. The partner units also collaborate on research studies examining faculty development, institutional change, cultural change, student engagement and student learning. Additional ongoing scholarship of teaching and learning (SoTL) conducted in partnership with IMPACT faculty fellows contributes to a greater understanding and use of empirically derived effective learning and teaching practices institution wide. In this chapter, I will provide an overview of the comprehensive IMPACT assessment plan, with examples of surveys and measures we used to assess the different target areas. This presentation of the ways in which we assess IMPACT is not meant to be exhaustive, but it is intended to be a guide to provide assessment ideas to those who would like to engage in similar work and are interested in how to measures such constructs.

Faculty Change and Professional Development

The first area of the overall assessment plan focuses on faculty change and professional development. It draws from multiple sources of information, including self-report surveys and focus groups. This assessment area provides information on the effectiveness of the professional development program from the instructors' perspective.

Data Collected: Preparticipation, Post-FLC, and Postimplementation Self-Report Surveys and Post-FLC Focus Group Interviews

To evaluate the faculty development process, the ELRC obtains data from all IMPACT faculty fellows prior to the start of their participation in the program, on the last FLC session, and following the fellows' first implementation of their course transformation. Before the start of the program, following their participation in the FLC, and after the implementation of the transformation, faculty fellows complete self-report surveys. These surveys include measures of instructors' perceptions of learning and self-efficacy (e.g., ability to develop clear learning outcomes, self-efficacy for student-centered instruction), teaching and learning practices (e.g., satisfaction with teaching and assessment methods), and perceived student engagement and development of skills. During the final FLC session, the ELRC conducts focus groups with all IMPACT fellows. These focus groups engage faculty fellows in discussions about the benefits of participation as well as unanticipated outcomes and allow faculty fellows the opportunity to provide constructive feedback about the program and share their perceptions of the institutional climate for teaching and learning.

Data collected from the preparticipation and postimplementation self-report surveys show that the faculty fellows view IMPACT as a valuable source of professional development that positively influences their level of self-efficacy, their teaching practices, perceived student engagement, and student outcomes. Conducting the FLCs in an autonomy-supportive way following SDT motivation principles fosters engagement in faculty. As they create those autonomy-supportive environments, they notice change in their students in line with SDT principles and the effect of an autonomy-supportive environment on student outcomes. Based on data gathered from IMPACT faculty fellows (n = 100), we note significant increases in the areas of perceived student engagement, satisfaction with their teaching, their pedagogical practices, and experience with classroom learning spaces after implementing their IMPACT transformations (Impact Management Team and IMPACT Evaluation Team, 2017, 2018, 2019; Levesque-Bristol, Flierl, et al., 2019; Levesque-Bristol, Maybee, et al., 2019; Parker & Nelson, 2019). The IMPACT annual reports are made available on the IMPACT website. As seen in Figure 7.1, faculty fellows report increased engagement and active learning in their students following the implementation of their transformation. In addition, faculty fellows report that their students are demonstrating improved critical thinking skills and study habits.

Faculty fellows also report increased satisfaction with their teaching following the implementation of their transformation. Notably, fellows report significant increases in their satisfaction with the support they receive from their teaching assistants as well as their assessment methods (see Figure 7.2).

Very interestingly and importantly, IMPACT faculty fellows also report significant improvements in their pedagogical practices, including their ability to create clear learning outcomes and provide individualized feedback to students (see Figure 7.3). In addition, although technology is not a focus

Figure 7.1. Student engagement as reported by faculty fellows pre-IMPACT and post-IMPACT implementation.

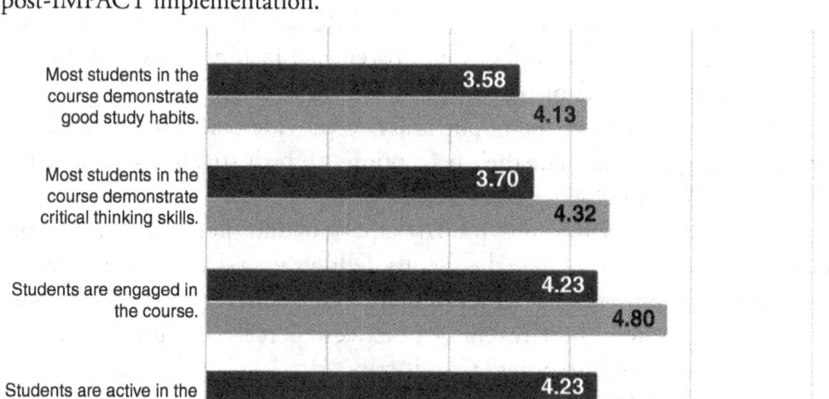

Figure 7.2. Teaching satisfaction as reported by faculty fellows pre-IMPACT and post-IMPACT implementation.

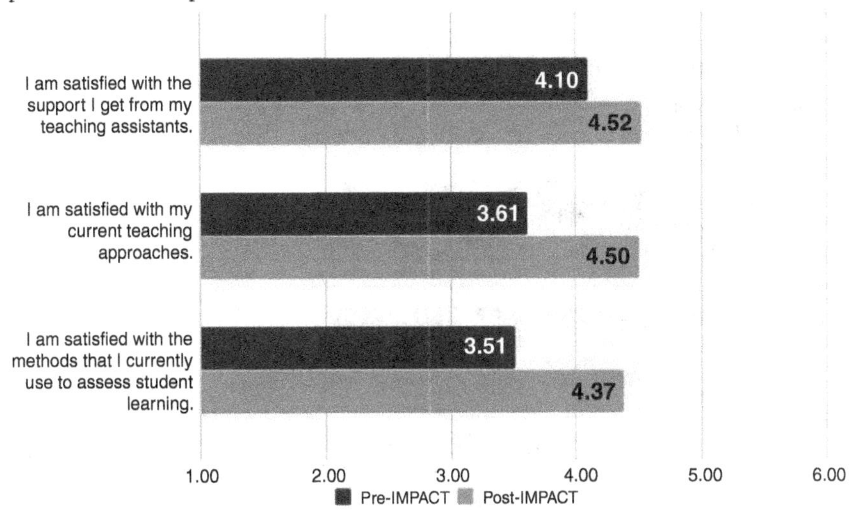

of the IMPACT redesigns, the appropriate use of technology tools to foster student engagement is. As seen in Figure 7.3, faculty fellows report significant improvement in their ability to incorporate instructional technology effortlessly in order to support student engagement.

Figure 7.3. Pedagogical practices as reported by faculty fellows pre-IMPACT and post-IMPACT implementation.

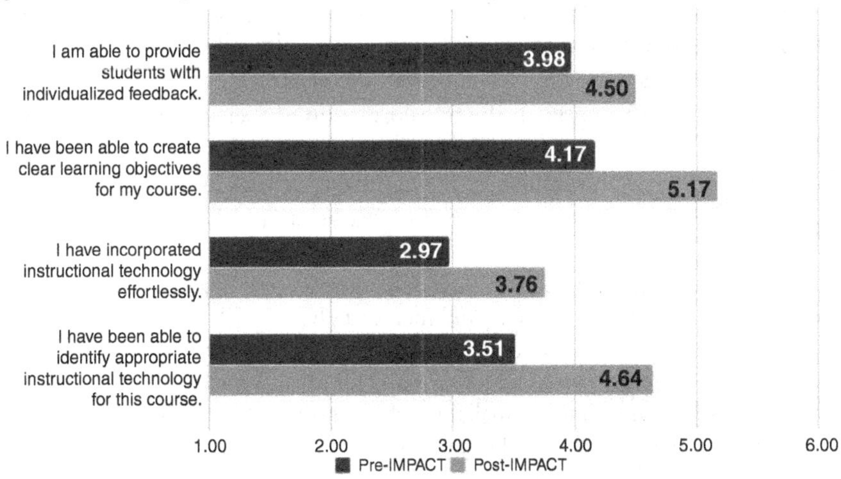

Figure 7.4. Learning space satisfaction as reported by faculty fellows pre-IMPACT and post-IMPACT implementation.

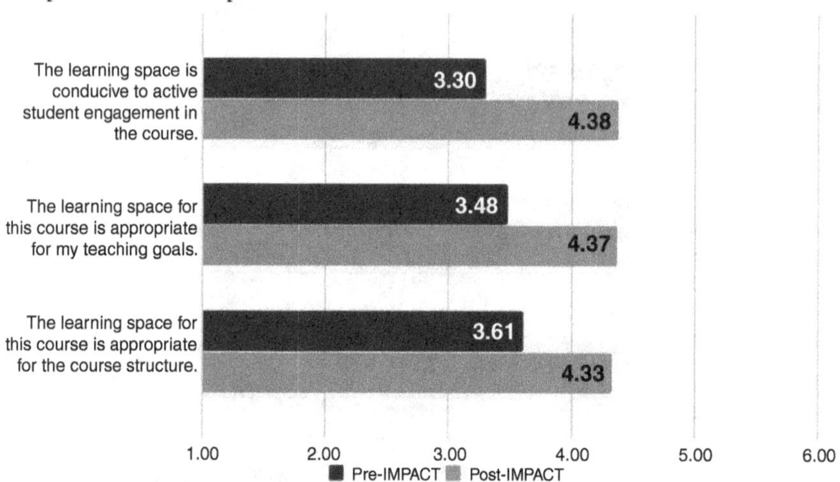

IMPACT faculty fellows also report improvements in their perceptions of the learning spaces that they are assigned to teach in after their experience with the IMPACT program (see Figure 7.4.). Sometimes these are active learning spaces, but sometimes they are not, depending on availability of classroom spaces on campus. Nonetheless, after the IMPACT professional development experience, faculty fellows are more comfortable teaching in any learning space on campus.

The data collected during the in-depth focus groups conducted on the last FLC session reinforce the quantitative data obtained from the self-report surveys and those presented previously (Parker & Nelson, 2019; Zywicki & Beaudoin, 2016). When asked to describe their experiences, faculty fellows report investing significant time reflecting about their course, their learning outcomes, and learning objectives as they engage in the transformation of their course. It turns out that working on clarifying learning outcomes is an important process that, when done well, transpires and influences the entire course transformation. As stated by a faculty fellow interviewed as part of the Parker and Nelson (2019) study:

> [I] went to the learning, the learning outcomes were put together and then the specific learning objectives. And then that's how I planned my lectures. That's how I write every exam. That's how I write every quiz. Is looking at those learning objectives. And it's very easy for me to hand that over to my [teaching assistants] and say make sure that you're teaching to the learning objectives, the students see the learning objectives so they know what to expect. And it clarifies everything. (2013 post-implementation focus group participant; Parker & Nelson, 2019)

IMPACT faculty fellows also emphasize the importance of the support they receive from the support teams as they work on the course transformation and the collegiality of the FLC experience as important contributing factors to their success (IMPACT Management Team and Evaluation Team, 2017, 2018, 2019). When asked about the single most important aspect of their IMPACT experience, overwhelmingly faculty fellows mention the interactions with other fellows and/or the IMPACT support teams and program facilitators (Zywicki & Beaudoin, 2016). They also indicate that opportunities to engage in dialogue and interact with supportive peers and colleagues regarding teaching and learning, share knowledge, obtain new ideas, and hear about successes or challenges are extremely valuable aspects of the IMPACT program (IMPACT Management Team and IMPACT Evaluation Team, 2017). The faculty fellows also highlight the importance of the flexibility and autonomy they are afforded as they engage in course transformation, so the changes made are based on and guided by what the instructors think is best for the students in their course. Throughout the results of the surveys and focus groups, clear themes emerge around the satisfaction of the basic psychological needs of autonomy, competence, and relatedness to explain and describe the effectiveness, influence, and success of the program for instructors' perceptions and teaching practices. The focus on student engagement was also paramount. Faculty fellows report that students are less likely to fall asleep while in the classroom and also less likely to be distracted by technology gadgets. As expressed by one faculty fellow:

> One of our biggest hurdles is getting the students engaged. And even to the point that they want to learn what we're trying to teach them. So I think that going through this course redesign has helped me a lot with that. Giving the students more ways to get engaged. (2013 postimplementation focus group participant in Parker & Nelson, 2019)

Student Engagement

The second area of the overall assessment plan focuses on student engagement. It is drawing from classroom observations and self-report surveys. This assessment area provides information on the effectiveness of the IMPACT course transformation from the students' perspective.

Data Collected: Classroom Observations and Self-Report Surveys

As faculty create environments that are autonomy supportive, we would expect to notice the effects on students who would experience and demonstrate a greater level of self-determined motivation, satisfaction of basic psychological needs, and a greater level of engagement. In order to evaluate this component in the beginning of the IMPACT program, when only a handful of faculty fellows and courses were part of the program, the ELRC conducted classroom observations based on an adaptation of the Reformed Teaching Observation Protocol (RTOP) (Piburn et al., 2000; Sawada et al., 2002, 2020). The RTOP requires observers to evaluate the pedagogical practices of instructors against best practices for engagement that are specific to STEM disciplines. Although the use of such a protocol to gather information regarding the classroom learning environment provides rich and detailed data, significant time and money are required to train observers and conduct the observations using such protocols (Meyer et al., 2011). As the IMPACT program grew and expanded to all the colleges at Purdue, the use of the RTOP procedure quickly became unsustainable and not easily applicable to non-STEM disciplines. The team began to explore the use of nonobservation protocols based in self-report surveys (Morris et al., 2014). Eventually, focusing on the goal of IMPACT to create student-centered learning environments and the scaling of IMPACT based on SDT principles, we made a complete shift in our assessment of student engagement toward the use of multiple validated measures capturing the various motivational constructs associated with the SDT framework.

Currently, in order to assess student engagement in IMPACT courses, CIE administers student self-report perception surveys at the end of each semester. All students enrolled in a course that has been transformed through the IMPACT program in the last 3 years receive the IMPACT survey containing measures based on the SDT framework (Deci & Ryan, 1985) and informed learning (Maybee et al., 2019). This survey is sent through the use of the Qualtrics software to over 12,000 students each semester. Specifically, the survey includes measures of the learning climate (Williams & Deci, 1996); satisfaction of the basic psychological needs of autonomy, competence, and relatedness (Chen et al., 2015; Wang et al., 2019); levels of self-determined motivation (Guay et al., 2000); perceived knowledge transfer (Levesque-Bristol et al., in press); and informed learning (Flierl et al., in press). This IMPACT survey is included in Appendix C, and the informed learning scale is presented in Appendix D.

In the first few years of the IMPACT program, when the focus on redesign types was still prevalent (Twigg, 2003), we examined whether different course redesign models tended to produce learning environments that were more student centered than others. Results suggested that the courses transformed through IMPACT, regardless of whether the redesign followed the supplemental or the replacement "flipped" model, were associated with equivalent levels of student engagement, as assessed by student perceptions on the learning climate scale (see Appendix C). The student perception data suggest that any transformation model can be effective as long as it contributes to the creation of a student-centered (autonomy-supportive) environment by fostering the fulfillment of the basic psychological needs of autonomy, competence, and relatedness. Almost 85% of the undergraduate students taking an IMPACT course perceived the course to be autonomy supportive. This is measured by scores on the learning climate scale, which generally captures the extent to which the instructor in the course is perceived to be autonomy supportive.

The IDA+A, CIE, and ELRC units collaborate during IMPACT assessment to correlate individual students' academic performance to their perceptions of the autonomy supportiveness of the learning environment. For IMPACT courses surveyed between spring 2014 and summer 2019, a small positive correlation of .20, regardless of redesign model, between students' rating of the learning environment and their mean final grade was observed. Figure 7.5 shows the mean ratings of perceived autonomy support (on a scale of 1 to 7) within final course grade groups.

In addition, Table 7.1 presents the means of student perceptions for key aggregate motivational constructs based in SDT and informed learning constructs, as assessed with the IMPACT self-report survey. These data were gathered from students taking IMPACT courses taught in fall 2019. All the scores range from 1 = strongly disagree to 7 = strongly agree.

As can be seen by examining the averages for the motivational and informed learning constructs, all the basic psychological needs and the self-determined forms of motivation are above the midpoint of the scale, whereas all the non-self-determined forms of motivation are generally low and below the midpoint of the scale. This is true with the exception of extrinsic motivation, with a mean of almost 5 on the 7-point Likert scale. This makes

Figure 7.5. Mean autonomy-support ratings by final grade group.

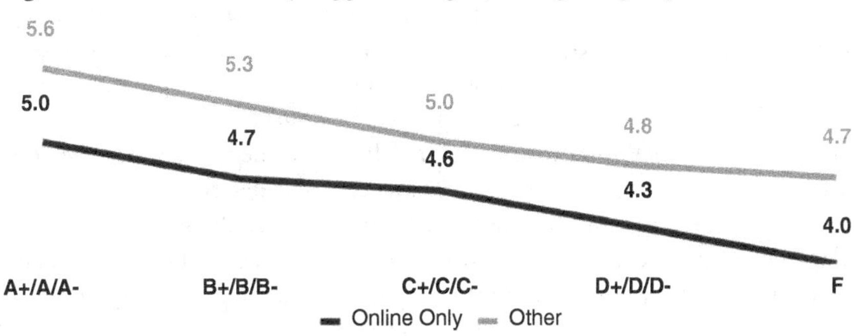

TABLE 7.1
Means for Motivational and Informed Learning Constructs

	N	*IMPACT Mean*	*Standard Deviation*
Learning Climate	3,216	5.50	1.35
Basic Psychological Needs			
Autonomy	3,064	4.25	1.19
Competence	3,065	5.11	1.25
Relatedness	3,064	5.03	.98
Motivation Continuum			
Self-Determined Forms			
Intrinsic	3,137	4.27	1.72
Integration	3,136	5.01	1.29
Identification	3,137	4.97	1.44
Non-Self-Determined Forms			
Introjection	3,136	3.03	1.51
External	3,136	4.94	1.46
Amotivation	3,136	2.61	1.44
Informed Learning	3,033	5.41	1.03

Note. Means can range from 1 = strongly disagree to 7 = strongly agree.

sense considering that we are asking students about their reasons for taking classes, which are often required as part of their program of study. Therefore, in a class that has been transformed through the IMPACT program, even though the class is required and can activate extrinsic reasons for participation in the class, the other forms of non-self-determined motivation are low (introjection and amotivation) and the forms of self-determined motivation and basic psychological needs are high. In other words, the students are able to see the value and importance in the class and perceive the environment to be autonomy supportive and satisfying of their basic psychological needs and informed learning experiences, even though the class is required. The students understand why they are taking the class and see the benefit in these classes, and are not engaging in these classes out of guilt or other internal pressures. These demonstrate the advantages from the students' perspective of creating learning environments that are autonomy supportive.

In regard to students' perception of informed learning (Flierl et al., in press), research on the validation of the scale has demonstrated that informed learning is moderately and positively associated with motivational constructs such as the autonomy supportiveness of the learning climate and self-determined motivation. In addition, a small but significant correlation between informed learning and overall course grade was found. The findings support the importance of examining the ways in which students perceive how they use information in a broad view of their motivation and perceptions of the autonomy supportiveness of the classroom environment. Research on informed learning also supports the benefits of synthesizing and communicating information. The frequency with which faculty asked students to synthesize and communicate information did significantly correlate with student self-determined motivation and academic performance in the course (Flierl et al., 2018).

Furthermore, in regard to the motivational outcomes, when we examine the correlational models assessing the relationships between the motivational constructs and learning outcomes, we find that fulfillment of the basic psychological needs of autonomy, competence, and relatedness fosters student self-determined motivation, which can then lead to positive outcomes such as well-being, student success, learning, retention, academic performance, and ultimately progress toward degree completion. We found support for these hypotheses, based in SDT, in several studies conducted as part of the IMPACT assessment. Students who perceived their instructors and classrooms to be autonomy supportive reported significantly higher levels of perceived competence and other basic psychological needs, higher levels of self-determined motivation, ability to transfer knowledge to other relevant courses and experiences, and higher perceived learning gains (Levesque-Bristol, in press; Yu & Levesque-Bristol, 2020). These results are consistent with the results of studies I reviewed in chapter 3 that focused on the application of SDT motivational principles to education.

Some of our findings seem to point to the prevalence of the need for competence and the importance of the development of skills and knowledge in an environment that is autonomy supportive and in which connections between people can be made (Yu & Levesque-Bristol, 2018, 2020). These findings were particularly evident for students from underrepresented minorities or low socioeconomic status (Wang et al., 2020). In other words, it appears that the creation of student-centered environments can reduce the achievement gaps found in certain groups of students.

Student Academic Outcomes and Retention

The third area of the overall assessment plan focuses on student academic outcomes and retention. It is drawing from data captured at the institutional level. This assessment area provides information on the effectiveness of the IMPACT course transformation in terms of student academic success and performance.

Data Collected: Institutional Data

As faculty create environments that are autonomy supportive, we would expect to notice the effects on students who would experience improved academic outcomes and retention rates. An initial goal of IMPACT was to increase student academic success and decrease time to degree by transforming traditionally difficult courses. Each academic year, IDA+A examines these metrics for courses that are large (i.e., enrollment exceeding 100 students) or foundational (course number of 299 or below) and with high failure rates (i.e., pre-IMPACT DFW rates of 20% or higher).

For many of these IMPACT courses, we observe an improvement in the mean final grade and/or a reduction in the DFW rate. For example, in the 2016–2017 academic year, 12 courses met the high failure criterion and at least one of the large enrollment or foundational criteria. DFW rates improved in IMPACT sections for nine of these 12 courses (IMPACT Management Team and IMPACT Evaluation Team, 2017). In the 2017–2018 academic year, 15 courses met the high failure criteria and at least one of the large enrollment or foundational criteria, and DFW rates improved for 11 of the 15 courses in the IMPACT sections (IMPACT Management Team and IMPACT Evaluation Team, 2018). In the 2018–2019 academic year, 16 courses met the high failure criteria and at least one of the large enrollment or foundational criteria, and DFW rates improved for 12 of the 16 courses in the IMPACT sections (IMPACT Management Team and IMPACT Evaluation Team, 2019). Overall, the DFW rates decreased an average of almost 6% when compared to the pre-IMPACT DFW rate. This rate of change corresponds to an additional 404 students passing the courses with a C- or higher in the 2016–2017 academic year, 590 students in the 2017–2018 academic year, and 587 students in the 2018–2019 academic year. These students are then able to be retained in their major or at the university and continue with their studies without the need to retake these foundational courses. These data support a positive role of IMPACT in increasing student academic success and decreasing time to degree. In some of the large gateway courses with high levels of DFW rates, such as introductory chemistry, calculus, and mechanical engineering, the DFW rate decreased by as much as 30%.

Student Learning Outcomes

The fourth area of the overall assessment plan focuses on student learning outcomes. It draws from multiple sources of information, including self-report surveys and focus groups. This assessment area provides information on the effectiveness of the professional development program at influencing the learning outcomes instructors create and the attainment of those outcomes from the students' perspective.

Data Collected: Self-Report Surveys and Post-FLC Focus Group Interviews

The learning outcomes faculty fellows create during the IMPACT FLC are presented to students at the end of the semester for them to evaluate in one of two ways. They either appear at the end-of-semester course evaluation for each IMPACT course or at the end of the IMPACT survey sent to students toward the end of the semester (see Appendix C). Students then evaluate the extent to which each of the course learning outcomes have been met over the course of the semester, using a 0 to 4 Likert scale. Data gathered during all the semesters assessed between spring 2015 and fall 2017 demonstrated that when students perceive the learning environment as autonomy supportive, they also report significantly greater attainment of the identified learning outcomes (M = 3.85) compared to when the learning environment is not perceived to be autonomy supportive (M = 2.85) (Lott & Nunes, 2018).

Furthermore, our emphasis on developing clear, specific, and measurable learning outcomes resulted in an overall reduction in the number of course-level learning outcomes faculty fellows keep for their courses, from an average of 5.37 before the IMPACT program to an average of 3.75 after the IMPACT program (Lott & Nunes, 2018). In addition, the coding of these learning outcomes based on Bloom's taxonomy for the cognitive domain (Anderson et al., 2001) revealed that the final learning outcomes created by faculty fellows, with the help of their support team members, featured more specific and measurable wording and more frequently focused on higher-order cognitive processes during all semesters assessed (Lott & Nunes, 2018). IMPACT fellows were able to articulate more cognitively demanding and complex learning outcomes as a result of their participation in the IMPACT program, shifting from a predominance on "remembering," a less complex cognitive domain, toward a predominance on the more complex cognitive domains such as "evaluate" and "create" (Lott & Nunes, 2018).

As described in the IDA+A briefing (Zywicki & Beaudoin, 2016), the faculty interviewed during the focus groups conducted on the last session of the FLC reported learning much about how to create, adequately use, and assess the learning outcomes in their courses. They reported that the IMPACT program helped them understand the value and importance of writing good learning outcomes, becoming more knowledgeable about the various types of learning outcomes they could use, and then utilizing that knowledge to guide their decisions about course content and pedagogical choices. This qualitative work on learning outcomes suggests that the IMPACT program and the guidance faculty receive from the support teams help faculty fellows in four broad categories: (a) planning to achieve course outcomes, (b) using outcomes appropriately, (c) communicating outcomes to students, and (d) assessing outcomes. This is also reflected in the approach the IMPACT management team follows when delivering the FLC to faculty fellows (see also chapter 4 for a discussion).

The faculty fellows interviewed described creating learning outcomes to guide their course decisions. This is a significant change resulting from the IMPACT program. In interviews before the start of the IMPACT program, only a fraction of the faculty fellows reported creating and using learning outcomes to plan their course content and guide their pedagogical decisions. Importantly, these learning outcomes are clearly defined and are explicitly written down. Before the IMPACT program, faculty may have reported using learning outcomes, but these were not explicitly written or used in course planning or the creation of assessment. As mentioned in chapter 4, IMPACT faculty spend a significant amount of time working with their support teams in order to make revisions and improve their learning outcomes and when these learning outcomes are introduced and reinforced during the semester. These learning outcomes become the blueprint for the course redesign decisions, focusing the attention of the faculty on what it is that they want their students to do, know, and appreciate by the end of the course.

The IMPACT fellows interviewed reported creating and selecting learning activities for students that align best with the course learning outcomes or a series of outcomes. The work the faculty do during the IMPACT program fosters this intentional alignment between learning activities and course learning outcomes. As discussed in chapter 4, this is another very important component of the FLC and the work the faculty conduct with the support teams. Following their experience with IMPACT, faculty fellows actually make use of their learning outcomes in order to plan their entire course from start to finish. Importantly, the instructors report being willing to make adjustments to their CDPs based on what unfolds during a learning activity. This flexibility is also something that is fostered by the autonomy-supportive professional development.

The faculty interviewed reported communicating their outcomes and expectations to students either verbally or in writing in their syllabus or both. This is also a significant result of the IMPACT professional development program, since not all faculty consistently followed this practice before participating in IMPACT. The support team members encourage the faculty to become explicit about sharing their learning outcomes with students. However, the faculty still have the choice to do so in a manner that makes sense for them and their course. Some faculty reported that they chose not to share the learning outcomes with the students on the first day of class but instead chose to model the engagement with the learning outcomes and introduce them one at a time throughout the course of the semester. In contrast, some faculty elect to introduce in writing the learning outcomes for each class session and use these to promote informal and regular self-assessment by the student. Either way, the learning outcomes are clearly communicated to students as part of an overall course plan and strategy designed to be transparent and explicit with students. This fosters the creation of an environment that is autonomy supportive and student centered.

Although IMPACT faculty fellows report using typical assessment methods in their courses such as assignments, projects, quizzes, and/or exams to assess learning, they tend to do so in unique or creative ways that foster engagement and deep learning. For example, some of the faculty interviewed reported using a pre-/postassessment to evaluate the knowledge of the students before presenting the course content for a certain topic in order to adapt their teaching and specifically address knowledge gaps or misconceptions. Some use pre-/postassessments in order to evaluate the change in knowledge in their students and explicitly examine improvement in knowledge and skills. The use of the minute paper, discussed in chapter 5, could be a good small teaching strategy to meet this goal. Some faculty make a conscious decision to focus on higher-order learning outcomes and use lower-level learning outcomes (Bloom's taxonomy) to build toward these higher-level learning outcomes. In these cases, the lower-level learning outcomes serve as stackable building blocks or as scaffolding toward higher-level learning outcomes.

Institutional Change, Culture Change, and Sustainability

The fifth and final area of the overall assessment plan focuses on institutional change, culture change, and sustainability. It is drawing from multiple sources of information, including institutional data and program data. This is the most challenging area to assess, and it provides information on the broad impact of the program on instructors and students beyond the immediate influence of the professional development program.

Data Collected: Institutional Data, Program Data, and Counts of Faculty Fellows and Students

Institutional change, culture change, and sustainability is the most challenging area to assess and document, perhaps because it encompasses areas beyond the immediate influence of the program on faculty fellows and students. Although broad and difficult to capture, over the years the IMPACT team has attempted to do so by using a number of metrics as indicators of institutional and culture change including faculty efficacy, faculty career progression and recognition, departmental incentives and policies, investment in institutional infrastructure, and the development of an IMPACT network. This broad topic necessitates a separate chapter and will be the focus of chapter 9. In this section, I will be focusing on the quantitative evidence of the breadth and scope of the IMPACT program as a way to demonstrate its institutional impact and reach.

From fall 2011 to spring 2020, 397 instructors from every one of the 12 academic colleges or schools from over 50 academic departments at the Purdue West Lafayette campus participated in the IMPACT program, transforming 350 courses, sometimes as a working team. IMPACT as a professional development program has empowered and encouraged faculty fellows to transform not only the course they are bringing to the IMPACT FLC initially but also other courses they teach. We have referred to these courses as "influenced courses." These influenced, transformed courses emanate from faculty confidence and efficacy in applying the principles of IMPACT to other courses they teach and are a direct result of our focus on professional development as opposed to course redesign.

Between 5% and 10% of all faculty have participated in the program depending on which faculty are included in the denominator (e.g., all faculty, only faculty teaching undergraduate classes, etc.). Each semester around 30 support staff members from three of the units—CIE, TLT, and PULSIS—work with faculty fellows in consultation on the redesigns. By targeting faculty who teach foundational courses, we have been able to reach the majority of students with a relatively small percentage of faculty. In terms of the students, we can say that more than 88% of undergraduate students registered for at least one undergraduate IMPACT course during any one of the academic terms from the inception of the program in fall 2011 through summer 2019. In some semesters, this number went up to 95.6%, showing that almost 100% of the undergraduate students had taken at least one IMPACT class during their academic career at Purdue.

Figure 7.6 shows a summary of the overall scope and growth of IMPACT in terms of the college representation (IMPACT Management and IMPACT Evaluation Team, 2019). As seen in the figure, the college with the greatest level of participation in IMPACT is the Purdue Polytechnic Institute PPI College of Technology. I will discuss in greater detail the involvement and

Figure 7.6. Colleges' representation in IMPACT.

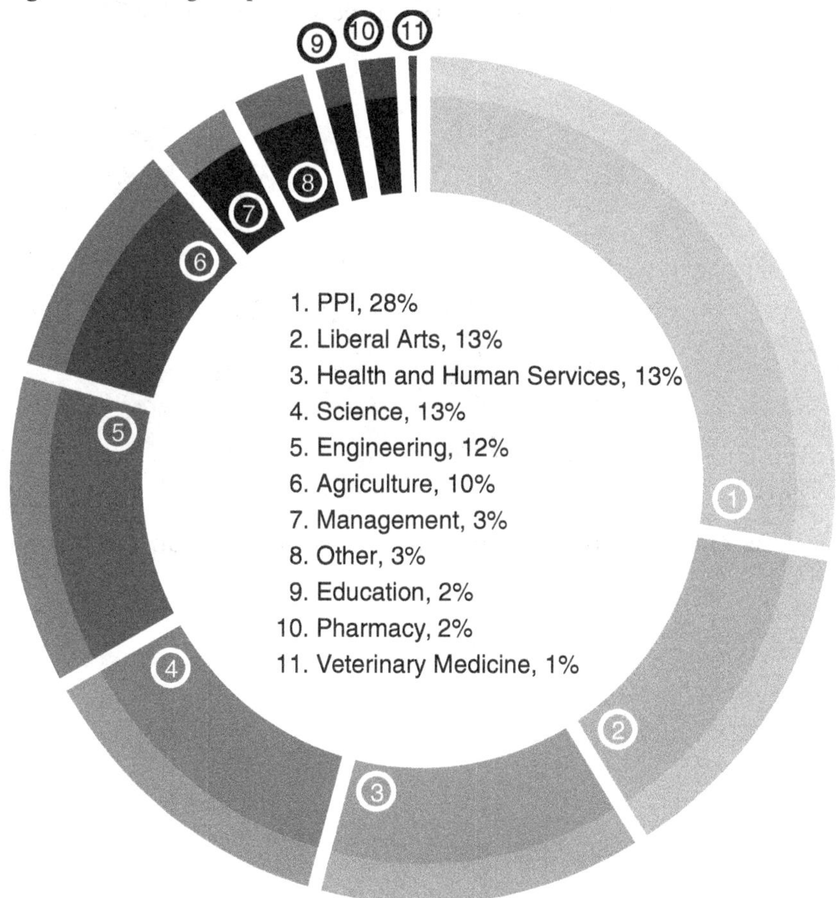

Note. Reprinted with permission of A. M. Allred.

commitment of PPI to active and transformative learning at Purdue, but it is not surprising that PPI is the most heavily represented with over 70% of their instructors in the college having taken part in IMPACT professional development. This represents almost 30% of the total number of faculty fellows who have participated in IMPACT.

The growth of IMPACT in terms of number of faculty fellows is presented in Figure 7.7 (IMPACT Management Team and IMPACT Evaluation Team, 2019).

Finally, Figure 7.8 presents the growth of IMPACT in terms of the number of courses that have been part of the IMPACT program since its inception in 2011 ((IMPACT Management Team and IMPACT Evaluation Team, 2019).

Figure 7.7. Total number of faculty fellows participating in the IMPACT program.

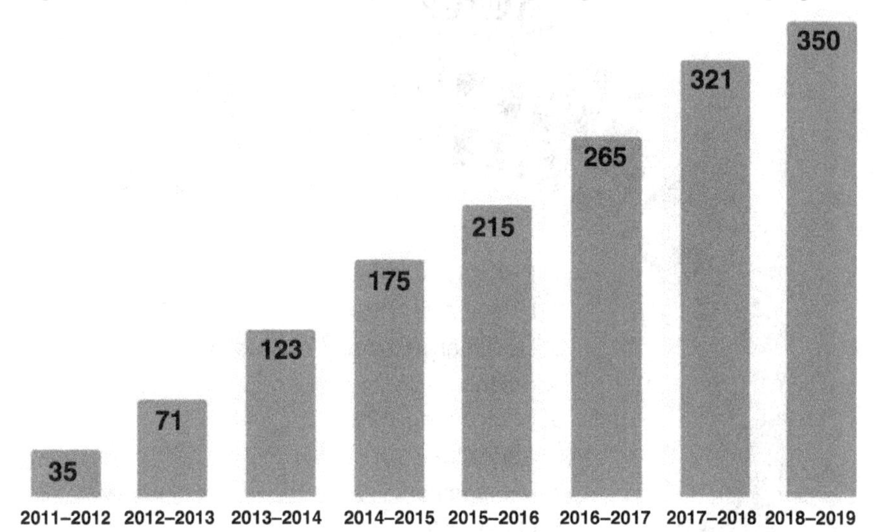

Figure 7.8. Total number of IMPACT courses, including influenced courses.

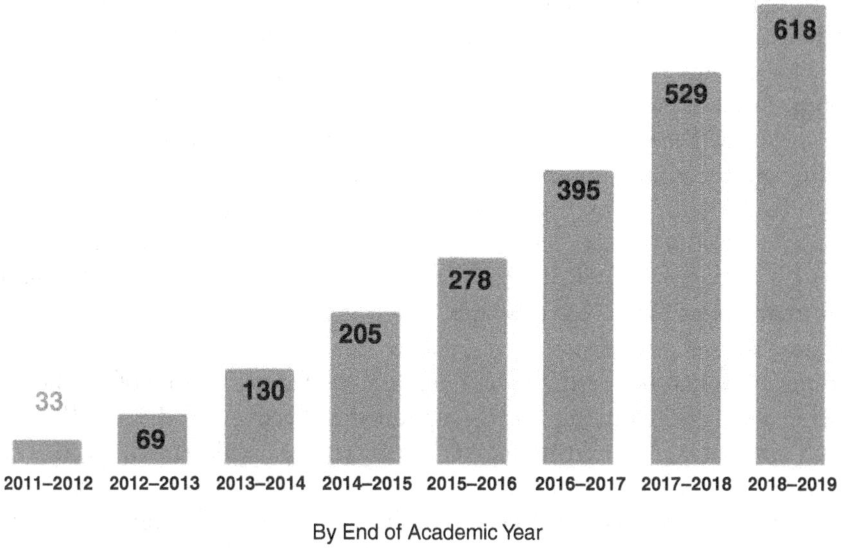

618
529
395
278
205
130
33
69
2011–2012 2012–2013 2013–2014 2014–2015 2015–2016 2016–2017 2017–2018 2018–2019
By End of Academic Year

General Implications for Assessment

Having a strong theoretical framework to guide the design and assessment of the course transformation and overall assessment plan allowed us to be more intentional and systematic in the kinds of research questions we examined and program areas we assessed.

Under this general framework, the IMPACT team has used multiple indicators of success to gauge the effectiveness of the IMPACT program. We examined professional development and faculty change; student engagement; student academic outcomes; student learning outcomes; and institutional change, culture change, and sustainability.

One important note in terms of assessment is that it is very difficult to systematically assess professional development such as IMPACT, in part because of the scope and breadth of the program, but also because of the lack of control groups or course sections. As IMPACT is a professional development program, instructors taking part in IMPACT are committed to engage in the change and the transformation. They are not bringing colleagues along with them that are interested in offering their course sections as control sections. In addition, even though in the beginning of the program, the IMPACT team encouraged faculty fellows to use their semester in IMPACT as their baseline semester and refrain from engaging in transformations, it proved almost impossible to do so. Instructors find themselves so very excited to attempt to immediately implement the skills they learn during the program and begin creating environments that are autonomy supportive that we fail to capture the first semester as a baseline semester before changes are implemented. At best, we sometimes are able to compare the instructors' pre-IMPACT course outcomes to their post-IMPACT course outcomes, although these comparisons are very limited.

In 2014, my team and I were awarded a FITW grant from the DoE to systematically study the effects of the IMPACT intervention in a limited number of IMPACT STEM courses, such as Calculus I and II and Introductory Physics. For this grant, there was a requirement for instructors whose courses were part of the project to have control groups or control sections. Although the results are not yet published at the writing of this book, I can say that the findings clearly support the effectiveness of the IMPACT program, possibly contributing to a reduction in achievement gaps. The mechanisms explaining the effectiveness of the intervention are associated with the motivational constructs from SDT and the satisfaction of the basic psychological needs (Deci & Ryan, 1985; Ryan & Deci, 2017).

8

LEARNING SPACES

The physical space we find ourselves in matters. The way a room is configured can influence what we do, how we think, and how we feel in the space. In regard to learning spaces, it makes sense to assume that the way a space is designed and configured could influence instructors' course planning and teaching practices; the actual classroom that instructors find themselves assigned to could influence the pedagogies they use and the extent to which they engage their students in the space. Some teaching and learning spaces might make instructors feel more or less comfortable and even competent. If the space is familiar, instructors might feel more comfortable and could draw from prior knowledge and scripts. Instructor teaching practices, or their teaching repertoire, will be influenced by their prior experiences, the way they have been taught, or their professional development experiences (Beaudoin, Zywicki, Doan et al., 2016; Zywicki & Beaudoin, 2016). In fact, it is very common for instructors to teach the way they were taught (Oleson & Hora, 2014), and most instructors do not receive professional development before they begin teaching. Research on learning space design has demonstrated that the layout of a classroom has an impact on the way in which students and instructors interact and engage in teaching and learning (Baepler et al., 2014, 2016).

The most common classroom space is the large lecture hall. This space triggers a familiar script in instructors' minds because of the amount of experience gathered in these spaces both as a student and an instructor. The instructor stands at the front of the room behind the podium and proceeds to lecture. Copious amounts of slides are shown while the instructor typically reads off the slides, and the students diligently take notes. In many instances, the instructor does not even face the students; they turn to face the slides and read them off to students. The students in the front are perceived to be the diligent, dedicated, and motivated students, while the students in the back are perceived as, and often are, disengaged, sometimes catching up on some needed sleep. Often, the slides are made available to students at the end of the lectures. Although perceived to be a positive and useful pedagogical strategy, by itself this practice may encourage disengagement and lack of participation from students who may not feel the need to go to class in order to receive the classroom content. In addition, if interactions are not encouraged and fostered in the large lecture classroom, why would students be motivated to participate or engage in class? If attendance is required, but questions and student engagement are not fostered and encouraged during class time, only warm bodies are required in the classroom. In these cases, especially in very large classrooms, a technology tool such as the SRS or clickers might be used to record attendance at the beginning of the class, or a short quiz might be administered with the use of the clickers in order to see who is attending. It is well known that the use of technology for this purpose does not foster engagement and instead tends to annoy the students who feel compelled to purchase the technology with no clear pedagogical purpose for their use in class (Bruff, 2009). The large lecture hall is still the most common type of physical classroom space, and therefore this type of interaction around teaching and learning is still the norm rather than the exception. So, is a move to active learning spaces the answer? If we build more active learning spaces, will instructors use the space? Will active learning spaces lead to a magical increase in attainment of student learning outcomes? Or more accurately, if we build active collaborative learning spaces, will instructors know how to effectively make use of the space to foster student engagement and student learning?

When ALCs are available at an institution, the underlying assumption is that instructors will utilize these spaces to their maximum potential. Although some researchers portray classroom space as an independent and direct predictor of student learning outcomes, it is more probable that the combined use of active learning spaces and student-centered practices fosters attainment of student learning outcomes (Baepler et al., 2014, 2016).

If instructors have received professional development in order to increase their ability to use student-centered practices and create environments that are engaging and autonomy supportive, the results are even better. After receiving professional development, instructors might expect their classroom space to support those pedagogical practices and be more comfortable teaching in those spaces. Alternatively, instructors might be more likely to adapt the skills they have learned through professional development and apply them to any teaching and learning spaces. However, a possible downside is that if active learning spaces are not available, but instructors have received professional development to use them, they might be disappointed in their lack of availability.

IMPACT provided us with a natural way to examine these questions, as the growth of IMPACT created the need for a greater number of ALCs. When IMPACT was created in 2011, the aim was to challenge the traditional way of teaching in order to improve student success by using pedagogical practices that would take into consideration how people learn and foster the creation of student-centered learning environments. These learning environments would foster success and growth through improvement in learning gains, attainment of course-specific learning outcomes and higher-order thinking skills, student engagement, confidence, and competence. The original mission of the IMPACT program was to improve student competency and confidence through the redesign of foundational courses by using research findings on sound student-centered teaching and learning. The general expectation was that IMPACT would improve student success as well as completion in large foundational courses. As mentioned in chapter 4, we have since expanded our reach to a variety of undergraduate courses, not only the large foundational courses, and the mission of the IMPACT program has evolved accordingly to simply state that through collaboration and research-based practices, IMPACT at Purdue creates student-centered teaching and learning environments (IMPACT, 2020). The focus on student-centered learning put an emphasis on the creation of active or collaborative learning spaces. Back in 2011, very few of these types of spaces existed at Purdue.

As alluded to in chapter 1, in the second year of the program, the involvement of the libraries was instrumental in the growth and expansion of the program. As the collaboration among the units working on the IMPACT program increased and the reputation of the program itself grew simultaneously, the need for active learning spaces quickly mounted. At that time, the libraries at Purdue had begun to think about and conceptualize space differently. To address the changing needs of the 21st-century student learner, academic libraries in higher education were reconceptualizing their formal and informal learning spaces, and Purdue libraries were leading the way. Academic libraries are dramatically reinventing their physical spaces. The traditional model of dark rooms separated by stacks of books is incompatible with the digital age. As expectations for library resources and physical facilities have changed, stakeholders have been called on to transform campus libraries in innovative ways (Head et al., 2020). Today at Purdue, library space is no longer considered a repository for books and microfiche, but a space to learn, think, create, grow, collaborate, discuss, and exchange ideas. The reconceptualization of library space into a collaborative student learning place changes the essence of the traditional library, moving from a book-centered to a learning-centered space. The libraries at Purdue took many of the book collections off the shelves and collaborated with other institutions of higher education to exchange books, reducing the number of physical books needing to be stored in multiple physical locations. In addition, books were digitized where possible, which saved a tremendous amount of space. This newly available physical space could then be repurposed and converted into flexible, active learning spaces in order to enhance the teaching and learning mission. The involvement of the Purdue libraries as a partner in the IMPACT program initially provided access to the needed space to accommodate IMPACT's ambitious transformation timetable.

The first space designed by the libraries was The Learn Lab located in the Roland G. Parrish Library of Management and Economics in the Krannert School of Management. This was a 40-seat high-tech computer lab. Next, three additional library spaces in the basement of the existing Hicks Undergraduate Library were redesigned into active learning collaborative spaces. These classrooms were redesigned based on the scale-up model, which was developed and popularized by a group of physics educators at North Carolina State University (Beichner et al., 2007). These four classroom spaces were made available to the IMPACT fellows in 2012, the 2nd year of the program. However, almost more compelling than the availability of these classroom spaces is how the accessibility of study and social gathering spaces directly outside the classroom spaces changed the way students interacted with each other and with instructors, and what they did and how long they stayed in the space before or after classes. In both the Parrish and the Hicks libraries, the number of visits dramatically increased, and the types of interactions changed. The availability of a coffee shop in both locations and a variety of attractive and comfortable spaces to study and informally gather drew students and instructors to the space, blurring the lines between formal and informal study spaces. This was especially true in the Parrish Library, which was completely redesigned based on this concept of juxtaposition of formal and informal learning spaces. Over the last decade, the terms *formal learning spaces* and *informal learning spaces* have become commonly accepted in space planning to refer to scheduled instructional and unscheduled or user-scheduled activities, respectively (DEGW, 2012). The scheduled instructional activities typically take place in a classroom, whereas unscheduled activities can take place anywhere, such as in cafés, libraries, lounges, or any other type of space across campus.

In the Parrish Library, it was common to observe students studying not only individually but also in groups, as well as eating, drinking, and occasionally resting in the library spaces. And that was exactly what we wanted to see: a space where students would feel free and comfortable to gather, work on group projects and individual homework, meet with instructors before and after class, have lunch and a coffee, and take a nap in between classes if they needed to. These spaces catered to how students, instructors, and staff, people in general, choose to live and learn; these spaces helped foster autonomy-supportive learning environments where students and instructors grow and develop.

These new collaborative spaces on campus primarily served the IMPACT fellows who were engaging in course transformation. It provided the necessary collaborative and active learning spaces, allowing the faculty fellows the opportunity to teach in these new spaces and apply the skills they had learned going through the IMPACT program. The availability of these spaces was sufficient in the early years of IMPACT when the scope of the program was still relatively small, in comparison to what it is today (IMPACT Management Team and IMPACT Evaluation Team, 2013). Being part of the IMPACT program gave instructors priority access to these active learning spaces. For the IMPACT fellows who received professional development through IMPACT, the use of the space worked hand in hand with the skills and knowledge they developed and the transformation they achieved toward greater student engagement. However, the demand for the number of active and collaborative spaces quickly grew. Faculty fellows were seeing the value in IMPACT and the influence of the program on their teaching practices. They were talking about the value and benefit of the IMPACT program to their colleagues, and more people wanted to take part in the program. This began to put pressure on the available active learning spaces on campus. The engagement and commitment of Purdue to promote active learning and transform teaching university, wide, which began in 2011 with the initiative from the Provost's Office, was continuing to gain momentum.

In January 2013, Mitch Daniels became the 12th president of Purdue, after serving two terms as governor of the state of Indiana. Daniels designated IMPACT as part of Purdue Moves (more on the Moves in chapter 9). This led to the need to double the IMPACT program from working with no more than 30 instructors a year to up to 60 instructors a year and secure physical spaces to foster this growth in active and collaborative teaching and learning. The way in which we scaled the program is described in chapter 4. To support this ambitious expansion goal, Mitch Daniels and James L. Mullins, the dean of the library, worked collaboratively to seek funds from potential donors and the Indiana State Legislature for a colossal transformation project: converting the old Smoke Stack at Purdue, which sat in a prime location at the center of campus, into an active learning center. The success of the Parrish and Hicks libraries fueled the vision for this new active learning center, as well as the results of the studies conducted the previous year.

On August 7, 2017, the Thomas S. and Harvey D. Wilmeth Active Learning Center (WALC) opened in the heart of campus. This 170,390-square-foot facility serves as a central location for classroom and library space housing the Library of Engineering and Science (LoES) and 27 classrooms designed for active learning. The LoES is a consolidation of six of the nine science libraries formerly located across the entire campus. The WALC is a state-of-the-art, innovative building, designed based on research conducted on the Parrish and Hicks collaborative spaces. Throughout the WALC, study and collaborative spaces are blended seamlessly with classrooms, creating a highly collaborative and educational use of space.

In the WALC building there are six different types of ALCs (BoilerUp, Eye2Eye, Flexible, Scale-Up, 6 Round, and Turn2Team; four are highlighted in the following paragraphs) and one large traditional 329-seat performance room. These different classroom configurations foster certain types of pedagogical strategies, and some of the classrooms feature more or less technology. Some of the classrooms are set up with round tables seating six students or with smaller collaborative tables seating three students, which can be grouped together in order to foster collaborations among larger groups of up to nine students. The amount of technology varies in these collaborative rooms from a few flat-screen panels in the room, power on the walls, and whiteboards, to power at each table for laptops as well as one flat-screen panel per large collaborative table.

In preparation for the opening of the WALC, the IMPACT partners collaborated to offer professional development, tours of the WALC, and just-in-time support. The IMPACT team realized that in order to be successful in the active learning spaces, instructors needed support to understand how to best use the different classroom configurations and feel comfortable in the new space. One of the very successful initiatives offered to instructors as a partnership between CIE, TLT, and the faculty fellows is the Active Learning Community of Practice or ALCoP. Led by past IMPACT faculty fellows and supported by CIE and TLT, ALCoP fosters community building and an exchange of ideas in an informal setting in regard to active learning pedagogical practices. Topics range from how to creatively use some of the active learning spaces in the WALC to how to foster inclusivity and diversity in ALCs.

The most high-tech of these classrooms is labeled the Scale-Up classroom. (The low-tech version of this classroom is called the 6 Round.) Two IMPACT fellows have been particularly successful in using these classrooms: Andrew Hirsch, emeritus faculty, professor of physics and astronomy, as well as Robert (Bob) Herrick, professor and the Robert A. Hoffer Distinguished Professor of Electrical Engineering Technology.

Hirsch teaches his introductory physics class in a Scale-Up classroom, seating 108 students arranged in 12 tables seating nine students each. He arranges students in groups of three, each group with their own whiteboard. During class, Hirsch puts problems up on the screen one at a time. While in their groups, students work on these problems, instead of working on them outside of class as homework assignments. The room configuration allows Hirsch and his five teaching assistants to move around easily, answer student questions in real time, and observe where students are encountering issues and bottlenecks. After each problem, the class reconvenes for a general debrief and the opportunity to ask questions about the problem that was just worked on. When several groups of students get stuck on the same issue or make common mistakes, Hirsch stops the class to review or clarify the problem in question. Physics demonstrations are recorded and played on the multiple monitors in the high-tech Scale-Up classroom. This allows him to pause the presentation of the demonstration and highlight points of interest. Overall, this pedagogical approach fosters an autonomy-supportive environment that meets all three of the basic psychological needs of students—autonomy, competence, and relatedness.

Bob Herrick also teaches in a Scale-Up classroom, this one seating 72 students arranged in eight tables seating nine students each. Herrick was not originally scheduled to teach in the Scale-Up classroom in the WALC. However, after one of the WALC tours and a demonstration of the capability and the pedagogical advantages of teaching in this classroom, he asked to be scheduled into a Scale-Up room and has been teaching there ever since. The two large-screen displays in the classroom, one at the front and one at the back, in addition to the computer displays available for each of the tables with HDMI and VGA connections, allow Herrick to begin the class with a hot topic discussion by projecting a video on both screens and the computer displays. A short online quiz inspired by the Readiness Assurance Test (iRAT and tRAT) of TBL (see chapter 5) follows the discussion. The first four questions test students' individual knowledge and preparation for the lecture that day, while the fifth question is a question that is solved as a team. The questions are projected on the computer display at each table, and when the team question is up, students physically gather around the computer display and use the whiteboard directly underneath the display to work the problem until a successful resolution. Herrick walks around the room to answer students' questions and takes note of the challenging concepts for students. During that time, the students work together, interacting and collaborating to solve the problem, with support and guidance from the instructor. When the problem is solved or the time is up, one student in each group takes a picture of the solution on their whiteboard and emails the picture to the instructor with the names of all the students in their group. The whiteboard pictures of the solution are then posted on the LMS for other team members to review. The classroom configuration allows Herrick to freely move throughout the classroom, interacting easily with all the students, answering questions in real time when students get stuck or encounter a problem. The physical space allows Herrick to create a learning environment that facilitates individual, paired, or group activities. In a different space, before access to the Scale-Up room in the WALC, Herrick struggled with making group work a consistent feature of his classes. He believes that the configuration of the WALC Scale-Up classroom has allowed him to effectively foster collaboration among students and with him as an instructor, which then carries outside of the classroom. Once again, this pedagogical approach fosters an autonomy-supportive environment that meets all three of students' basic psychological needs—autonomy, competence, and relatedness.

Another room configuration found in the WALC is called Turn2Team. It is set up with pairs of wide and narrow long tables. The chairs are movable and typically face forward for presentations. When instructors first enter this classroom, they are at first confused by the different widths of the tables. Many instructors wonder whether the architects made a mistake. Why would you have a room set up like this, with tables with different widths? This is one clear example where we note the importance of professional development in collaborative spaces. Without professional development, instructors and students will use the room in a very traditional way. All students will be sitting at a table, facing forward toward the instructor at the front of the room. When instructors are shown how the room can easily accommodate group work of four or more (e.g., having the students sitting at the narrow tables turn their chairs back toward the wide tables, then facing the other students in their group), many instructors who make frequent use of group), work then request to teach in this Turn2Team classroom. This room provides instructors with both structure and flexibility. With professional development, what was originally perceived as a design flaw is turned into a powerful flexible element of this collaborative classroom, which can easily support both group work and individual work.

The Flexible classroom type in the WALC appears as though it hasn't been thought through at all. Frankly, when you first enter the classroom, it looks like unorganized chaos. It is composed of between 45 to 126 single mobile tablet armchairs. That's it! Picture in your mind 126 mobile chairs in a large open space. Following their participation in IMPACT, some instructors, discovered how this room could meet their specific course goals and learning outcomes and objectives and have been able to make effective use of the room. Larry Nies, professor of civil and environmental and ecological engineering, is one such example. He uses the highly flexible nature of the classroom in order to quickly and creatively engage students in a variety of small group discussions in order to develop their critical thinking and problem-solving skills. Each small group has a discussion leader with a short list of guided questions related to the learning objectives of the day. Nies uses the classroom time to walk around the different groups and listen to the conversations, and he only occasionally intervenes and redirects the conversations when he finds the students are not engaging deeply enough with the material or missing the point of the guided question. He creates an autonomy-supportive environment where students are encouraged to take ownership of the learning space. Following conversations with his IMPACT support team members, Nies created maps of the various classroom configurations he uses at different points in the class to foster the completion of the guided group discussions. When it is time for the students to get into a certain type of configuration to complete an exercise, Nies projects the configurations on the screens and asks the students to organize themselves into the pictured configuration. Within seconds the students are able to reorganize themselves, following the particular configuration map displayed, and are ready to work in small groups. This flexibility allows Nies to meet the learning objectives for the class. This classroom is not for every instructor; not all instructors would feel comfortable in this type of physical environment, especially without professional development. However, with the appropriate guidance and instructional support, instructors are able to successfully and effectively use this room to meet their needs. Without professional development, instructors may either refuse to teach in this room or organize the room like a traditional classroom, with all the single mobile armchairs facing forward toward the "front of the room" and the instructor.

The last classroom configuration I would like to highlight is the BoilerUp classroom. This tiered fan-shaped classroom is composed of wedge-shaped tables with six chairs, each accommodating teams of six students. There are three projectors at the front of the room with some confidence monitors for the instructor on the tier wall in front of the instructor station. This allows the instructor to face the classroom without having to constantly turn to look at what is projecting on the screens. All tables have access to small personal portable whiteboards, which they can display at the table. The clear advantage of this room, beside the confidence monitors that allow instructors to stay engaged with the entire classroom, is that the tiered configuration allows up to 180 students to collaborate together at tables of six students each and still allows the groups of students in the back to be relatively close to the instructor in the front of the room.

Research on Active Learning Spaces

The design work leading to the opening of the WALC and the opening of the WALC itself created many opportunities for research and development. For some of this research, the Purdue libraries partnered with the Office of Institutional Research (OIRAE, recently renamed IDA+A; pronounced IDATA), ELRC, and CIE (Beaudoin, Zywicki, Doan et al., 2016; Beaudoin, Zywicki, Uche et al., 2016; Zywicki & Beaudoin, 2016). Some of the other research was conducted in partnership with an outside consulting firm (DEGW, 2012). This research would pave the way for future assessment of learning experiences in the WALC following its opening. This section summarizes some of the research that has been conducted in order to better understand the use and impact of active learning spaces from the instructors' perspective as well as the students' perspective. This work enables us to improve active learning spaces on campus and plan for the construction of future ALCs. The growth and interest in learning spaces as a way to foster innovative pedagogies, as part of a much larger institutional and culture change, are discussed in chapter 9.

The research conducted with instructors focused on perceived importance of active learning spaces, perceived teaching effectiveness, satisfaction with teaching, and the instructor and learning space match in active learning spaces. The research conducted with students focused on perception of engagement in active learning spaces and attainment of learning outcomes. One of the overarching findings of this research is that although the physical space influences teaching practices and learning experiences and outcomes, it is not as universally important as commonly assumed. In other words, the physical classroom space, like technology, is a tool, which when used well can support effective and engaging teaching and learning practices. Going back to the opening discussion in this chapter, the availability and use of an ALC space does not by itself guarantee improvements in teaching practices or learning outcomes (Beaudoin, Zywicki, Doan et al., 2016; Beaudoin, Zywicki, Uche et al., 2016; Zywicki & Beaudoin, 2016).

Experience of Instructors

Most of the research reported in this section focuses on the experience and perceptions of instructors in active learning spaces. In the studies discussed here, 148 instructors who taught in active learning spaces during the 2014 to 2015 academic year and who were interested in research in the development of these types of spaces were invited to participate in focus groups. From the interviews during the focus groups, compelling themes emerged.

Importance of Active Learning Spaces

The degree to which instructors attempt to use student-centered teaching practices strongly influences the perceived importance of learning spaces. That is, instructors who seek to or indeed do integrate student-centered teaching practices as a way to create environments that are engaging or autonomy supportive for students reported that these efforts were enhanced and maximized when they were scheduled to teach in an active learning space. Instructors who mainly relied on lectures as their teaching practice de-emphasized the importance of the physical classroom space.

Teaching Effectiveness

Related to the importance of active learning spaces, instructors' attitudes and perceptions regarding active and collaborative learning spaces, as well as their pedagogical skills, strongly guide their teaching practices. Instructors who feel confident and comfortable teaching in a traditional lecture-style classroom are more concerned about their teaching effectiveness in active learning spaces and more skeptical about their ability to engage students in active learning spaces. Other research has come to similar conclusions. Instructors who are uncomfortable teaching with new pedagogical practices are more likely to reorganize furniture to resemble a traditional learning space when teaching in an active learning space (Hunley & Schaller, 2009). These instructors are also more likely to report that the layout of the room is affecting their perceived ability to teach effectively in active learning spaces (Michael, 2007; Petersen & Gorman, 2014).

In a related study conducted with 151 instructors teaching in ALCs instructors were asked about the features of the room that most fostered or hindered their teaching (Nelson et al., 2019). The most frequently mentioned elements for helping learning were seating configuration (75% of instructors) and technology configuration (63% of instructors). Interestingly, instructors mentioned the exact same features as hindering their teaching: technology configuration (35% of instructors) and seating configuration (29% of instructors). What transpires from this study is that it is not the physical space per se that is most important for teaching effectiveness, but instructors' ability to adapt to the space they find themselves teaching in.

Fortunately, instructors' attitudes, skills, and confidence can be enhanced through professional development such as IMPACT. Formalized and institutionalized programs like IMPACT foster the development of teaching and learning strategies, optimal instructional design, and sharing of ideas among instructors with common teaching and learning challenges. The importance of professional development cannot be overstated. Instructors scheduled to teach in collaborative and active learning spaces, such as the ones found in the WALC, need support in order to use the space most effectively and extract the benefits from the space. In this body of research, instructors who were interviewed also emphasized the need for support, training, and professional development (see chapter 6 for a discussion regarding the importance of professional development and how it can be guided by SDT). As we suspected, instructors reported that transitioning their courses to include more active learning strategies to create learning environments that are more student centered require additional time and effort to plan and implement. However, the benefits of such an investment in professional development are marked for instructors. IMPACT faculty fellows were significantly more likely to say that teaching in an active learning space positively affected student learning compared to instructors who did not take part in the IMPACT program (Nelson et al., 2019).

Satisfaction With Teaching

When ALCs are not available for instructors for a variety of reasons (e.g. lack of space, scheduling conflicts), instructors need pedagogical strategies they can rely on in order to transform the teaching and learning spaces in which they find themselves into more active, engaging, and autonomy-supportive learning environments. They need to develop or build on skills they already have in order to make use of student-centered pedagogical strategies independent of space. The extent to which instructors make efficient use of a space and the technology in it, are satisfied with their teaching in the space, or find ways to overcome perceived and actual limitations of a space depends on instructors' knowledge, skills, and perceived self-efficacy and locus of control (McDavid et al., 2018). Instructors with a greater level of perceived self-efficacy and an internal locus of control (also see chapters 2 and 3) are more likely to find ways to adapt their active learning pedagogical strategies successfully, and as a result are more likely to be satisfied teaching in the space (McDavid et al., 2018). Instructors who have received professional development in student-centered practices will acknowledge the limitations of the room, but then be able to adapt more easily. Instructors will be able to articulate the importance of student-centered learning and find ways to foster it regardless of the physical teaching space (Nelson et al., 2019). In a traditional lecture hall, active learning strategies become more difficult to implement since the space is by design less conducive to group work or peer-to-peer engagement (Beaudoin, Zywicki, Doan et al., 2016).

Nonetheless, instructors who have been through IMPACT are more likely to use active learning strategies even in large lecture classrooms. The following quote from an instructor interviewed as part of the study highlights this point:

> I make do with any classroom I get. I tell my students that I don't lecture. I facilitate discussions, and we have a lot of discussions. If I'm in a typical lecture hall, even stadium seating, I make students turn their chairs or at least twist to talk to other people. I teach one course that has demonstrations, and not just for the students to watch. But I've had students have to stand up in their seats and do different things, and I just make do with it. In some of my smaller class sizes, when I'm in the active learning space and definitely walking around, the students are moving around [and] switching up seats. So that style actually helps facilitate what I'm trying to do, but I'm all about active learning. I manage to figure out how to do that in a constrained environment. (Beaudoin, Zywicki, Doan, et al., 2016, p. 9)

Instructors' Skills–Active Learning Space Match

Instructors perceive active learning spaces to be in high demand, but not every active learning space is perceived as meeting the instructors' specific pedagogical needs. Therefore, the research team came up with a way to describe the optimal match between instructors' skill level and interest in using active learning strategies and the extent to which features in a physical space enable active learning.

The ideal situation is one in which there is a match between instructors' skills and interest and the type of physical classroom they are scheduled to teach in. Instructors wanting to integrate active and student-centered pedagogical practices are scheduled in active learning spaces. In contrast, instructors who rely on or prefer to lecture are scheduled in traditional learning spaces. The following quote from an instructor is illustrative:

> Having been in a very good active learning type of environment you can really do the most things. If I had to go back into a room where the chairs are all bolted to the ground or whatever, then I feel like I've been compromised as an instructor because I can't tap into a lot of things that I think are very beneficial to students and that would be frustrating. On the other hand, I have a number of colleagues that love that environment because that is what they've always been comfortable with. So, moving to an environment and even thinking about trying something with cooperative learning is a scary thing for them. So, you're likely to see people going both ways. (Beaudoin, Zywicki, Doan, et al., 2016, p. 8)

The first type of space–instructor mismatch occurs when instructors with high levels of skills and interests to teach using active learning and student-centered pedagogical practices are assigned to teach in traditional learning spaces. This mismatch represents a waste of skills. The following quotes are illustrative:

> So typically in our courses we have 150 students, and I like to do group work and active learning but I'm always placed in a room that is not conducive to that. It is usually a large lecture class that doesn't have anything movable. A lot of it is more theater type seating. (Beaudoin, Zywicki, Doan, et al., 2016, p. 9)

> I've had to give up on some things that I wanted to be able to do or the quality of the interaction. I would do my best to try and adapt but there is only so much you can do in a space. . . . But it's not enough to say I want an active learning room. We need to be able to specify which active learning rooms meet our needs. (Beaudoin, Zywicki, Doan, et al., 2016, p. 7)

The second type of space–instructor mismatch occurs when instructors are not interested or equipped to teach using student-centered or active learning pedagogical strategies but are assigned to teach in active learning spaces. This mismatch represents a waste of space. The following quote is illustrative:

> We're fighting for active learning classrooms. And the other frustrating part to me is that sometimes some of my colleagues want to use this space because it's a nice space but they don't use any of the active learning facets of it. They just like it because it's a new classroom and it's really nice and things like that. They don't want to go in the old 1950s-looking classroom. And that's frustrating. If they're not taking advantage of what this is designed for that's problematic. (Beaudoin, Zywicki, Doan, et al., 2016, p. 9)

Experience of Students

The research reported in this section focused on the experience and perceptions of students in active learning spaces. Over 2,000 students registered in the classes of 21 instructors teaching in ALCs reported on their perceptions of engagement in active learning spaces and attainment of learning outcomes (Beaudoin, Zywicki, Uche, et al., 2016).

Engagement in Active Learning Spaces

In working with faculty to create environments that are autonomy supportive and student centered, IMPACT makes connections with the principles of good practice from Chickering and Gamson (1987), since these principles align well with SDT. These seven principles are (a) encouraging contacts between students and faculty, (b) developing reciprocity and cooperation among students, (c) using active learning techniques, (d) giving prompt feedback, (e) emphasizing time on task, (f) communicating high expectations, and (g) respecting diverse talents and ways of learning. Results suggest that students taking classes in active learning spaces rated their experience along the seven principles of good practice as significantly greater for six of the seven principles. These were compared to their perceptions when taking classes in a traditional space. The only nonsignificant difference was found for the element of time on task, which was rated equally (Beaudoin, Zywicki, Uche, et al., 2016).

Another series of survey items asked about perceptions related to course competencies, feedback, and course preparation. Students reported feeling significantly more confident in being able to achieve their academic goals, adapt how to learn in order to be successful, and articulate course content in their own words when taking classes in active learning spaces. In regard to feedback, students taught in active learning spaces reported knowing their instructors and teaching assistants better and receiving more feedback from them as well as their fellow classmates. Finally, students in active learning spaces also reported being significantly more likely to be held accountable to be prepared for class. Although not all of the instructors teaching in active learning spaces have participated in the IMPACT professional development program, many have been exposed to some form of professional development, either through IMPACT or ALCoP. This suggests that the instructors teaching in ALCs are better equipped at creating environments that are autonomy supportive and that foster greater attainment of academic and learning outcomes.

Attainment of Learning Outcomes

Furthermore, during the IMPACT FLC, as described in chapter 4, instructors are introduced to Bloom's taxonomy as they work on creating and revising learning outcomes for their redesigned course. The six original domains of Bloom's taxonomy are (a) knowledge, (b) comprehension, (c) application, (d) analysis, (e) synthesis, and (f) evaluation. In the study described here, students were again asked to rate statements, this time aligning with the six domains of the original Bloom's taxonomy. They rated these statements for their experience in a course taught in an ALC and for their experience in a course taught in a traditional manner, typically in a traditional learning classroom. Results show that students perceived significantly greater attainment of all six domains of Bloom's taxonomy in ALCs compared to traditional classrooms, although the effect sizes were small. Interestingly, the greatest difference between the perceptions in the active versus traditional classrooms was observed for the two highest levels of the taxonomy: synthesis and evaluation (Beaudoin, Zywicki, Uche et al., 2016). Although many factors could influence these results, and keeping in mind that the effect sizes are small, these results may nonetheless suggest that when provided with the appropriate support and professional development resources, instructors are able to create environments that are fostering the attainment of all cognitive domains, especially the ones at the highest level of complexity. Once again, the effect of space needs to be taken into consideration in combination with the influence of the instructor facilitating the attainment of the established learning outcomes by using pedagogical practices that are student centered and autonomy supportive.

The professional development provided through IMPACT also helps instructors understand that learning environments are not necessarily experienced in the same way by all students. The round tables commonly found in active learning spaces and the group work they foster, if overused, may not always be perceived as autonomy supportive, under all situations, for some groups of students. For example, publicly discussing and sharing ideas may not align with the cultural norms and values of some Eastern cultures. This way of collaborating is common in Western societies but may not be as common in Eastern societies. This cultural piece needs to be taken into consideration as faculty are introduced to active learning pedagogies. In order to maximize the potential of all students, developers must help instructors seek to appreciate and understand how active learning pedagogies will influence the diversity of students in their classes. This, again, is where SDT could offer some insights. Offering a mix of learning activities and choices for student engagement may be part of the answer. Some students can take the lead discussing in groups, while others could choose to express their opinions on a discussion board (autonomy). Frequently seeking feedback from students regarding the effectiveness of new pedagogies at fostering their learning is also desirable (competence). Avoiding assumptions and generalizations is also essential. Building a sense of trust, belongingness, and community early on and throughout the semester is also a good strategy (relatedness). More research is definitely needed in this area, but these ideas can serve as a starting point.

Purdue is a leader among peer institutions in design, development, and use of learning spaces. The dedication of physical resources and personnel to the improvement of teaching and learning is remarkable. The contribution of the Purdue libraries as a catalyst for changing the way space is designed and used is revolutionary and follows recommendations for partnership as discussed in a recent information literacy research project (Head et al., 2020). Purdue has heavily invested in professional development for transformative education in the IMPACT program and the building of the WALC, this innovative academic library learning space. The commitment from Purdue to the transformation of teaching and learning spaces into more active and collaborative places of learning and the investment in professional development through the IMPACT program propelled instructors to adopt more student-centered teaching practices and examine their teaching in a scholarly way with support from the IMPACT team. Some of this research was featured in this chapter. More work needs to be done in this area, especially to understand the intersection of physical and developmental factors, which can foster success for all students. If we have ALCs on our campus, we all need to contribute and add to this work as well as provide support to instructors teaching in active learning spaces. We need to support instructors as they transform their courses, engage in teaching in ALCs, and engage in research to understand the influence of active learning and student-centered pedagogies on their teaching. This work is very important as teaching and learning spaces are transformed in many institutions of higher education. Let's remember the human factor of the transformations. That is the innovation.

9

INSTITUTIONAL, CULTURAL, AND ORGANIZATIONAL CHANGE

The IMPACT program has had a profound and deep influence at Purdue in several areas. I have addressed some of these, such as the influence on professional development, the active learning spaces, and the growth of the program, in (chapters 6, 7, and 8). In the current chapter, I want to contextualize these areas of influence among many others, which may or may not be as evident but are nonetheless part of a broader picture of the work of the IMPACT program on the institutional and culture change. This is the result of the work that we have been doing together as a team toward institutional and culture change.

Instructional Support and Learning Spaces

The work of the management team is where I would like to begin this discussion. When IMPACT was created back in 2011, the partnering units did not have the strong working relationship and common vision for professional development and teaching and learning that we have today. The partnering units now share a common goal, a common vision toward professional development based in SDT motivational principles and informed learning through their work on IMPACT (Flierl et al., 2019). The strengthening of the collaboration among the partnering units has fostered a culture change. It took time and systematic work to get where we are today with a strong spirit of collaboration among the partnering units. Today, the units regularly collaborate on supporting teaching, so much so that it has now become the norm.

Furthermore, in recent years a manifestation of this common vision toward teaching and learning has influenced hiring decisions. The TLT unit and the libraries have committed to hire staff members and faculty whose roles incorporate instructional design and professional development as part of their commitment to IMPACT. The way in which we have worked together toward a common mission and goal, for a university priority, has become a hallmark of collaboration at the institution. We continue to meet once a week as a management team and discuss the topics related to the IMPACT program, as well as the mission and vision of the program. IMPACT, and the way we foster the creation of working teams and learning communities, has been hailed as the standard for collaboration at the institution. In university provost's meetings, town hall meetings, and community gatherings, IMPACT is often referenced as a successful institutional program with far-reaching positive results for the institution. In fall 2018, this collaboration was broadened into a formalized team, the Innovative Learning Team. The Innovative Learning Team is a formal collaboration among CIE, TLT, Purdue Online, and the libraries, all partners in IMPACT. The Innovative Learning Team collaboration is based on the principles that make the IMPACT collaboration productive and successful, and it focuses on innovative and transformative teaching and learning projects. In addition, as discussed in chapter 8, the work of IMPACT in collaboration with PULSIS has been instrumental in the growth of active learning spaces on campus and ultimately the creation of the WALC. Since 2011, Purdue has been engaged in and committed to university-wide initiatives to promote active learning and transformation toward more student-centered practices, and the IMPACT team has been an integral part of these initiatives. The construction and opening of the WALC has helped spread the IMPACT transformation and curriculum. The collaborative classrooms in the WALC are colloquially referred to as the IMPACT classrooms. This commitment is continuing today and is manifested in plans and strategies for the conceptualization and design of future active learning buildings and physical facilities fostering student learning and engagement (DEGW, 2012; Head et al., 2020). The IMPACT team is currently working with entire departments and colleges in preparation for their move to new active learning facilities in the upcoming years. IMPACT professional development is spreading into other types of professional developmental initiatives and support for instructors, such as the ALCoP, and tailored curriculum design offerings for entire departments such as nursing and the PPI. IMPACT is also an important program mentioned in the Purdue Road Map for Transformative Undergraduate Education. This road map is in essence the provost's strategic plan for the years ahead, looking toward the most important outcomes of a university degree in 2030. IMPACT is hailed as a vehicle to foster transformative education and scale up effective research-based pedagogies.

Growth and Student Outcomes

As discussed in chapter 6, a focus on instructors as human beings and their motivational needs has allowed us to engage them in professional development and release their natural growth and creativity, beginning a process of individual change and fostering institutional transformation. This allowed us to shift the focus of the program from a perspective aligned with course redesign to one aligned with professional development. IMPACT fellows talk to their colleagues about their experience and encourage them to participate in the program. The focus on professional development has created ripple effects, where instructors not only transform the course they took through the IMPACT program but also apply the motivational principles they learned to other courses they are teaching. These influenced courses are a hallmark of the success of IMPACT as a professional development program. We have now reached the point where we count more influenced courses than courses that have formally gone through the IMPACT program. An interesting point to support this notion is that the IMPACT management team has essentially stopped actively recruiting in recent years. Instructors come to us to participate, and we effortlessly fill the cohort every semester. They have been referred by their colleagues or have heard about the program from a town hall meeting, a provost-level meeting, or a dean's or departmental meeting. IMPACT faculty fellows, deans, and department heads are strong allies of the IMPACT program and transformative education.

The IMPACT program has reached every college at Purdue and over 350 instructors teaching over 600 courses. In some colleges, the impact of the transformation has been so profound that some of the departments in these colleges have almost achieved 100% participation. The PPI and the nursing department are great examples of this phenomenon at Purdue. For example, at this time, almost 75% of the instructors in the PPI have been through the IMPACT program and transformation experience in one way or another. In addition, PPI has a goal to offer the IMPACT experience to 100% of their instructors in the next few years. The IMPACT team is working very closely with the PPI in order to make this a reality, accelerating the rate of change, and offering IMPACT program variations which would be tailored to the needs of the remaining faculty as well as new faculty hired into the college. In the words of Gary Bertoline, dean of the PPI:

> About 7 years ago, the undergraduate learning transformation of the college I lead, the Polytechnic Institute, was chosen as one of the Purdue Moves by President Mitch Daniels and the Board of Trustees at Purdue. The transformation of teaching and learning in the college was centered around 10 high-impact educational practices. One of the foundational high-impact practices we adopted was to convert all of our courses to an active learning format. Although our college had historically supplemented our lectures with hands-on laboratories, the lecture portion of our courses were almost entirely delivered through a traditional 50-minute lecture by the professor. Our goal was to disrupt this teaching methodology and adopt active learning in the lecture portion of our courses. This was a daunting task that faced our college. The IMPACT program was the key in our conversion efforts. We started to work directly with the leadership of the IMPACT program so that we could provide as many of our faculty with IMPACT training as possible. We also worked on creating special programs with IMPACT leadership to give some of our faculty training in the summer. Through these efforts we were able to quickly accelerate the conversion of many of our undergraduate lecture courses to an active learning format. (Personal communication, February 21, 2020)

Institutional Culture

As mentioned, Mitch Daniels created the Purdue Moves as a way to strategically move Purdue forward in four strategic areas of focus and growth in higher education. Still in place today at Purdue, the four strategic areas are affordability and accessibility, STEM leadership, world-changing research, and transformative education. As briefly discussed in chapter 4, when IMPACT was identified as a Purdue Move, we were called to scale up the program, and we drew on the principles of SDT, more specifically the satisfaction of the need for relatedness, to build the FLC into a true learning community with scaling potential. Building trust and meaningful relationships in the teams is very important and can't be overstated. It is at the core of the IMPACT philosophy driven by the principles of SDT, and the cornerstone of a successful scale-up. Today, IMPACT is reaching over 90% of the students over the course of their studies at Purdue and up to 96% of the students in certain semesters (Levesque-Bristol, Flierl et al., 2019; Levesque-Bristol, Maybee, et al., 2019). For some students, the effect of the transformation on their academic success has been dramatic. In certain STEM courses, such as introduction to chemistry, calculus, or mechanical engineering, the drop in DFW rates has been up to 30%! For any one of these large gateway courses, the significant reduction of these failure rates has translated into over 500 students on average every academic year passing their classes and staying on track to degree completion (IMPACT Management Team and IMPACT Evaluation Team, 2019).

The significance of the improvements in student learning outcomes at the level of an entire college is expressed by Gary Bertoline:

> The results have made a remarkable positive difference in our courses, our faculty, and our student learning outcomes. Students are more engaged and we believe that our improved first-year retention and improved graduation rates are in part because of our adopting the IMPACT way of teaching. We also believe that having our faculty take the IMPACT program, they have become much more receptive to the other high impact education practices. The IMPACT program has opened their minds and hearts to recognize that a focus on their teaching will have a direct benefit to their students and their own satisfaction as a teacher. (Personal communication, February 21, 2020)

When I began this work early in my faculty development career thinking about a course transformation program based in motivational principles, I encountered some resistance from university administration. Guided by the motivational theory of SDT, I had a sense that to build and grow a course transformation program that could be scaled across all disciplines and impact a large number of instructors with a diversity of training, backgrounds, and interests throughout the institution, a rigid approach was not the answer. The common course transformation programs at the time were rigid, inflexible, and prescriptive. In SDT terms, they were controlling or pressuring faculty who participated in these course transformation programs to enact a transformation in a certain way and forego their autonomy as an instructor. These transformations were requiring instructors to use a certain amount of technology or select an online textbook, and to approach their redesign with the specific goals of increasing retention rates and lowering costs (Twigg, 2003). Although these models were effective for certain faculty who were teaching certain disciplines and who could get behind the idea of a certain redesign model with certain fixed features, it was clear to me that this strategy would not foster pedagogical changes that would be broad, far-reaching, and felt throughout the institution. It was too prescriptive. In other words, this approach would not foster the kind of culture change we were ultimately seeking. It could not foster deep and broad institutional change around teaching and learning, because it did not provide choices, options, and flexibility to instructors engaging in the transformation. The choices and options were very limited, and instructors were not fully involved in the transformation process. The administrative burden of participating and then successfully completing the transformation program was significant. It involved the completion of spreadsheets demonstrating the cost savings of the course redesign for the proposed increase in student success defined heavily by completion rates. As part of the cost-saving demonstration, the integration of an online pedagogical tool or technology in the redesign was mandatory. In SDT motivational terms, it did not foster the satisfaction of the need for autonomy. It did not offer an autonomy-supportive environment to engage in these demanding transformations and therefore failed to provide the conditions necessary for the satisfaction of basic psychological needs in order to foster deep, lasting, broad, and meaningful changes. It did not provide the conditions necessary for culture and institutional change.

Addressing the instructors' need for autonomy is an essential part of the FLC process of scholarly inquiry and discovery. In working with the fellows, the support team members create environments that are autonomy supportive and satisfy the three basic psychological needs of autonomy, competence, and relatedness. As SDT is a theory of human motivation, the principles apply to all human beings; not only students but also instructors. The instructors are central to the transformation process. When working with the instructors, the support team members ask what the instructors want to do with their course; they listen to their needs and interests; they provide choices and options; and they do not force, prescribe, or pressure instructors to move their transformation in a certain direction, or toward a certain redesign model, or to adopt a certain technological tool. The instructors are being empowered in the process and find themselves at the center of the transformation work, which allows them to feel supported and to enact the transformation the way they want to following the SDT motivational principles. If a certain technological tool or redesign model is selected, it is because it can support the overall learning and engagement goals identified in the course. It serves a purpose and functions to further engage the students in the learning process and support the learning outcomes and objectives identified by the instructor. The provision of an autonomy-supportive environment leads to endorsement by the instructors and long-lasting change, because it allows the instructors to internalize and endorse the reasons for the course transformation and to focus on their own transformation goals through the satisfaction of basic psychological needs. This approach that supports the basic needs and the internalization process is a cornerstone of SDT, and the process by which deep and lasting institutional and culture change is possible.

Because this autonomy-supportive process fostered through the IMPACT FLC is aligned with the satisfaction of basic psychological needs, instructors participating in the program feel energized and engaged in the program.

They report gaining a lot of knowledge and value from their participation in the FLC. This allows the program to grow and be scaled in very meaningful ways and affect the larger institutional and organizational culture. It makes it possible for instructors from a variety of disciplines, STEM and non-STEM fields, to equally engage in the transformation process. The central innovation of the program is the focus on human motivation and basic psychological needs as a way to create an engaging and student-centered learning environment, as opposed to a certain model or redesign type to achieve student engagement and success.

Our most important assets are people: the students taking the classes, the instructors teaching the classes and researching at the institution, the academic administrators influencing educational policies, and all other stakeholders. We all need to be engaged in the process for culture and organizational change to be fostered and sustained (Levesque-Bristol, Flierl, et al., 2019; Levesque-Bristol, Maybee, et al., 2019).

What instructors have learned going through IMPACT has broadly influenced not only the courses they teach but also their teaching philosophy, their ability to foster innovation inside and outside of their classrooms, and their ability to describe these teaching innovations as part of their application process for tenure and promotion as well as various teaching awards and grants. The focus on human needs has allowed instructors to integrate these principles in their teaching philosophy and view and present their teaching differently. If an instructor has been a participant in IMPACT, their application packet for teaching and learning awards will reference and highlight their IMPACT work. The Charles B. Murphy Outstanding Undergraduate Teaching and Exceptional Early Teaching Award is the highest university teaching award at Purdue, and induction into the Teaching Academy is a highly selective process. In recent years, for both of these honors, a large proportion of the nominees have been IMPACT fellows, and their application portfolios include the result of their work with IMPACT and the influence of this work on the courses they teach, their teaching philosophy, and teaching and learning innovations they engaged in.

In addition to the role of IMPACT in teaching and learning awards, participation in IMPACT is also highlighted in tenure and promotion portfolios. Overall, about 17% of faculty fellows have been promoted since going through IMPACT. This is especially true in certain colleges who have fully endorsed the transformation culture focused on student engagement. This large-scale departmental involvement indicates buy-in by both faculty and administrators. One such college is PPI, whose requirements for promotion and tenure include participation in IMPACT. In many colleges, research and scholarly pursuits include SoTL. IMPACT faculty fellows are encouraged and provided resources and financial support in order to turn their redesign/transformation goal into a research question. A small but meaningful proportion of them have done so and have even had the opportunity to present their work at research or teaching and learning conferences, as well as publish the results of their inquiry in peer-reviewed journals.

To meet an even greater proportion of the instructional community at Purdue and beyond, new professional development opportunities have been created in conjunction with IMPACT by the IMPACT management team. As discussed previously, a SoTL community of IMPACT faculty fellows has formed for those who want to more deeply pursue scholarship emanating from their IMPACT experience. In addition, similar communities around informed learning, data science, and course portfolios have emerged from the IMPACT program and are supported with funds and personnel resources. These additional opportunities are met with excitement; instructors want and welcome more of these opportunities coming from IMPACT. The IMPACT team has also created a mostly online offering of the 14-week FLC, called IMPACT ACCESS. The IMPACT ecosystem is growing in many ways and influencing more of the lives of instructors and students at Purdue and beyond. This expansion based on the specific needs of instructors is definitely an important marker of culture and institutional change.

Teaching and Learning Higher Education Culture and Beyond

The research and scholarly work of the IMPACT team, conducted nationally and internationally, has contributed to influence the conversation in higher education more broadly, regionally, nationally, and internationally. The IMPACT management team has worked with several institutions of higher education who have been interested in reproducing and adapting the IMPACT professional development model at their own institution. Some actually did very successfully. The national recognition the program has received also contributes to its successful dissemination. In October 2018, IMPACT was featured as one of six programs to change classroom culture in the special "Innovator" issue of *The Chronicle of Higher Education*. In February 2019, IMPACT was once again featured in *The Chronicle of Higher Education*, this time in the context of their special report on "The Truth About Student Success." Internationally, IMPACT is also gaining traction and has been implemented or is being considered in institutions of higher education in Europe, South America, and Africa, creating a network of institutions interested in the IMPACT model for professional development and course transformation.

In general, the conversations about IMPACT are not solely focused on the program itself and the content of the program but tend to gravitate toward the broad implications of the programs for higher education. In engaging in conversations with other institutions nationally and internationally, the most important factors for successful application emerged to be the collaboration and partnership among multiple units on campus, ensuring autonomy in selecting redesign models and elements of the transformation, and the use of a theoretical framework to guide the design and assessment of the course transformation program.

The extent to which instructors are able to create environments that are autonomy supportive is influenced by not only the professional development support that instructors receive but also instructors' own motivational orientation at the beginning of the process and the larger educational context. Instructors bring their own motivation and personality characteristics to a professional development program like IMPACT as well as the classroom. Instructors who are autonomy supportive are more likely to create environments that are engaging and autonomy supportive and be perceived by students as such. In contrast, more controlling instructors tend to create environments that are less flexible and more controlling (Ryan & Deci, 2017). In addition, the institutional and administrative context can also either foster or thwart instructors' level of motivation. Administrative controls, inflexible curriculum, or a stringent and controlling educational context at the level of the institution can all undermine the satisfaction of instructors' basic psychological needs of autonomy, competence, and relatedness. The lack of recognition and support for instructors, the lack of time to invest in course transformation efforts in the midst of other demands and priorities, high-stakes environments for tenure-track faculty, and lack of clear standards for promotion and tenure are only a few of the most common types of pressures faced by instructors. Instructors experience many pressures and constraints as they attempt to engage in transformative education. In certain situations, some of these pressures are experienced from above, and in other cases some of these pressures are experienced from below, and these challenges are very real (Pelletier et al., 2002).

The "pressures from below" stem from the students' perceptions regarding active learning. Although active learning is effective and beneficial when implemented well, as I describe in this book, students may still feel very hesitant when they walk into their first ALC. To students used to passively listening in a lecture, active learning can feel very unfamiliar and unsettling at first. Students may not understand how to behave in this type of classroom and may be concerned about how to best perform in a classroom environment like this and how this will affect their grades. The high-stakes testing for students may contribute to these fears regarding change. Students understand how crucial good performance on high-stakes tests is. They may have developed strategies to help them succeed in these environments. It may put pressure on them, but the pressures you know are sometimes more comforting then the fear of change. It takes time for students to trust and adapt to change, even if these changes are ultimately beneficial, as with autonomy-supportive environments.

In a qualitative study conducted by the IMPACT team (Parker et al., 2015) in the first few years of the program, some of these pressures were highlighted by faculty fellows as significant barriers for implementation and sustainability of their transformation. In this study, 27 faculty fellows were interviewed one on one or in small groups, and they highlighted student resistance to active learning as an important barrier. There is a great discrepancy between students and instructors in their understanding and expectations regarding the roles and responsibilities of students and instructors in higher education, especially if students have not been exposed to this transformed model. In addition, students may not understand the importance of communication and the expectation of instructors regarding group work in an ALC. Students might be scared to fail. As mentioned previously, controlling environments tend to produce fear responses and lead to inflexibility in students. International students and students from underrepresented minorities may not feel comfortable in environments in which they need to communicate extensively. In our work with faculty fellows, we highlight these differences and challenges and invite them to clearly communicate, on day one, the purpose of active learning and their expectations around this type of pedagogy. Essentially, we emphasize the importance of providing a meaningful rationale for the transformation.

The "pressures from above" are created by the institution itself or upper administration. Under many inflexible and top-down policies, institutions have become extremely focused on a very narrow definition of student success, pressuring faculty, staff, and students to emphasize only certain cognitive goals and neglecting the development of the students as individuals with their diverse interests, talents, and psychological needs. Evidence demonstrates that when teachers are empowered, provided opportunities to be creative, supported, and trusted, students benefit through the provision of autonomy-supportive environments. As discussed in chapter 2, humans naturally are drawn to environments and behaviors that support the satisfaction of their basic psychological needs. In optimal environments, humans are oriented toward growth and development. Being supported in the larger educational context provides the conditions under which instructors can also create autonomy-supportive environments that will foster and support the satisfaction of their students' basic psychological needs. The creation of a motivational educational climate provides all sorts of positive affordances in terms of instructor and staff well-being and educational outcomes; however, it is not an easy task. Policymakers, stakeholders, and university administrators are called to create and foster an educational climate that supports instructors so they can implement and sustain institutional transformations, educational reforms, and curricular changes through the creation of student-centered, autonomy-supportive, and inclusive learning environments that support the growth and success of all students. SDT provides a framework to stimulate reflection and suggest changes in educational policy and practices that thwart the basic psychological needs of instructors, staff, and students and undermine intrinsic motivation, self-determined motivation, and internalization.

The many pressures that instructors face in the larger educational context make it more difficult to enact and sustain educational transformations that foster the success of students. Instructors may see and understand the value of creating environments that are more engaging, student centered, and autonomy supportive. They may wish to engage in this meaningful and important work; however, they may feel constrained in their ability to do so. Should they focus on submitting a grant proposal, writing an article in their academic field, or engaging in growing their teaching and learning practices? Should instructors be more concerned about setting up their research lab, or can they spend the time to reflect on their teaching practices and engage in creating student-centered environments? Should they stick with the traditional format commonly adopted in their field using a limited number of high-stakes, multiple-choice machine-graded tests, or should they transform their courses and use more student-centered autonomy-supportive assessment practices, which require reflection, provision of meaningful feedback, and more time to implement well? Instructors often wonder, and rightly so, whether engaging in teaching and learning professional development and developing their practices will be valued in their academic department, college, and university when it comes time for tenure and promotion decisions or renewal of a work contract. Just like students, instructors may fear this changing landscape and what it will mean to them and their careers (Palmer, 1998).

In a qualitative study conducted by Parker et al. (2015), the faculty fellows interviewed highlighted their colleagues' and administrators' perceptions of the value of teaching and learning as another important barrier to transformation and sustainability. Instructors reported that spending too much time on their teaching could be perceived negatively and put them at risk of being perceived as a less than stellar researcher. In other words, instructors emphasized their concerns that spending too much time on teaching could send the message that they were not great researchers and needed to invest their energies and time elsewhere. Although both men and women talked about this issue, women felt that their gender increased the risk of their colleagues and administrators minimizing their research accomplishments because of the time they invested in their teaching.

Too often, instructors face these challenges and question how they should spend and invest their time. Their desire to engage in growing their teaching practice and fostering the learning and development of all of their students is pitted against the demands of the academic institutions. The focus on "publish or perish" may limit instructors' time and focus on the students who are perceived to be the most successful and talented—those who obtain the best grades with apparently little effort, who are retained in the most competitive majors, and achieve at the highest level. Instructors may feel torn between satisfying their need for autonomy and their need for relatedness and competence, especially if instructors have chosen to work in academic institutions for the love of teaching and learning. In academic institutions, the need for relatedness and competence may involve securing tenure and being accepted and valued by senior colleagues and academic administrators. Situations in the workplace in which autonomy is pitted against relatedness and competence can lead to illness, compulsions, burnout, and the lack of vitality, energy, and motivation to engage fully, passionately, and creatively in the work that one is doing. It leads to disengagement in employees and lack of focus, which translates to lack of productivity.

An institutional culture focused on professional development based in SDT can help. We have seen changes at Purdue that are making me hopeful about what can be accomplished in higher education, if we truly work together and focus on human needs and potential. We have seen changes that more equally align the focus on research and teaching. I have seen instructors speak up in a public venue for the positive changes IMPACT has brought to their teaching and advocate for more of this culture and institutional change. Deans have also endorsed the transformational and professional development power of IMPACT.

> I am convinced that without the IMPACT program we would have fallen far short in our goal to transform undergraduate teaching and learning in our college. One of the lessons we learned early on in our transformation efforts was that you have to start with the faculty when making change. You do that through a carefully crafted professional development program and provide faculty with the time and support necessary to make the change. The IMPACT programs does all of that. (G. Bertoline, 2020, personal communication, February 21, 2020)

More work certainly needs to be done, but this deep, broad, and meaningful culture change is possible. If we all work together and commit to the growth and development of human potential, change and true transformation is possible. Inertia is not an excuse for lack of transformation. It's not acceptable to stay where we are because this is how it's always been done. Heart work is hard work, but it's possible. Let's focus on human potential, the potential of students, educators, faculty developers, and administrators—all of us, together, toward the transformation of higher education. Embrace change, not fear.

10

IMPACT AND THE COVID-19 PANDEMIC

Implications for Faculty Development

Before the Pandemic

On March 2, 2020, I delivered a full draft of this book to John von Knorring, editor at Stylus. I was tired but satisfied. I had been sick for about a month—since Febuary 8th—and was very much looking forward to some time off to rest, heal, and recharge. I had some down time scheduled that week and vacation planned with family for spring break 2020. That evening, I received a call from Frank Dooley, at the time Purdue's vice provost for teaching and learning, telling me that we needed to be ready for the possibility of shutting down the IMPACT program so we could divert all resources toward helping faculty prepare for emergency remote teaching (ERT).

As we sat in a meeting the next day with Frank Dooley and a small core group of the IMPACT leadership team, we began to think about how we could support faculty in the event we would need to shut down campus and teach remotely. The idea of not finishing the spring 2020 semester face to face for the full IMPACT FLC seemed such a far-fetched and distant idea. At that time, we thought we could use the IMPACT team and the resources in order to support faculty making the move to the possibility of ERT and, at the same time, continue to deliver the IMPACT program face to face. It is bizarre to say this, but on that day, most of us did not think we were going to have to shut down campus. As we all know now, we were only 11 days away from this new reality—the physical closure of the campus and the end of face-to-face instruction for the remainder of the spring 2020 semester.

Nonetheless, the IMPACT team, as part of the broader Innovative Learning Team, mobilized immediately and began meeting daily to discuss what faculty needed during this period of uncertainty and possible transition and how we could marshal the IMPACT team to build resources for faculty and instructional staff. The strong collaboration built over the past 9 years, and described in previous chapters, allowed us to immediately put our skills, resources, and teamwork forward to support instructors in this time of transition, uncertainty, and questioning. I quickly redirected the resources of two team members, one to lead the strategic communication plan and create a web presence related to supporting ERT and the other one to lead a "Tiger Team" made of IMPACT team members to begin creating an emergency professional development plan. We also began hosting face-to-face drop-in sessions in the WALC to discuss with faculty what this remote teaching environment would look like and feel like. As the days progressed and the looming realization of a physical shutdown of the campus became more of a distinct reality, we drew on the IMPACT model to understand how we could adapt not only this model to the remote and online environment but also our own IMPACT program. On March 4, during the IMPACT FLC, we shared the possibility for the first time with the IMPACT faculty fellows.

In less than a week, the strategic communication team had created a web presence with a Teaching Remotely page (https://www.purdue.edu/innovativelearning/teaching-remotely/). This page was full of resources guiding the entire instructional community of faculty and instructors to put their content online, revise their syllabus, and rethink their assessments for the online remote environment. The content on the page was designed to support faculty as they began to think about what a remote teaching and learning environment could look like and prepared to make the quick pivot to teach remotely. In less than a week, we brought important pedagogical principles to bear to help faculty make a successful transition to the ERT environment.

On March 6, the Teaching Remotely page was launched on the Innovative Learning website. The Teaching Remotely page featured two quick-start guides, orienting instructors to one of the two LMSs available at that time, Blackboard and Brightspace, and walked instructors through uploading content and establishing a presence into one of the LMS systems. To add to the complexity of the situation, Purdue was also in the middle of an LMS transition.

By March 10, over 700 visits had been logged to the new Teaching Remotely web page. Obviously, instructors were actively looking for information from the Innovative Learning team in order to meet the remote teaching challenge successfully.

The Pandemic

On March 11, 2020, the novel coronavirus disease COVID-19 was declared a pandemic by the World Health Organization. Purdue also announced that we were not returning after spring break and to prepare to move all remaining course content online. That same day, we had our last in-person IMPACT FLC. During this session, I announced to the faculty fellows that we were going to finish the semester remotely. We were dedicated to leading by example, and instead of canceling the face-to-face IMPACT FLC, we chose to adapt the recommendations for remote teaching to the IMPACT FLC. In fact, these recommendations for remote teaching were emanating from the work that we were doing together as the IMPACT team, drawing on the SDT principles and research-informed pedagogical recommendations. I'll focus on these principles and how we adapted them in the following section.

The next morning, March 12, at 8:00 a.m., 4,912 visitors had logged into the Teaching Remotely web page! There was a big gasp during the morning meeting. There was not merely a need; instructors were desperate to find information on how to adapt their teaching to the pandemic crisis and the need to teach remotely for the remainder of the semester. We had our work cut out for us.

On March 13, 2020, I, along with my colleagues in the Center for Instructional Excellence and Innovative Learning, started working remotely, knowing that we were not coming back to face-to-face campus after spring break. Now well into June, I am still working remotely and planning for fall 2020, when students will be returning to campus. But I digress.

All the remote meetings were very taxing at first. Staring at a screen all day without the benefit of being able to walk down the hallway to engage in conversation with my colleagues was jarring. My ability to meet my need for relatedness was definitely suffering. My need for competence was high, however. I was engaged in a very important and meaningful task. We were now working remotely; the entire instructional community was being called to move to remote teaching and very quickly. We were going to be remote following spring break 2020. We had to let that sink in.

But we could not rest or reflect for too long. We had an exceptionally important task to do, and faculty and instructors were counting on us to help them successfully navigate this transition. To be successful during this transition, we drew on the IMPACT model and our strong collaboration to continue to work as a team and adapt very quickly and effectively to the remote environment. As we learned to adapt the skills and strengths we had developed to the remote environment, we brought those same ideas forward to help instructors do the same by drawing on our experience.

Drawing on the principles of SDT, we focused on how we could foster engagement in this new work and learning environment. We began by intentionally bringing more relatedness to our work. We used the WebEx meeting rooms as a way to spontaneously connect with each other throughout the day, and we hosted happy hour on Friday afternoons, just as we would have done in a face-to-face environment. We quickly realized what I had suspected, that the IMPACT collaboration and model we had used were applicable in this context as well, and they were invaluable in helping us pivot very quickly to a remote environment.

As we continued to build content and provide resources on the Teaching Remotely web page of the Innovative Learning website and develop a regular communication channel with faculty and instructors through the provost's office, we continued to see the request for consultations and the views to the Teaching Remotely page grow daily, as you can see in the following:

On March 13: 9,320 views
On March 16: 13,353 views
On March 20: 17,346 views

On Monday, March 23, the first day of ERT classes following spring break, the number of views on the website hit 19,518! As of June 2020, we had passed 40,000 views! Simply outstanding.

The significance of the IMPACT model and what we had built over the years became evidently important for conducting faculty development face to face and online and with implications for future practice. The model was scalable and important not only in times of crisis such as the current pandemic but also as a standard practice of professional development. The IMPACT model continued to inform our pedagogical practices as we moved to ERT and working remotely as a team. We were able to continue to effectively work together as a team and collaborate while supporting the instructional community, because the same principles we had used to build and scale the IMPACT model across various teaching and delivery modalities were applicable in this time of crisis as we worked with faculty and instructors to shift to remote instruction. What we had built with the IMPACT program, and what I described in the previous chapters of this book, allowed us to increase our reach as professional developers for not only for brick-and-mortar institutions but also institutions who have or plan to implement a significant online presence.

ERT

March 23 marked the first day of ERT at Purdue. What did that look like for us at Purdue? How did we, as professional developers, foster the transition to remote teaching, and what guiding principles did we emphasize in our work and communication with faculty and instructors?

Focusing on Engagement and Student-Centered Learning

As I describe in this book, and as supported by research evidence, a cornerstone of effective teaching is a focus on student engagement and student-centered learning. When learning environments are engaging and student centered, positive personal and academic outcomes follow. Students, in what we have described in this book as autonomy-supportive environments, are more likely to report that their basic psychological needs of autonomy, competence, and relatedness are met. In turn, when students' basic psychological needs are met, more positive learning outcomes follow. In the move to ERT, it was extremely important to preserve this level of engagement with students and help faculty find ways to continue to foster the students' basic psychological needs. In our role as professional developers, we in turn had to find ways to support faculty and instructors' basic psychological needs so they could provide this level of support and care to their students (consult chapters 2 and 3 for a detailed discussion of SDT, autonomy-supportive environments, and basic psychological needs). How did we do that? As a group of professional developers, we held weekly drop-in sessions, first in person in the WALC and then remotely through WebEx, in order to consult with faculty and instructors about strategies to maintain student engagement. We made ourselves available to instructors and provided a host of resources on the Teaching Remotely web page. In particular we encouraged faculty and instructors to find ways to stay connected with their students and pay attention to students who were not engaged in the course. This could be done through the use of the discussion board or a WebEx call. We encouraged instructors to do so in a variety of ways, using synchronous and asynchronous ways of connecting, since students were now in various times zones all around the United States and the world. Even among those students who were still in the United States, many reported facing various challenges from poor internet connection, to crowded houses, to a lack of available devices enabling students to engage with the content and with others and complete their work on time. We encouraged faculty to carefully pay attention to a sudden lack of engagement. Did they have students who used to be timely with their assignments suddenly missing deadlines or not turning in work altogether? These signs of disengagement were often symptoms of greater underlying problems during this stressful time. Some students reported stress from financial difficulty due to loss of family income or emotional burden due to the illness of a parent testing positive for COVID-19 and being admitted to the hospital. Some students lost the ability to communicate with their peers and instructors after being placed in a quarantine camp with essentially nonexistent access to the internet. Many reported a general sense of anxiety and confusion from the overall situation and the need to now do their work all remotely without the face-to-face support of others and the schools' infrastructure (advising, dining, residence hall). Some students found themselves with no safe place to go and not enough to eat once the campus physically shut down. This discussion leads us to the second guiding principle we emphasized in our work supporting faculty through ERT: the need to be flexible and understanding in our work with faculty and, in turn, in their work with students.

Focusing on Flexibility, Understanding, and Adaptability

We encouraged faculty and instructors to be flexible and understanding. It was not only difficult for instructors to make the quick pivot to remote teaching; it was difficult for students. Everyone was feeling the stress and the anxiety of the situation. Some instructors were finding themselves having to teach online for the first time in their career; some students were finding themselves in the same learning situation. We discovered that although many students are digital natives, using a cell phone for communication with friends you can also see, meet, and engage with face to face is not the same as working, learning, and engaging completely remotely. Some students reported not being able to find their motivation and lost entire days scrolling through social media on their phones or watching the news mindlessly. The loss of relatedness and the feeling of isolation that ensue are powerful paralyzing factors. Focusing on engagement and relatedness became a crucial piece of our work with faculty during ERT. Building, fostering, and maintaining the sense of belongingness and relatedness in the online remote environment was necessary in order to help students engage in their course work. Creating environments to continue to engage with students and meet the need for relatedness energized students to get through the course work, complete the semester, and find ways to succeed, allowing them to meet their need for competence.

Again, maintaining engagement was our most important task. With this backdrop in mind, maintaining the current course schedule as outlined in the syllabus, with the same assignments and deadlines, was simply impossible in most cases because of not only the nature of the work to do but also mental, emotional, and physical burdens students and instructors were facing. The multiple face-to-face labs, the group field work, the in-class presentations, the small group discussions, which were all scheduled as part of the regular semester and outlined in the syllabus for points earned toward the course grade, could not be conducted as originally planned. Much of the work with faculty involved coming up with alternatives for these in-class activities while emphasizing flexibility, understanding, and adaptability. Some assignments or activities had to be eliminated while others were completely restructured. For example, one faculty member in forestry and natural science showed video footage of controlled forest burns and asked his students to write an analysis of the burn procedure and what they would do differently. This remote activity replaced the planned field trip and on-site participation that was originally scheduled. Face-to-face labs had to be modified and conducted at home with common household products, or videos of labs readily available on the internet were used for demonstration purposes while students were asked to write an analysis of the lab procedure. Exams, especially the final exam period, were remarkably challenging, particularly for the courses that typically hold large high-stakes, proctored, evening exams, such as is typical in the introduction STEM courses. In some cases, the final exams were replaced with a number of lower-stakes assessments or some term papers or projects that were more easily completed remotely. This is such an important issue in our current teaching and learning environment that I will come back to the issue of academic integrity in a later section.

Focusing on Course Learning Outcomes and Objectives

As we worked with faculty and instructors and helped them rethink their course syllabus and requirements for the remainder of the semester, we emphasized the need to focus on course learning outcomes and objectives. We focused on the following questions: What do you want the students to still gain from your course from now until the end of the semester, before the course is completed? What learning outcomes do the students still need to meet? What we really needed to establish, and specifically write down, in partnership with the faculty were the learning outcomes that still needed to be met in order for the course to be completed. In doing this work, some faculty realized that the learning outcomes for the course were mostly met. They may have had one more to meet; in some cases, meeting this last learning outcome didn't require a high-stakes final exam. In those cases, we encouraged instructors to restructure the final exam to be a lower-stakes assessment specifically designed to meet the remaining learning outcome. As instructors completed this exercise, some recognized that the unmet learning outcomes could be achieved in a different way, which reduced the experience of stress and was more appropriate to the remote learning environment. For example, in introduction to chemistry, instead of testing foundational chemistry concepts in a high-stakes comprehensive final exam, the understanding of these concepts was examined in a series of smaller, lower-stakes assessments, which allowed students to explain their answers and expand on their understanding of the concepts. The assessment was untimed and could be completed over a week.

Online Exams and Academic Integrity

In spring 2020, the conversation and questions around ERT quickly spilled into how we would conduct large-scale, high-stakes exams online and maintain academic integrity. As professional developers, we engaged in some difficult conversations. Our goal was to steer the dialogue to and foster meaningful conversations around the purpose of exams and in particular the use of high-stakes exams in meeting learning outcomes. In all our conversations and support material, we encouraged faculty and instructors to think about alternative ways of assessing students that would be lower stakes; foster collaboration among students; engage them in meaningful problems to solve; and not necessitate extensive proctoring methods, tools, and technologies. In the ERT environment, high-stakes, multiple-choice, timed exams, requiring the use of proctoring or very high levels of control in order to administer it properly, were encouraged only as a last resort. Why did we choose such an approach? As I discussed in chapter 3, high-stakes exams, because of their high level of control, already undermine autonomous motivation. In addition, the pressures associated with high-stakes exams tend to disproportionately affect women (Ballen et al., 2017) and underrepresented students (Harris et al., 2020). In the context of the quick pivot to ERT, the controlling and demotivating nature of high-stakes exams was further enhanced and magnified, especially for women and underrepresented students. As discussed in chapter 6, there are ways to de-emphasize the controlling aspect of exams and instead emphasize their informational nature or the opportunity for exams to provide feedback on the students' ability or attainment of important course learning outcomes related to critical course concepts. When we encourage instructors to think about exams in this way, as we did during the shift to ERT, we encourage a focus on the learning outcomes and objectives of the course. We guided the conversation toward the meaning of exams and assessments as a way to provide information on the development of skills and knowledge associated with course content. To achieve these goals does not require a high-stakes, high-pressure, highly controlled environment. As described in the previous section, some instructors chose this approach with great success. The approach was very rigorous, as it was connected to learning outcomes and objectives for the course, and it had the advantage of being sensitive to the new pressures, constraints, and realities of the COVID-19 teaching and learning context. In instances where high-stakes exams were nonetheless utilized and proctoring obviously could not be conducted with the level of control afforded in the face-to-face environment, a number of problems occurred related to academic integrity. In those instances, we did experience a significant increase in the numbers of reported instances of academic dishonesty to the Office of Students' Rights and Responsibilities. For the 2019–2020 academic year to date, over 1,000 cases had been reported, with 1 more month to go of data capturing, compared to a little less than 500 cases in the past academic year. This is on average about double the cases reported over the past 4 academic years. Of those 1,000 cases, 700 of them were reported since March 23, when we began remote instruction. The vast majority of the cases involved some form of unauthorized use of online resources. This occurred even though we offered the following common recommendations to foster academic integrity when conducting high-stakes multiple-choice exams (Purdue University, n.d.).

Begin the exam with a nongraded "prequestion" about the Purdue Honor Pledge, set as a gateway to be able to access the actual exam. At Purdue, this statement reads as follows: "I agree with this statement: As a Boilermaker pursuing academic excellence, I pledge to be honest and true in all that I do. Accountable together—we are Purdue" (Purdue University, n.d., p. 3). Make use of a large question bank comprising questions of various levels of difficulty for different topics and concepts in order to create multiple equivalent versions of the exams. Then, randomize the order of the questions and set the exam to display only one question at a time. Assign a time limit for the completion of the exam once the student starts the exam; however, consider providing a generous amount of additional time to complete the exam, for example double the time, to account for internet connectivity issues. In addition, consider leaving the exam open and available for at least a 24-hour period, so students in widely different time zones can take the exam at a convenient time. We also recommended that instructors avoid using the forced completion function in the LMS, which prevents students from getting back into the exam if they get kicked out because of connectivity issues. Finally, as a general recommendation, we strongly encouraged instructors to avoid grading on a curve, which increases the likelihood of students cheating, as they feel the pressure of competing with other students in the class in order to succeed. All these and more recommendations can be found in Purdue University's (n.d.) Exams and Academic Integrity Considerations document.

As this point, I would like to engage in a broader conversation as to why students feel motivated to cheat. The high-stakes pressured exams create environments that are highly controlling, in which the desired outcome (good grades) is highly valued and its importance heightened. In these situations, pressure is very high to obtain these desired outcomes, and if the support and resources needed to foster learning is not present (e.g., cannot find relevant course material to study before an exam), some students will seek ways to obtain the desired outcomes by any means available under those highly pressured environments. Although most students will choose to do the right thing, some will seek these nonoptimal routes.

How could academic integrity be truly enhanced and fostered, especially but not only in times of remote teaching? Let's begin by giving real problems to students to solve. In this time of pandemic, there are so many real problems to solve and to ponder, problems that the students are already thinking about and grappling with. Why not ask them to apply the content, knowledge, and skills developed in the course to those real problems they are already trying to solve? I believe, and research in SDT supports this assertion, that humans are not lazy. As I have discussed in this book, all humans, including students, are motivated and have a natural tendency to grow and develop. When students appear unmotivated, it is most often because the environment is not compelling enough to grab their attention, curiosity, and interest. Students appear disinterested, unmotivated, and are more susceptible to thinking about cheating when the problems we as educators are asking them to solve are not engaging or meaningful. When problems are real, even though a clear solution to the problem is not known, and students are asked to explain the process of arriving at their solution, critical thinking is fostered while we tap into the natural interest and curiosity of students. In addition, allowing or even encouraging students to work together collaboratively on the solution, bringing to bear different talents, strengths, and perspectives, teaches students important soft skills that are absolutely necessary and valued in a growing number of fields. Thinking about incorporating learning outcomes such as teamwork and collaboration into the course is also something we strongly encouraged in our work with faculty as we tackled the challenges of ERT. In fact, I would ask, how many situations do you face in your work as a professional developer or an instructor in which you have to complete a task absolutely on your own, without consulting any of the resources at your disposal, whether the internet or a book, and without consulting with any of your colleagues? Teamwork and the ability to work in teams and collaborate with others are actually essential skills we don't teach and emphasize enough. Along the same lines, allowing exams to be open book and open source makes a lot of sense and also eliminates the pressure to cheat. In an online remote environment that can't be controlled like the in-person exam can, assume that students will be naturally drawn to using the resources at their disposal. In fact, encourage them to do so. For reasons I mention previously, I would actually say that we want to teach students how to collaborate and draw on open resources effectively. Of course, when encouraging collaboration and open-book, open-source exams, you want to give students problems to solve or questions to answer that necessitate a deeper level of knowledge and understanding, as well as a deeper level of reflection, requiring them to apply, assess, and evaluate. That is, we want to encourage students to use higher levels of Bloom's taxonomy to arrive at their answers. Teach students how to properly cite the sources of information and resources they use.

I am also sensitive to the fact that the previous assessment recommendations could be very time consuming on the instructors, since in many instances, these types of questions or problems to solve will require open-ended responses from the students. The use of a good rubric focusing on the level of critical thinking, reflection, analysis, and application the students demonstrated would be useful as a way to save time in grading. In addition, allowing the students to work collaboratively in groups and submit one response or project per group would help when it comes to time spent grading. Also consider that the students may not necessarily need individualized feedback for every single piece of work they submit. Providing summary feedback on the responses of the entire class, based on common challenges or particularly good responses, is often useful and fosters learning and engagement. Alternatively, we have also suggested that instructors ask students to post their work for each other on the LMS and assess each other's work using peer grading.

In instances where the size of the class is too large to allow anything but multiple-choice exams, asking students to create and submit answers to be included on the exams, essentially allowing the students to participate in the construction of the exam or assessment, fosters their sense of autonomy and competence and ultimately deeper engagement. Finally, we encouraged instructors to consider types of questions that would provide students with the opportunity to submit their answers in various formats such as essays, pictures, videos, or other creative mediums.

Beyond ERT—The New Normal in the New World: IMPACT X Professional Development

We survived the spring 2020 semester. Now what? After barely any time to take a deep breath, we turned our attention to summer 2020. With the spread of the virus continuing, and campus remaining closed for the summer, the questions became, "How can we move beyond ERT? How can we do better with remote instruction?" We stopped the bleeding in spring 2020 and pivoted very quickly, but now we had to think more deeply about the support we were providing to faculty and instructors and the way remote teaching could look with a bit more planning and support. The situation was not changing. We were facing the need to continue teaching remotely. In the spirit of the hero's journey, popularized by Joseph Campbell (1949), we continued to answer the call; we had to cross the threshold and continue to move forward although we knew we would face many other challenges ahead. The IMPACT team indeed continued to move forward, pushing the limit and boundaries of professional development and working to adapt the 16-week, face-to-face FLC described in chapter 4 to create what would become a portfolio of professional development opportunities based on the IMPACT model.

IMPACT X

IMPACT X was created in response to the need to move all summer 2020 courses online. Its aim and purpose was to go beyond the quick and sudden pivot of the spring 2020 caused by the closure of the physical campuses due to COVID-19. Through IMPACT X, faculty and instructors were guided to move their content online and into the Brightspace LMS. In addition to the COVID-19 pandemic, Purdue was confronted with the need to move all courses from Blackboard to Brightspace, Purdue's new LMS system. As many of you will be able to appreciate, transitioning to a new LMS is difficult enough; doing so during a pandemic where all instruction needs to be conducted online is . . . well, exponentially more difficult. In its original form, over 400 instructors participated in this program. In the creation of IMPACT X and our work with faculty and instructors, we further emphasized the pedagogical principles described previously and broadened the discussion around engagement and student-centered learning.

IMPACT X compressed the IMPACT FLC into five modules that could be completed in 1 week:

- Module 1: Creating a Student-Centered Learning Environment
- Module 2: Creating Learning Outcomes and Objectives
- Module 3: Creating Assessments and Grading in Brightspace
- Module 4: Connecting the Dots: Design and Develop in Brightspace
- Module 5: Drawing It All Together: Course Delivery Structure, Schedule, and Syllabus in Brightspace

In developing and delivering IMPACT X for courses to be taught fully remotely and online in summer 2020, we focused on and emphasized the satisfaction of the need for relatedness in the context of satisfying the other two basic psychological needs of autonomy and competence. It was crucial to do so, because as I described previously, a major struggle for students in spring 2020 was the lack of belongingness, relatedness, and community felt by the quick pivot to ERT. So much of the connection with others was lost that it paralyzed students and some instructors alike. Emphasizing ways to engage in the remote learning and teaching environment was the key to success in meeting course goals, outcomes, and objectives. In our work with faculty, we helped them develop an online presence for their course and with their students. We encouraged them to communicate often and in a multitude of ways with their students and their colleagues, using synchronous and asynchronous tools such as WebEx, discussion boards, video messages, social media, and back channels such as Slack and Hotseat.

On May 5, President Mitch Daniels, guided by the recommendations of the Safe Campus Task Force based in scientific evidence, announced that the campus would be open in the fall 2020, students who could do so would return to campus, and classes would be offered face to face. This was going to present additional challenges but also afford some opportunities to re-engage in a face-to-face environment in some form or another, though it was uncertain as to how at this point. A few days later, the Board of Trustees approved dedensification measures and an alternative fall calendar, which would move all instruction to be remote after Thanksgiving break beginning on November 24. Again, this meant that final exams were going to be conducted fully online. We knew that we would face the continued difficult but inspiring conversation of how to conduct final assessments in alternative ways, one that would de-emphasize the focus on high-stakes exams.

IMPACT X+

Once again, our professional development role was called to be extended even further and our work to be scaled even more. All faculty and instructors teaching in the fall needed to think about how to deliver instruction in a hybrid fashion with some elements of their courses being delivered face to face. As professional developers, we are very familiar with the hybrid model. We also know that the hybrid mode of delivery is one of the most difficult ones to implement well. The connections between the face-to-face and online components of the course need to be very well and intentionally aligned in order to foster engagement and meet learning outcomes. In the world of COVID-19, the hybrid delivery is even more critical and difficult to implement well, especially because all faculty and instructors are called to engage in this mode of delivery regardless of interest or skill level. Furthermore, in the time of COVID-19, the hybrid model needs to be highly flexible, adaptable, and robust, which means that it needs to be resilient to the perturbations caused by the COVID-19 pandemic and special circumstances. As professional developers, this means that we need to conduct our work with instructors and faculty while being mindful of the need to create course design that is flexible enough to account for a variety of circumstances: students testing positive for COVID-19 and needing to be quarantined, students who are feeling ill or experiencing symptoms and not certain whether they have been exposed to COVID-19 and should remain home or in the dorm, or instructors becoming sick or testing positive and needing to be quarantined.

IMPACT X+ was developed in collaboration with a team of 22 Purdue faculty and the instructional developers and designers and other staff members of the Innovative Learning Team. It also followed IMPACT's underlying theoretical framework and design principles discussed throughout this book. Focusing on the concept of resilient pedagogy as a design principle, the professional developers in collaboration with the faculty worked to provide exemplars of what instruction could look like in five major common course archetypes: large lectures, labs, discussion based, writing intensive, and experiential/clinical/field work. The IMPACT X+ program is designed to be completed in a 2-week period.

Both IMPACT X and IMPACT X+ are facilitated and centrally funded programs. Faculty and instructors worked through the programs, during the summer, in preparation for the delivery of the courses in the fall 2020. An important focus in IMPACT X and IMPACT X+ is the development of high-quality courses. The additional time we had to prepare for fall 2020 compelled us to move beyond the quick pivot, ERT, and sometimes "bandaged-stop-the-bleeding" instruction of the spring and summer 2020. These temporary emergency solutions were not going to be an acceptable design and delivery modality for fall 2020. For this reason, IMPACT X and IMPACT X+ are more about course development than professional development, because the work is much more course specific. In many cases, the professional developers worked with teams of faculty and instructors, with a faculty lead identified in order to reach consistency in course learning outcomes and objectives and assessment strategies. In addition, the professional developers led WebEx calls twice a day every day for the 1-week or 2-week period of the program and provided feedback to materials that instructors submitted as they went through and built their courses in Brightspace as they completed the program.

But what about the other instructors—those who might be teaching a smaller discussion-based course, or those who are not teaching a high-priority course with high enrollment, or graduate teaching assistants who typically do not have responsibility for the course or the course coordination? That is when the pendulum swung again toward a concern about professional development and our desire with IMPACT to meet the needs of the faculty and instructors, including graduate students, through broad professional development. To meet this aim, IMPACT X Access was developed in order to open the resources and content of IMPACT X and IMPACT X+ to all who needed or wanted to learn about how to deliver their courses in a hybrid fashion that was flexible, adaptable, and resilient to any perturbations, whether they are COVID-19 related or not.

IMPACT X Access

IMPACT X Access is an asynchronous, fully online professional development program designed to house all the content and resources found in IMPACT X and IMPACT X+. It is a nonfacilitated version of the IMPACT X and IMPACT X+ program. This means that there is no support staff facilitator assigned to the program or actively monitoring the discussion boards or providing feedback; however, the faculty, instructors, and graduate teaching assistants who are part of IMPACT X Access serve as support for each other. In addition, when instructors complete either the IMPACT X or X+ program, they are placed into the X Access program to continue to benefit from the resources and contribute to the growing online learning community of faculty, instructors, and teaching assistants. Therefore, as they go through the content, instructors can draw on the experience of others in the program and connect directly through the discussion board with others who completed the program for advice and support. To date, over 500 faculty and instructors, including graduate teaching assistants, are in the IMPACT X Access course. Across the various professional development opportunities offered this summer, we have worked with over 1,000 instructors. They use the discussion boards to comment on their redesign experiences and ask questions of other instructors. As instructors review the content and reflect on the course elements in preparation for a hybrid or fully online delivery, they are using the platform to create an Online Learning Community of Practice (OLCoP) in order to discuss design and delivery strategies for all the courses they are teaching and the way they engage and assess their students. The instructors leading the OLCoP encourage and welcome engagement from other faculty, instructors, and teaching assistants in the IMPACT X Access program with each other to share ideas and provide feedback in an online learning community.

The Return to Campus in Fall 2020

As I complete the writing of this chapter, we are deep in the planning of the return to campus in fall 2020. We still don't know exactly how students, faculty, instructors, and staff will react to the new world and our new reality. The Innovative Learning Team and the IMPACT team are intricately absorbed in this work, collaborating with the registrar's office, enrollment management, physical facilities, residence halls, student life, and student services in order to make the residential on-campus experience in fall 2020 a successful reality.

What the Residential Experience Will Look Like in Fall 2020

Although all the details are not yet known of what the residential experience will be like in the fall, one thing is for certain: It will be very different! As we return to campus, the message is that the residential classroom experience will necessarily be hybrid, where only a portion of the face-to-face content is maintained. These face-to-face components will be added where it makes sense and where it adds the most value to the student experience as a way to foster student engagement. This means that although each student will be able to experience some face to face classroom engagement and some amount of face-to-face instruction, the amount and type will vary depending on the courses they are taking. For some courses, the majority of the instruction could be conducted face to face. This might be the case for experiential learning courses, labs, or smaller discussion-based courses. For other courses, only a limited portion of the course or certain specific components of the course will be delivered face to face. For example, the lecture portion of a large lecture course might be delivered online, whereas the labs associated with that large lecture course could be delivered face to face. The traditional large 50-minute lecture could be chunked into several recordings of 10 to 15 minutes, each focusing on one important concept or an important learning outcome. In our work with faculty and instructors, we emphasize the following guiding principles: (a) Create courses that are student centered and engaging, and (b) create designs that are flexible, adaptable, and robust to the disturbances in the environment (e.g., a student needing to be quarantined, or a faculty needing to be quarantined and move their teaching online, or another outbreak necessitating another shutdown of the physical campus).

Moving beyond hybrid, the Hy-Flex delivery model takes the hybrid model and adds even greater flexibility to this delivery mode, especially for large lecture courses. In the Hy-Flex model, students are given the option to attend the face-to-face class components, in person or online, or to engage in a mix of both. As the environment changes, as the situation changes, students can choose to attend, for example, the lecture face to face on certain established days, or watch the recorded lecture synchronously, or watch it later asynchronously when it is posted on the LMS. All the class components can be done online if need be, for example in the situation in which a student tests positive and needs to be quarantined, or in the event that a new outbreak requires once again the physical shutdown of the campus. These Hy-Flex models are intentionally designed to allow us to quickly, easily, and seamlessly move to an alternative delivery option or move all aspects of the course online, at any point in the semester if necessary.

Resilient Pedagogy

In other words, in the times of COVID-19, as we are preparing to return to campus in the fall, we need to think of our course designs as fostering a resilient pedagogy, one that is student centered while also being robust, flexible, and adaptable in the face of disturbances outside of our control. This resilient pedagogy is based in hybrid and Hy-Flex models allowing students to move easily between face-to-face and online components, immediately and seamlessly. This resilient pedagogy needs to have a robust online backdrop and incorporate face-to-face components where it makes the most sense, where those face-to-face components enhance student engagement and motivation. In this hybrid residential model, the face-to-face components need to add value to the overall course experience and serve to foster student engagement. Throughout the book, especially in chapters 1, 4, 5, and 9, I discussed the importance of being intentional about using and integrating technology in our course design. I talked about the importance of not using technology simply for the sake of using the new tool or the new technology gadget available. Just as tools and technology need to be integrated intentionally in course designs as a way to foster engagement and the three basic psychological needs of autonomy, competence, and relatedness, now, in the times of COVID-19 as we prepare to return to campus, the face-to-face components are the ones that need to be integrated intentionally to enhance student engagement and overall learning outcomes. We can't mindlessly integrate face-to-face components for the sake of meeting face to face. We need to ask ourselves as developers and instructors, what course elements or activities would be done much more poorly and would hinder student engagement if they were conducted online? For example, a lecture could easily be delivered online without much loss in engagement. In fact, using available lecture capture tools embedded in the LMS or video express rooms on campus, quality short lectures can be recorded and made available online to students and provide an experience equivalent to the face-to-face lecture. In contrast, engaging discussions, with question-and-answer (Q&A) sessions that typically follow a powerful lecture, would be harder to replicate online. In that case, holding multiple smaller face-to-face discussions, Q&A, or "office hour" sessions in rooms large enough to allow appropriate social distancing makes sense to maintain a high level of engagement in the course. The same appears to be true for field work or some labs. Although some of these were conducted fully online during the shift to ERT as discussed previously, instructors reported great loss in engagement and learning by attempting to conduct these course components remotely. Some faculty had to cancel these experiences during ERT because we could not find a good way to deliver those remotely during the quick pivot to ERT. In fall 2020, there might be fewer labs offered in STEM disciplines or they might be shorter, in order to allow all students to experience the labs face to face in smaller lab groups, allowing us to meet the social distancing dedensification requirements.

In short, the principles I discuss in this book remain the same: We need to foster student-centered, engaging, and autonomy-supportive learning environments; however, the way in which we implement these principles is necessarily changing in the world of COVID-19 and the context of fall 2020. Everything we do in course design is intentional and intended to foster enhanced student engagement and attainment of learning outcomes. In the times of COVID-19, where social distancing and wearing a face covering is essential for our safety and well-being, the face-to-face components are the ones we now need to very intentionally integrate and think about. Face-to-face components, integrated into the course well and with intentionality, will serve to enhance student engagement while preserving safety.

In planning for the in-class face-to-face components, a few more considerations need to be mentioned. In a hybrid resilient pedagogy model, the face-to-face class components and activities necessarily need to be integrated while also planning for alternative online options for the students. The last thing we want to do as developers and instructors is incentivize the in-class, face-to-face components so students feel forced to come to class, even if they are feeling sick or suspect a potential exposure to someone with COVID-19. Among other things, this means that we need to carefully rethink our attendance policy and strongly avoid giving points or requiring students to be in class to participate. A student who wakes up feeling sick needs to feel absolutely comfortable staying home and completing the class activity using the alternative online option. This goes back to the need to create a strong online backbone for each course so that all activities can be completed online if necessary. The necessity could be driven by many factors and situations: A student tests positive for COVID-19 and needs to be quarantined; a student feels sick without necessarily having tested positive for COVID-19; a student is concerned they may have been in contact with a person who had COVID-19; a student exhibits symptoms associated with COVID-19; or an instructor tests positive for COVID-19 or is ill, or falls into one of the situations described here and can't come to class. In the fall, as we enter the regular common flu season, many of the symptoms of the flu will easily be confounded with the symptoms of COVID-19. This means that on any given day of the fall 2020 semester, many students may need to stay home and complete their work online.

Most definitely, following the previous discussion, assessments and exams should not be offered only face to face. Providing online alternatives for completing assessments, exams, and anything tied to obtaining points toward a grade in the class should have an equivalent online alternative for completion. If not, we are incentivizing students to come to class sick, and we absolutely *do not want* to be in this situation and create scenarios where sick students are taking exams and assessments face to face while sick or possibly sick. In this process, in this new world, it will be even more important for instructors to be understanding and flexible and build in their course multiple choice points for students and the ability to move easily and seamlessly between the online and the face-to-face environment as the situation evolves and changes. Without those choice points allowing students to complete the course and meet learning outcomes fully online *if* the situation warrants it, too many students will be placed in a position of failing the course. If students can't come to class for a significant portion of the semester, in order to complete an assessment that met a learning outcome of the course and obtain the grade to succeed in the class, they will either be faced with the consequence of not succeeding in the course or having to request a grade of Incomplete for the course. In our work with instructors, we are also encouraging them to not see the Incomplete grade as the answer to the attendance issue, since a large proportion of Incomplete grades will add a grading burden to the following semester. Another important consideration as we work with instructors to prepare for the fall 2020 is to reflect on the role of the entire instructional team and devise contingency plans that would allow instruction to continue under a variety of circumstances. How can the members of the instructional team, including teaching assistants and other instructors teaching the same or similar courses, contribute to the delivery of the instruction in a variety of modalities? Could a teaching assistant or another instructor take over the section of a course if the primary instructor needed to be quarantined or became too sick to teach even remotely? As we prepare for fall 2020, it is not only the students who need to have choices and options in how they learn and complete courses; the instructors and teaching assistants also need choices and options in how to offer the course and deliver the instruction.

Implications for Higher Education and Faculty Development

Although, as I said previously, we are still deep into the fall 2020 preparations, and only time will tell how successful we will be as we transition to the new world of hybrid face-to-face learning in times of COVID-19, a few wider implications for faculty development and higher education are emerging.

Importance of Choices and Options

As I discussed throughout this book, the provision of choices and options as a way to create teaching and learning environments that are autonomy supportive and engaging turns out to be even more crucial in times of crises, such as the one we are experiencing now. The creation of autonomy-supportive environments as a way to satisfy the basic psychological needs of autonomy, competence, and relatedness in higher education is important for all human beings involved in the educational endeavor, students and instructors alike.

Sense of Control Over the Environment and Health and Well-Being

Although in this book I have primarily emphasized the perception of agency and choice from the motivational perspective of SDT, what I'm hearing consistently from faculty, instructors, staff, and teaching assistants in addition to the importance of the ability to choose is the need to have a sense of control over their environment and well-being. In chapter 2, I discussed the work of Heider (1958) and De Charms (1968), which greatly influenced SDT. In particular, De Charms (1968) coined the term *I-PLOC* to refer to behaviors or actions that are intentional or personally caused and experienced as freely chosen or endorsed. In contrast, he referred to behaviors or actions that are personally caused but experienced as externally pressured or coerced as having an *E-PLOC.* Although both types of behaviors are carried out by the person, only the ones with an I-PLOC are truly experienced as intentional and volitional by people. Only in those situations do people feel like they are agents in their own life or at the origin of their actions. Behaviors with an E-PLOC are experienced as compelled or pressured and alien to the self. The preceding sentence could just as easily read, In these instances, people feel obligated to behave in a certain way and experience their behaviors as pressured and easily swayed by others. The concept of I-PLOC versus E-PLOC is crucial in understanding the quality of the outcomes that will follow from the behaviors and the resultant effects on personal growth, mental health, and well-being. In the current context, as faculty, instructors, and staff contemplate the return to campus in fall 2020 and what teaching in the residential experience will look like, they need to feel a sense of agency or an I-PLOC in order to embrace the return to campus. Instructors and staff need to feel heard and need to feel a sense of choice in deciding how they will deliver instruction in this new world. Without this sense of choice, as I have described in this book, but even more so now because the stakes are so high, instructors, staff, and students will feel disengaged, alienated, and disenfranchised. Without the sense of choice and personal agency, the instructional community is much more likely to feel forced to return to campus and learn and teach in a certain way.

The sense of control, as described by Rotter (1966), is about the expectation that a person's behavior is associated with the desired outcomes. Here, having an I-PLOC is important—the belief that people can control their own outcomes or have control in most situations. In contrast, an E-PLOC is associated with the perception and the belief that others, fate, or external forces control the outcomes. Only an I-PLOC is associated with positive outcomes such as happiness, well-being, creativity, and ideation (Pannells & Claxton, 2008). Although an I-PLOC is important in general, in the current context, as the instructional community contemplates what will it mean to teach and learn in a hybrid classroom and campus in fall 2020, and how to do so safely, feeling and believing that one has control over the outcome is even more important. Unfortunately, because there is so much unknown in the context surrounding COVID-19, and so many varied and often competing and inconsistent views and messages around the spread and containment of the virus, it is very difficult for the instructional community to feel in control of the consequences. The likelihood of believing that others or fate will determine the consequences, as opposed to their own behaviors, is very high. In the current context, we are heavily relying on the decision of others, whether they are students, other instructors, staff, and administrators, to ensure our perceived and actual safety. Will students wear their masks on campus? What will I do if they do not comply? Will my colleagues respect the school policy? Will students and instructors comply with social distancing guidelines when they are not on campus? Why can't I continue to teach my class fully online? Do I have to offer face-to-face components? Why?

Involve Faculty and Instructors in the Conversation in Order to Change the Culture

To increase the sense and perception of choice and control, it is crucially important to involve the instructional community in the conversation and ideally the decision-making process. This is true whether or not we are in a state of crisis, like we currently are, but it certainly is even more important in times of stress and uncertainty. As discussed in chapter 9, an increase in the perception of choice and the inclusion and involvement of faculty in the developmental process related to IMPACT fostered a culture change at Purdue. The same process needs to be followed if we want to foster a culture change on our campus, one where it is the new normal for students and instructors to follow the safety guidelines around the reopening of campus, such as wearing their masks and social distancing while in the classrooms or other campus buildings. In the same way that instructors were central to the IMPACT transformation process and our role as faculty developers was to listen to instructors' needs, interests, and goals for their course and support them in their process, it is now our aim to involve instructors in the process and the conversation so they do not feel forced, prescribed, or pressured to move their teaching in a certain direction, follow a certain pedagogical model, or require a specific amount of face-to-face components. For the past few months, the IMPACT team has been involved in multiple and regular communications (written or through live forums) in order to provide information to instructors as well as answer their questions about what fall 2020 will look like. The most important benefit of involving instructors in the process and the conversation is that it reinforces and helps internalize the rationale and the why for reopening campus and going back to a residential environment. Not freely and transparently opening the conversation with faculty and instructors, in any contexts but especially in times of anxiety, uncertainty, and stress, fosters a controlling environment, which tends to enhance the already present fear responses and lead to inflexibility and resistance.

Student and Instructor Engagement Regardless of Modality

Throughout this book, I spoke of the importance of engagement, for students and for instructors alike. In the book, I certainly focused much more on face-to-face engagement and why active learning works when done well (chapter 5). This was framed to mean that it fostered the satisfaction of the basic psychological needs of autonomy, competence, and relatedness and contributed to the creation of an autonomy-supportive learning environment. Throughout the book, I spoke very little of online learning, and as discussed previously, I de-emphasized the importance of technology for the sake of technology. I instead highlighted the usefulness of technology when used to create an environment that is autonomy supportive and engaging. In this final chapter, now that the tables have turned and the use of online learning tools and technology is paramount, I want to emphasize something

I mentioned briefly in chapter 7; regardless of teaching modality and redesign model, engagement can be fostered when the redesigns are done well. The shift to ERT, and now online learning and hybrid learning, can certainly be considered a massive course redesign project that we are all involved in. A focus on student and instructor engagement regardless of modality is certainly one of the broad implications we can derive from the work over the past 4 months and what is yet to come. There are many ways of engaging students as they learn, and there are many ways of engaging faculty through professional development and as they teach. I would reiterate that our focus is to create learning and teaching environments that are autonomy supportive, engaging, and inclusive and that support and foster the success of all students, regardless of race, age, sexual orientation, or generational status. A focus on the learning outcomes of the course will be very useful here and now and as we look to the future of higher education. It will matter less where instruction occurs, as it will take place face to face and remotely, but more how it takes place and why we even engage in learning. I predict that in the future, course learning outcomes will be further broadened to include soft skills such as teamwork, collaboration, emotional intelligence, respect, inclusivity, cultural understanding, and responsiveness. It is not sufficient to mainly focus on content knowledge related to a specific discipline. Interdisciplinary work, across academic disciplines but also across institutional units, will become more and more important so we can tackle and solve problems and challenges that were highlighted by the pandemic.

In closing this chapter and book, I will end in the same way I did when I thought I was writing the last paragraphs of this book on March 2, 2020, with a quote from the dean of the PPI, Gary Bertoline, and my own words. These closing words still feel very relevant today.

> I am convinced that without the IMPACT program we would have fallen far short in our goal to transform undergraduate teaching and learning in our college. One of the lessons we learned early on in our transformation efforts was that you have to start with the faculty when making change. You do that through a carefully crafted professional development program and provide faculty with the time and support necessary to make the change. The IMPACT program does all of that. (G. Bertoline, personal communication, February 21, 2020)

The IMPACT program and the faculty developers and staff associated with the program have pushed the envelope during the time of the COVID-19 pandemic and, in doing so, forged ahead to create even greater transformational and culture change.

To quote myself from the end of the last chapter,

> More work certainly needs to be done, but this deep, broad, and meaningful culture change is possible. If we all work together, and commit to the growth and development of human potential, change and true transformation is possible. Inertia is not an excuse for lack of transformation. It's not acceptable to stay where we are because this is how it's always been done. Heart work is hard work, but it's possible. (p. 148, this volume)

Here's to a successful fall 2020, a continued transformational journey, and a deep process of evaluation, transformation, and reflection. Here's to the difficult heart work we are called to do and need more than ever before.

APPENDIX A: FACULTY LEARNING COMMUNITY SYLLABUS

Faculty Learning Community Description

The weekly faculty learning community (FLC) sessions will help you design and/or redesign your course in a way that focuses on student-centered learning. The sessions present research-based, pedagogically sound approaches to course design, guiding you through the design process from which you will be able to purposefully create a course that meets your unique needs.

Learning Outcomes

After participation in Instruction Matters: Purdue Academic Course Transformation (IMPACT), faculty fellows will be able to develop or refine the following:

- Learning outcomes and learning objectives
- Appropriate pedagogical approaches for increasing engagement and achieving student learning outcomes
- Integration of motivation principles in order to create inclusive, student-centered learning environments
- Course assessments that align with and measure learning outcomes
- Components of the course design plan

FLC Materials

IMPACT is excited to be participating as part of the soft launch of Desire to Learn's Brightspace this semester. We will use this site to share, collect, and archive information. To access the Brightspace IMPACT course, type "https://purdue.brightspace.com" into your web browser and log on using your Purdue career account. We will demonstrate and learn the new system together in the FLC, so don't worry if you are unfamiliar with it, as we all are!

Please log on to the Brightspace site weekly to see what materials you will need to read, watch, or listen to, as well as any exercises or activities you may need to complete for the following week's FLC session.

FLC Participation Requirements

In order to maximize your experience, the completion of specific items is necessary to move to the next phase of your redesign work. For example, you will need learning outcomes and objectives to develop an assessment plan and learning activities. You will learn more about each of these items in specific FLC sessions.

As an IMPACT faculty fellow, it is expected that you will do the following:

- Attend and participate in the FLC sessions
    - **You may miss only three (3) sessions.**
    - **For each session you miss, you must complete a reflection activity.**
- Notify your team primary and the IMPACT coordinator if you plan to be absent from an FLC session
- Complete all prework prior to each session, and upload artifacts to the Brightspace before the due date
- Outside the FLC, meet regularly (at least every other week) with your IMPACT support team to work through the course design plan (CDP) as you develop content for your course. See Table A.1 for suggested scheduling.

TABLE A.1
Spring 2020 IMPACT FLC Schedule

Welcoming Session				
Session	*Date*	*Topic*	*Facilitator(s)*	*Major Deliverables Due*
1st	1/15	Welcome and IMPACT Kickoff Guest: Past Fellows	Chantal & Allison	
Motivating Learners				
2nd	1/22	Motivation Framework for Learning Guests: Students	Chantal	Initial Redesign Goal
3rd	1/29	Student Characteristics Guests: John Gates & Students	Clarence	
Learning Outcomes				
4th	2/5	Learning Outcomes	David	Initial Learning Outcomes
5th	2/12	Informed and Inclusive Learning Objectives	Clarence & Rachel	

		Assessment		
6th	2/19	Assess Student Performance, Part 1	David	
7th	2/26	Assess Student Performance, Part 2	David	Revised Learning Outcomes and Specific Learning Objectives
		Learning Activities		
8th	3/4	Learning Activities, Part 1	Rachel	
9th	3/11	Learning Activities, Part 2	Rachel	Initial CDP
		Spring Break Week (No Class)		
10th	3/25	Connecting the Dots Guests: Students	Chantal	
		Drawing It All Together		
11th	4/1	Redesign Decisions	Chantal	Revised CDP and Redesign Goal
12th	4/8	Redesign Presentations Guests: Students	Allison	
13th	4/15	Scholarly Practitioner	Emily & Faculty Panel	
14th	4/22	Closing the Loop & Focus Group NOTE: FLC will be 15 minutes longer	ELRC & Chantal	Final CDP and Data Plan

APPENDIX B: IMPACT SERVICE-LEVEL AGREEMENT

Service-Level Agreement

This document constitutes an agreement between the IMPACT faculty fellow(s), (hereafter known as "faculty fellow(s)") and the Steering Committee of Instruction Matters: Purdue Academic Course Transformation (IMPACT) (hereafter known as "IMPACT Steering Committee").

1. Term

The term of this agreement is from the beginning of the term ________________ through ________________ (the end of the semester of the first time the redesigned course is offered; should be December 2020 or May 2021).

2. Definitions

IMPACT support staff—staff assigned to support the faculty fellows and faculty design teams by providing expertise in pedagogies, student-centered learning, assessment, instructional technologies, information literacy, and so on, consisting of staff from the Center for Instructional Excellence (CIE), Teaching and Learning Technologies (TLT), Purdue Online (PO), and the Libraries and School of Information Studies (LSIS).

Faculty fellow(s)—faculty member(s) responsible for the course redesign and approved by the department head to lead the course design

Faculty redesign team—small group of faculty either elected by the course instructors or assigned by the department head to work with the Faculty Fellow in developing the course redesign materials

Course redesign—the final redesign materials including (a) course-level learning outcomes, (b) course-level design plan, and (c) a student-centered learning environment

Single course section redesign—used when

- course is typically taught by the same one to three instructors OR one to three instructors and multiple teaching assistants *and*

- other sections are already redesigned or instructors are coordinating among themselves for adoption of redesign.

Multiple sections with course coordinator—used when

- single person responsible for managing all sections of course *and*
- course typically taught by many instructors and/or teaching assistants *and*
- coordinator responsibility includes control of all sections in determination of (a) course-level learning outcomes, (b) course-level design plan, and (c) a student-centered learning environment.

Multiple sections with collaborative faculty—used when

- multiple faculty teaching sections of same course with no controlling coordinator *and*
- small group (one to eight) of faculty either elected by the course instructors or assigned by the department head to work developing the course redesign materials (faculty redesign team) *and*
- single or small group (one to three) of faculty selected from faculty redesign team as responsible for final course redesign materials (designated faculty fellow[s]) *and*
- all instructors teaching the course will use the faculty redesign team's materials.

3. Service Overview

The IMPACT program, overseen by Provost Jay Akridge, is centrally funded and supported by CIE, PO, LSIS the Institutional Data Analytics and Assessment (IDA+A), and ELRC.

As outlined in this agreement, the IMPACT Steering Committee will oversee the provision of services by the IMPACT support staff to the faculty fellow(s) for instructional design services, professional development, assessment, and content development assistance, to redesign the Purdue University course, ______________________________. These services will be provided free of charge to the faculty fellow(s) for the period outlined in the Term section (Section 1).

In return for completion of course redesign activities outlined in Section 5, Faculty Fellow(s) Responsibilities (which include the development of a course redesign consisting of (a) course-level learning outcomes, (b) course-level design plan, and (c) a student-centered learning environment as determined by the

IMPACT student self-assessment survey), the IMPACT Steering Committee will provide funding in the amount of $10,000, distributed in accordance with the schedule outlined in Section 9, Milestone Funding. **There will be a 1-year limit in meeting these milestones to obtain full funding.**

4. IMPACT Responsibilities

The IMPACT support staff will appoint a team composed of IMPACT support staff to work with the faculty fellow(s) in their course redesign project. Four types of services are provided: instructional design, professional development, assessment, and content development.

4.1. Instructional Design Services

- Work as a team to assist in analysis of course goals and learning outcomes, student needs, and development of course design, content, and activities.
- Assist in choosing and implementing redesign strategies according to accepted instructional design principles.

4.2. Professional Development Services

- Prepare and deliver FLC sessions on topics related to course design to support active learning, such as student learning, pedagogy, teaching strategies, assessment, and technology.

4.3. Assessment Services

- Assist in developing learning outcomes and learning objectives for the course.
- Assist in developing and implementing an assessment plan for measuring whether learning outcomes were achieved.
- Coordinate an assessment plan that measures the effectiveness of various IMPACT course attributes (faculty development, student experience, existence and use of learning objectives, course data mining, cultural change, and student achievement).
- Coordinate analysis and reporting of data.

4.4. Content Development Assistance

- Assist the faculty fellow(s) in identifying which content items from among a group of instructor-supplied content may be appropriate for specific learning objectives.
- Assist the faculty fellow(s) by providing training on content creation in technologies that will be used for instruction in the course or directing the faculty fellow(s) to the appropriate source for training if needed.

- Assist the faculty fellow(s) in locating and procuring libraries electronic information resources to help create assignments using those resources to enhance student learning.
- Assist in creation of a set of common course materials to be used by current and future instructors of the course to help ensure the sustainability of the course redesign.

5. Faculty Fellow(s) Responsibilities

As described in the IMPACT Call for Proposals, faculty fellow(s) agree to do the following:

- Attend and participate in required FLC sessions and all activities associated with FLC meetings, which are facilitated by other faculty and IMPACT support staff for the cohort semester. Success of the FLC meetings and redesign process depends heavily on faculty participation; **absence from more than three FLC sessions in the curriculum may result in termination of this agreement.**
- Develop and follow a course design plan (CDP) and assessment strategy in consultation with IMPACT support staff.
- Work with the IMPACT support staff to refine learning outcomes and align course assessments and activities with learning outcomes for your course redesign project.
- Share the set of common course materials with other instructors of the course to help ensure the sustainability of the course redesign.
- Deliver the redesigned course within **1 calendar year** of acceptance into the program.

Faculty fellow(s) are strongly encouraged to do the following:

- Meet weekly or biweekly with IMPACT support staff outside of the FLC to work through their redesign plan and develop content for the course for at least the initial semester involved in FLCs.
- Attend and participate in other IMPACT events such as presentations by invited guest speakers.
- Present a brown bag seminar in the home department, college, and/or campus about the course redesign as part of the IMPACT project.
- More broadly, become leaders of continued improvement with respect to teaching on the Purdue campus. This includes providing feedback to the IMPACT Steering Committee about your experience, serving as a mentor to future IMPACT fellows, and sharing insights with colleagues.

- Because sustainability of the redesigned course is critical to the success of IMPACT, if at all possible, continue to teach the redesigned course for an additional three semesters, and pass redesign on to subsequent instructor.
- With the support of IMPACT support staff, share the redesign by participating in the scholarship of teaching and learning.
- Meet with the support team after the first semester of the course offering to identify additional redesign needs.
- Multiple sections with collaborate faculty: Consult with and communicate to the other members of the FRT throughout the course redesign process.

6. Multiple Sections With Course Coordinator: Additional Coordinator Responsibilities

As described in the IMPACT Call for Proposals, faculty fellow(s) agree to do the following:

- Commence and maintain regular communication concerning IMPACT course redesign activities with current instructors of the redesigned course throughout the redesign, assessment, and course delivery processes, soliciting and using input as needed.
- Utilize the input of current course instructors as appropriate and share the set of common course materials with current and future instructors of the course to help ensure the sustainability of the course redesign.

7. Multiple Sections With Collaborative Faculty: FRT Responsibilities

To help ensure the sustainability of the course redesign, the FRT agrees to work together to develop a common course redesign that can be applied by all instructors to all delivered sections of the redesigned course. To reach this goal, an IMPACT faculty fellow will be identified and will consult with the FRT to get input and make all efforts to reach consensus on issues surrounding the redesign. In addition, the FRT agrees that

- the group will designate a primary faculty member as faculty fellow to take the lead;
- the faculty fellow(s) will fulfill the responsibilities in the following section;

- members of the FRT will provide feedback and input to the faculty fellow(s) throughout the redesign process;
- members of the FRT will support and participate in the use of the course redesign when future sections of the redesigned course are delivered;
- members of the FRT will participate in IMPACT program assessment activities, which will include surveys and/or interviews with faculty fellows, as well as surveys and/or observations of the course and students; and
- all members of the FRT are invited but not required to attend IMPACT FLC sessions.

8. Department Support

Department support is critical to the success of the IMPACT program. Support of this application indicates the department's acknowledgement of and agreement with the following:

- While IMPACT is based on research in teaching and learning, it also involves *experimentation and innovation.* It is likely to require more than one iteration of delivery for a redesigned course before it will be possible to see the full effect of the transformation on student learning.
- Because course redesign will challenge student expectations of the learning process, students' initial feedback may reflect their discomfort or unfamiliarity with a new and challenging learning environment. The fellow and the department are strongly encouraged to discuss results of the course, including student evaluation results, with IMPACT team members to fully interpret them.
- To ensure that the redesigned course achieves the maximum positive results for the university, the IMPACT faculty fellow(s) will be provided the opportunity to **teach the redesigned course within a year of participating in IMPACT and for at least three additional semesters**, while allowing for normal departmental scheduling practices.
- The department will encourage and support the adoption of the redesigned course and materials by any additional and/or subsequent instructors of the redesigned course and mentorship by the IMPACT faculty fellow to ensure quality and sustainability of the redesign.

- The department will encourage current and future instructors of the course to attend IMPACT classroom implementation workshops to support their delivery of the redesigned course.
- Multiple sections with collaborative faculty: The department will select the FRT members to represent all instructors teaching the course and agree that all instructors will use the resulting course redesign.

9. Milestone Funding

IMPACT funds will be disbursed in accordance with completion of the following course redesign milestones. There will be a **1-year limit** in meeting these milestones to obtain funding.

Funds will be transferred directly to the department of the primary instructor, who will determine how funds will be spent. *Please be sure the memorandum of agreement is signed (last page) by the department head stating that the funds will be unrestricted as long as they are being used to support the redesign and the work of the faculty as part of the redesign.* Failure to achieve any of the milestones may result in the termination of this agreement. Unspent funds will be retracted if the instructor leaves the department and there are no plans to continue the redesigned course as transformed in IMPACT.

Milestone	*Estimated Completion Date*	*Funds Disbursed*
Service-level agreement signed and attendance of first FLC session, commencing participation	January 2020	$2,500
Attendance of fellow(s) at IMPACT FLCs and completion of all required activities, including clear learning outcomes established and mapped to activities (CDP).	May 2020	$2,500
Commencement of teaching and implementing the redesigned course within 1 year of FLC semester.	August 2020 or January 2021	$5,000
Total		$10,000

Please indicate the account number for disbursement of funds: __________

____

Please note: This account must be an unrestricted general funds account. It must be a WBSE '.06**' account number.*

10. Modifications to This Agreement

Modifications to this service-level agreement may only be made if mutually agreed on by all parties. Any modifications will be included in a written amendment to this agreement signed by all parties.

11. Reporting/Reviews

The faculty fellow or department head should contact Chantal Levesque-Bristol by telephone at 765-496-6424 or by email at cbristol@purdue.edu if there is a need to meet and discuss any problems or concerns with the terms or work covered under this agreement.

12. Service-Level Agreement Contact Information

Faculty fellow	IMPACT Steering Committee
Primary faculty fellow: __________________________ Career Account (Purdue Alias) __________________________	Chantal Levesque-Bristol, PhD Director, Center for Instructional Excellence 765-496-6424 cbristol@purdue.edu

13. Review and Approval

Faculty Fellow

__________________ __________________ __________________

Signature *Name (Please print)* *Date*

Course Department Head

__________________ __________________ __________________

Signature *Name (Please print)* *Date*

Faculty Department Head (if different from above)

__________________ __________________ __________________

Signature *Name (Please print)* *Date*

Faculty Course Redesign Team Members (if Multiple Sections With Collaborative Faculty)

Signature	*Name (Please print)/Date*	*Department*
Signature	*Name (Please print)/Date*	*Department*
Signature	*Name (Please print)/Date*	*Department*
Signature	*Name (Please print)/Date*	*Department*

IMPACT Steering Committee

	Chantal Levesque-Bristol	
Signature	*Name*	*Date*

IMPACT Spring 2020
Memorandum of Agreement

By signing this agreement, I acknowledge that I have read Part 8: Department Support of the service-level agreement for Purdue Academic Course Transformation (IMPACT) in the attached service-level agreement. I agree that IMPACT funds will be used to support the redesign of the course: ____________________, and the work of the instructor: ____________________ ____________________ as part of the redesign. Failure to achieve any of the IMPACT milestones may result in the termination of the agreement.

Department head signature	*Name*	*Date*

APPENDIX C: IMPACT STUDENT SURVEY

Learning Climate Questionnaire

Question Text: About the Learning Experience. The questions that follow are related to your learning experience in *Course Number: Course Name* thus far. The learning experience in different courses can vary and we would like to know more about how you generally feel about the overall learning experience in *Course Number: Course Name.* Your responses are confidential. Please be honest and candid. Use the scale provided to answer each item.

Answer Responses:

1. Strongly Disagree
2. Disagree
3. Somewhat Disagree
4. Neither Agree nor Disagree
5. Somewhat Agree
6. Agree
7. Strongly Agree

Individual Items:

1. I feel that my instructor provides me choices and options.
2. I feel understood by my instructor.
3. My instructor conveyed confidence in my ability to do well in the course.
4. My instructor encouraged me to ask questions.
5. My instructor listens to how I would like to do things.
6. My instructor tries to understand how I see things before suggesting a new way to do things.

Self-Determination Index

Question Text: Motivation for taking *Course Number: Course Name.* The questions that follow are related to your feelings of why you are taking *Course Number: Course Name.* Students have different motivations for taking different courses, and we are interested in your motivations for taking *Course Number: Course Name* thus far. Your responses are confidential. Please be honest and candid. Use the scale provided to answer each item.

Answer Responses:

1. Strongly Disagree
2. Disagree
3. Somewhat Disagree
4. Neither Agree nor Disagree
5. Somewhat Agree
6. Agree
7. Strongly Agree

Individual Items:

1. Intrinsic Regulation
   a. Because I really enjoy it.
   b. Because I really like it.
   c. Because it's really fun.
2. Integration
   a. Because learning all I can about academic work is really essential for me.
   b. Because acquiring all kinds of knowledge is fundamental for me.
   c. Because experiencing new things is a part of who I am.
3. Identification
   a. Because it allows me to develop skills that are important to me.
   b. Because it's a sensible way to get a meaningful experience.
   c. Because it's a practical way to acquire new knowledge.
4. Introjection
   a. Because I would feel bad if I didn't.
   b. Because I would feel guilty if I didn't.
   c. Because I would feel awful about myself if I didn't.
5. Extrinsic Regulation
   a. Because I feel I have to.
   b. Because that's what I'm supposed to do.
   c. Because that's what I was told to do.
6. Amotivation
   a. I don't know. I have the impression I'm wasting my time.
   b. I'm not sure anymore. I think that maybe I should quit (drop the class).
   c. I don't know. I wonder if I should continue.

Basic Psychological Needs Scale

Question Text: Your Overall Experience. The following questions concern your feelings about your experience in *Course Number: Course Name.* Please indicate how true each of the following statements is for you given your specific experiences with *Course Number: Course Name* thus far.

Answer Responses:

1. Strongly Disagree
2. Disagree
3. Somewhat Disagree
4. Neither Agree nor Disagree
5. Somewhat Agree
6. Agree
7. Strongly Agree

Individual Items:

1. Autonomy
   a. Satisfaction:
      i. I feel a sense of choice and freedom in the things I undertake in this course.
      ii. I feel that my decisions reflect what I really want in this course.
      iii. I feel my choices express who I really am in this course.
      iv. I feel I have been doing what really interests me in this course.
   b. Frustration
      i. Most of the things I do feel like "I have to" in this course.
      ii. I feel forced to do many things I wouldn't choose to do in this course.
      iii. I feel pressured to do too many things in this course.
      iv. My daily activities feel like a chain of obligations in this course.
2. Competence
   a. Satisfaction
      i. I feel confident that I can do things well in this course.
      ii. I feel capable at what I do in this course.
      iii. I feel competent to achieve my goals in this course.
      iv. I feel I can successfully complete difficult tasks in this course.
   b. Frustration
      i. I have serious doubts about whether I can do things well in this course.
      ii. I feel disappointed with many of my performances in this course.
      iii. I feel insecure about my abilities in this course.
      iv. I feel like a failure because of the mistakes I make in this course.

3. Relatedness
   a. Instructor
      i. I get along with the instructor(s) in this course.
      ii. I really like the instructor(s) in this course.
      iii. The instructor(s) in this course care(s) about me.
      iv. I am not close to the instructor(s) in this course.
      v. The instructor(s) in this course do(es) not seem to like me much.
   b. Peer
      i. I really like the other students in this course.
      ii. I get along with other students in this course.
      iii. The other students in this course do not seem to like me much.
      iv. The other students in this course care about me.
      v. There are not many students in this course that I am close to.

Cultural Responsiveness

Question Text: Your Overall Experience. The following questions concern your feelings about your experience in *Course Number: Course Name*. Please indicate how true each of the following statements is for you given your specific experiences with *Course Number: Course Name* thus far.

Answer Responses:

1. Strongly Disagree
2. Disagree
3. Somewhat Disagree
4. Neither Agree nor Disagree
5. Somewhat Agree
6. Agree
7. Strongly Agree

Individual Items:

1. My instructor is open to students expressing themselves in languages other than English.
2. My instructor uses examples from different cultures to explain concepts in the course.
3. My instructor seems to have an understanding of my culture.
4. My instructor is open to students using languages other than English in small group discussions.
5. My instructor seems to be aware of cultural differences among the students.

6. My instructor helps students think about ways to make changes in society.
7. My instructor provides opportunities to discuss different global issues in society.
8. My instructor talks about inequalities that exist in society during some lessons.

Perceived Knowledge Transfer Scale

Question Text: Your Overall Experience. The following questions concern your feelings about your experience in *Course Number: Course Name.* Please indicate how true each of the following statements is for you given your specific experiences with *Course Number: Course Name* thus far.

Answer Responses:

1. Strongly Disagree
2. Disagree
3. Somewhat Disagree
4. Neither Agree nor Disagree
5. Somewhat Agree
6. Agree
7. Strongly Agree

1. I feel confident in my ability to apply the course material in other classes that I have.
2. I feel confident in my ability to apply the course material in my professional life.
3. I feel as if the material covered in this course is relevant to my future career.
4. Given the future career that I have chosen, it is important for me to learn the information covered in this class.
5. I understand how I will use the information learned in this class in my professional life.
6. Information learned in this course will inform my future learning experiences.
7. I believe that it is important for me to learn the information included in this course.
8. The information learned in this course will help me become a more well-rounded individual.

Student Assessment of Learning Gains

Question Text (using your specific course-level outcomes):
Students respond on a 5-point scale from "0 = I gained nothing at all" to "4 = I gained a great deal."

1. As a result of your work in this class, what GAINS did you make in the SKILL of [enter your Learning Outcome 1]?
2. As a result of your work in this class, what GAINS did you make in the SKILL of [enter your Learning Outcome 2]?
3. As a result of your work in this class, what GAINS did you make in the SKILL of [enter your Learning Outcome 3]?

APPENDIX D: INFORMED LEARNING SCALE

Question Text: Using Information in *Course Number: Course Name*. The following questions concern your feelings about your experience using information to learn in *Course Number: Course Name*. Information could include many things such as websites, data, lab results, textbooks, journal articles, and so on.

Answer Responses:

1. Strongly Disagree
2. Disagree
3. Somewhat Disagree
4. Neither Agree nor Disagree
5. Somewhat Agree
6. Agree
7. Strongly Agree

Individual Items:

1. I believe it is important for me to carefully evaluate the information I use in this course.
2. I believe I can learn in this course by using information.
3. For this course my instructor encourages me to use my prior experiences of using information.
4. I build on my previous experiences of using information to learn subject content in this course.
5. My instructor encourages me to use information for specific purposes.
6. When I consider my life after college, I feel confident in my ability to learn when engaging with information sources.
7. I feel confident in my ability to synthesize information from different sources.
8. I feel confident in my ability to use information to learn subject content in this course.

REFERENCES

Anderson, L. W., Krathwohl, D. R., & Bloom, B. S. (2001). *A taxonomy for learning, teaching, and assessing: A revision of Bloom's taxonomy of educational objectives.* Longman.

Angelo, T. A, & Cross, K. P. (1993). *Classroom assessment techniques: A handbook for college teachers* (2nd ed.). Jossey Bass.

Arum, R., & Roska, J. (2011). *Academically adrift: Limited learning on college campuses.* University of Chicago Press.

Assor, A., Kaplan, H., Kanat-Maymon, Y., & Roth, G. (2005). Directly controlling teacher behaviors as predictors of poor motivation and engagement in girls and boys: The role of anger and anxiety. *Learning and Instruction, 15*(5), 397–413. https://doi.org/10.1016/j.learninstruc.2005.07.008

Baard, P. P., Deci, E. L., & Ryan, R. M. (2004). Intrinsic need satisfaction: A motivational basis of performance and well-being in two work settings. *Journal of Applied Social Psychology, 34*(10), 2045–2068. https://doi.org/10.1111/j.1559-1816.2004.tb02690.x

Baepler, P., Walker, J. D., Brooks, D. C., Saichaie, K., Petersen, C. I., & Cohen, B. A. (2016). *A guide to teaching in the active learning classroom: History, research, and practice.* Stylus.

Baepler, P., Walker, J. D., & Driessen, M. (2014). It's not about seat time: Blending, flipping, and efficiency in active learning classrooms. *Computers & Education, 78,* 227–236. https://doi.org/10.1016/j.compedu.2014.06.006

Bain, K. (2004). *What the best college teachers do.* Harvard University Press.

Ballen, C. J., Salehi, S., & Cotner, S. (2017). Exams disadvantage women in introductory biology. *PLoS ONE, 12*(10), e0186419. https://doi.org/10.1371/journal.pone.0186419

Bandura, A. (1977). Self-efficacy: Toward a unifying theory of behavioral change. *Psychological Review, 84*(2), 191–215. https://doi.org/10.1016/0146-6402(78)90002-4

Bandura, A. (1989). Human agency in social cognitive theory. *American Psychologist, 44*(9), 1175–1184. https://psycnet.apa.org/doi/10.1037/0003-066X.44.9.1175

Bandura, A. (1997). *Self-efficacy: The exercise of control.* Freeman.

Baumeister, R. F., & Leary, M. R. (1995). The need to belong: Desire for interpersonal attachments as a fundamental human motivation. *Psychological Bulletin, 117*(3), 497–529. https://psycnet.apa.org/doi/10.1037/0033-2909.117.3.497

Beaudoin, D., Zywicki, C., Doan, T., Flierl, M., Parker, L., & McDavid, L. (2016). *Faculty perceptions of learning spaces.* Purdue University Office of Institutional Research, Assessment, and Effectiveness. https://www.purdue.edu/idata/Products/Reports/whitePapers.html

Beaudoin, D., Zywicki, C., Uche, A., Flierl, M., & Doan, T. (2016). *Influence of learning space and physical design on students' interactive learning.* Purdue University Office of Institutional Research, Assessment, and Effectiveness. https://www.purdue.edu/idata/documents/White_Papers/ALS%20-%20Full.pdf

Beichner, R., Saul, J., Abbott, D., Morse, J., Deardorff, D., Allain, R., Bonham, S., Dancy, M., & Risley, J. (2007). Student-centered activities for large enrollment undergraduate program (SCALE-UP). In E. F. Redish & P. J. Cooney (Eds.), *Research-based reform of university physics.* American Association of Physics Teachers. https://www.per-central.org/document/ServeFile.cfm?ID=4517

Benware, C. A., & Deci, E. L. (1984). Quality of learning with an active versus passive motivational set. *American Educational Research Journal, 21*(4), 755–765. https://doi.org/10.3102%2F00028312021004755

Bitsko, R. H., Holbrook, J. R., Ghandour, R. M., Blumberg, S. J., Visser, S. N., Perou, R., & Walkup, J. (2018). Epidemiology and impact of healthcare provider diagnosed anxiety and depression among U.S. children. *Journal of Developmental and Behavioral Pediatrics, 39*, 395–401. https://doi.org/10.1097/DBP.0000000000000571

Black, A. E., & Deci, E. L. (2000). The effects of student self-regulation and instructor autonomy support on learning in a college-level natural science course: A self-determination theory perspective. *Science Education, 84*(6), 740–756. https://doi.org/10.1002/1098-237X(200011)84:6%3C740::AID-SCE4%3E3.0.CO;2-3

Bloom, B. S. (1956). *Taxonomy of educational objectives. The classification of educational goals. Handbook I: Cognitive domain.* McKay.

Bok, D. (2006). *Our underachieving colleges. A candid look at how much students learn and why they should be learning more.* Princeton University Press.

Bolin, A. U., Khramtsova, I., & Saarnio, D. (2005). Using student journals to stimulate authentic learning: Balancing Bloom's cognitive and affective domains. *Teaching of Psychology, 32*(3), 154–159. https://doi.org/10.1207%2Fs15328023top3203_3

Bonem, E. M., Fedesco, H. N., & Zissimopoulos, A. (2019). What you do is less important than how you do it: The effects of learning environment on student outcomes. *Learning Environments Research, 23*, 27–44. https://doi.org/10.1007/s10984-019-09289-8

Bonem, E. M., Levesque-Bristol, C., Zissimopoulos, A., Nelson, D., & Fedesco, H. (2016). *Modeling the effects of student-centeredness on student outcomes* [Presentation at the 6th International Conference on Self-Determination Theory, Victoria, British Columbia, Canada].

Bowlby J. (1979). *The making and breaking of affectional bonds.* Tavistock.

Bressoud, D., Mesa, V., & Rasmussen, C. (2015). *Insights and recommendations from the MAA National Study of college calculus.* MAA Press.

Brookfield, S. D. (2017). *Becoming a critically reflective teacher* (2nd ed.). Jossey-Bass.

Brown, P. C., Roediger, H. L., & McDaniel, M. A. (2014). *Make it stick: The science of successful learning.* Belknap.

Bruce, C. S. (2008). *Informed learning.* Association of College and Research Libraries.

Bruff, D. (2009). *Teaching with classroom response systems: Creative active learning environments.* Jossey-Bass.

Calder, B. J., & Staw, B. M. (1975). Self-perception of intrinsic and extrinsic motivation. *Journal of Personality and Social Psychology, 31*(4), 599–605. https://psycnet.apa.org/doi/10.1037/h0077100

Campbell, J. (1949). *The hero with a thousand faces.* Pantheon.

Carriveau, R. (2010). *Connecting the dots: Developing student learning outcomes and outcomes based assessments.* Fancy Fox.

Cavanagh, S. R. (2016). *The spark of learning: Energizing the college classroom with the science of emotion.* West Virginia University Press.

Centers for Disease Control and Prevention. (2019, September). *Anxiety and depression in children.* https://www.cdc.gov/childrensmentalhealth/depression.html

Chen, B., Vansteenkiste, M., Beyers, W., Boone, L., Deci, E. L., Van der Kaap-Deeder, J., Duriez, B., Lens, W., Matos, L., Mouratidis, A., Ryan, R. M., Sheldon, K. M., Soenens, B., Van Petegem, S., & Verstuyf, J. (2015). Basic psychological need satisfaction, need frustration, and need strength across four cultures. *Motivation and Emotion, 39,* 216–236. https://doi.org/10.1007/s11031-014-9450-1

Chen, B., Vansteenkiste, M., Beyers, W., Soenens, B., & Van Petegem, S. (2013). Autonomy in family decision making for Chinese adolescents: Disentangling the dual meaning of autonomy. *Journal of Cross-Cultural Psychology, 44*(7), 1184–1209. https://doi.org/10.1177%2F0022022113480038

Chen, K.-C., & Jang, S.-J. (2010). Motivation in online learning: Testing a model of self-determination theory. *Computers in Human Behavior, 26,* 741–752. https://www.researchgate.net/deref/http%3A%2F%2Fdx.doi.org%2F10.1016%2Fj.chb.2010.01.011

Chickering, A. W., & Gamson, Z. F. (1987). Seven principles for good practice in undergraduate education. *The Wingspread Journal, 9,* 1–10.

Chirkov, V. I., Ryan, R. M., Kim, Y., & Kaplan, U. (2003). Differentiating autonomy from individualism and independence: A self-determination theory perspective on internalization of cultural orientations and well-being. *Journal of Personality and Social Psychology, 84*(1), 97–110. https://psycnet.apa.org/doi/10.1037/0022-3514.84.1.97

Chirkov, V. I., Ryan, R. M., & Willness, C. (2005). Cultural context and psychological needs in Canada and Brazil: Testing a self-determination approach to the internalization of cultural practices, identity, and well-being. *Journal of Cross-Cultural Psychology, 36*(4), 423–443. https://doi.org/10.1177%2F0022022105275960

Cho, H. J., Melloch, M., & Levesque-Bristol, C. (2019). *Enhanced student perceptions of learning and performance using concept-point-recovery teaching sessions* [Manuscript submitted for publication].

Chua, A. (2011). *Battle hymn of the tiger mother.* Penguin.

Council for Aid to Education. (2008). *Collegiate Learning Assessment common scoring rubric.* Author.

Cox, M. D. (2004). Introduction to faculty learning communities. *New Directions for Teaching and Learning, 97*, 5–23. https://doi.org/10.1002/tl.129

Csikszentmihalyi, M. (1975). *Beyond boredom and anxiety*. Jossey-Bass.

Csikszentmihalyi, M. (1990). *Flow: The psychology of optimal experience*. Harper & Row.

Danner, F. W., & Lonky, E. (1981). A cognitive-developmental approach to the effects of rewards on intrinsic motivation. *Child Development, 52*(3), 1043–1052. https://psycnet.apa.org/doi/10.2307/1129110

de Charms, R. (1968). *Personal causation: The internal affective determinants of behavior*. Academic Press.

Deci, E. L. (1971). Effects of externally mediated rewards on intrinsic motivation. *Journal of Personality and Social Psychology, 18*(1), 105–115. https://psycnet.apa.org/doi/10.1037/h0030644

Deci, E. L. (1972a). The effects of contingent and non-contingent rewards and controls on intrinsic motivation. *Organizational Behavior and Human Performance, 8*(2), 217–229. https://doi.org/10.1016/0030-5073(72)90047-5

Deci, E. L. (1972b). Intrinsic motivation, extrinsic reinforcement, and inequity. *Journal of Personality and Social Psychology, 22*(1), 113–120. https://psycnet.apa.org/doi/10.1037/h0032355

Deci, E. L., Connell, J. P., & Ryan, R. M. (1989). Self-determination in a work organization. *Journal of Applied Psychology, 74(4)*, 580–590. https://psycnet.apa.org/doi/10.1037/0021-9010.74.4.580

Deci, E. L., Eghrari, H., Patrick, B. C., & Leone, D. R. (1994). Facilitating internalization: The self-determination theory perspective. *Journal of Personality, 62*(1), 119–142. https://psycnet.apa.org/doi/10.1111/j.1467-6494.1994.tb00797.x

Deci, E. L., Koestner, R., & Ryan, R. M. (1999). A meta-analytic review of experiments examining the effects of extrinsic rewards on intrinsic motivation. *Psychological Bulletin, 125*(6), 627–668. https://psycnet.apa.org/doi/10.1037/0033-2909.125.6.627

Deci, E. L., Nezlek, J., & Sheinman, L. (1981). Characteristics of the rewarder and intrinsic motivation of the rewardee. *Journal of Personality and Social Psychology, 40*(1), 1–10. https://psycnet.apa.org/doi/10.1037/0022-3514.40.1.1

Deci, E. L., & Ryan, R. M. (1980). The empirical exploration of intrinsic motivational processes. In L. Berkowitz (Ed.), *Advances in Experimental Social Psychology* (Vol. 13, pp. 39–80). Academic Press.

Deci, E. L., & Ryan, R. M. (1985). *Intrinsic motivation and self-determination in human behavior*. Plenum.

Deci, E. L., & Ryan, R. M. (2000). The "what" and "why" of goal pursuits: Human needs and the self-determination of behavior. *Psychological Inquiry, 11*(4), 227–268. https://psycnet.apa.org/doi/10.1207/S15327965PLI1104_01

Deci, E. L., Schwartz, A. J., Sheinman, L., & Ryan, R. M. (1981). An instrument to assess adults' orientations toward control versus autonomy with children: Reflections on intrinsic motivation and perceived competence. *Journal of Educational Psychology, 73*(5), 642–650. https://psycnet.apa.org/doi/10.1037/0022-0663.73.5.642

DEGW. (2012). A study of trends in pedagogy at Purdue. Analysis of the impact of changes in pedagogy and study needs on space planning. *Office of the Provost Publications and Reports*, Paper 2. http://docs.lib.purdue.edu/provost_pubs/2

Downie, M., Koestner, R., El Geledi, S., & Cree, K. (2004). The impact of cultural internalization and integration on well-being among tricultural individuals. *Personality and Social Psychology Bulletin, 30*(3), 305–314. https://doi.org/10.1177%2F0146167203261298

Elliot, A. J., McGregor, H. A., & Thrash, T. M. (2002). The need for competence. In E.L. Deci & R.M. Ryan (Eds.), *Handbook of self-determination research* (pp. 361–387). University of Rochester Press.

Eyler, J. R. (2018). *How humans learn: The science and stories behind effective college teaching.* West Virginia University Press.

Fedesco, H. N., Bonem, E. M., Wang, C., & Henares, R. (2019). Connections in the classroom: Separating the effects of instructor and peer relatedness in the basic needs satisfaction scale. *Motivation and Emotion, 43*, 758–770. https://doi.org/10.1007/s11031-019-09765-x

Fedesco, H. N., Kentner, A., & Natt, J. (2017). The effect of relevance strategies on student perceptions of introductory courses. *Communication Education, 66*(2), 196–209. https://doi.org/10.1080/03634523.2016.1268697

Felder, R. M., & Brent, R. (2009). Active learning: An introduction. *ASQ Higher Education Brief, 2*(4). www.ncsu.edu/felder-public-Papers/ALpaper(ASQ).pdf

Fink, L. D. (2013). *Creating significant learning experiences: An integrated approach to designing colleges courses.* Jossey-Bass.

Flierl, M., Bonem, E., & Maybee, C. (in press). Developing the Informed Learning Scale: Measuring information literacy in higher education. *College & Research Libraries.*

Flierl, M., Bonem, E., Maybee, C., & Fundator, R. (2018). Information literacy supporting student motivation and performance: Course-level analyses. *Library and Information Science Research, 40*(1), 30–37. https://doi.org/10.1016/j.lisr.2018.03.001

Flierl, M., Maybee, C., & Fundator, R. (2019). Academic librarians' experiences as faculty developers: A phenomenographic study. *Communications in Information Literacy, 13*(2), 184–204. https://doi.org/10.15760/comminfolit.2019.13.2.4

Forest, J., Gilbert, M.-H., Beaulieu, G., Le Brock, P., & Gagne, M. (2014). Translating research results in economic terms: An application of economic utility analysis using SDT-based interventions. In M. Gagne (Ed.), *Oxford handbook of work engagement, motivation, and self-determination theory* (pp. 335–346). Oxford University Press.

Freeman, S., Eddy, S. L., McDonough, M., Smith, M. K., Nnadozie, O., Jordt, H., & Wenderoth, M. P. (2014). Active learning increases student performance in science, engineering, and mathematics. *Proceedings of the National Academy of Sciences of the United States of America, 111*(23), 8410–8415. https://doi.org/10.1073/pnas.1319030111

Gagne, M. (2003). The role of autonomy support and autonomy orientation in prosocial behavior engagement. *Motivation and Emotion, 27*(3), 199–223. https://psycnet.apa.org/doi/10.1023/A:1025007614869

Gillet, N., Vallerand, R. J., & Lafreniere, M. K. (2012). Intrinsic and extrinsic school motivation as a function of age: The mediating role of autonomy support. *Social Psychology of Education, 15*, 77–95. https://doi.org/10.1007/s11218-011-9170-2

Grolnick, W. S., & Ryan, R. M. (1987). Autonomy in children's learning: An experimental and individual difference investigation. *Journal of Personality and Social Psychology, 52*(5), 890–898. https://psycnet.apa.org/doi/10.1037/0022-3514.52.5.890

Grolnick, W. S., & Ryan, R. M. (1989). Parent styles associated with children's self-regulation and competence in school. *Journal of Educational Psychology, 81*(2), 143–154. https://psycnet.apa.org/doi/10.1037/0022-0663.81.2.143

Guay, F., Vallerand, R. J., & Blanchard, C. (2000). On the assessment of situational intrinsic and extrinsic motivation: The situational motivation scale (SIMS). *Motivation and Emotion, 24*(3), 175–214. http://dx.doi.org/10.1023/A:1005614228250

Gundlach, E., Maybee, C., & O'Shea, K. (2015). Statistical literacy social media project for the masses. *The Journal of Faculty Development, 29*(2), 71–80. https://docs.lib.purdue.edu/impactpubs/2

Gundlach, E., Richards, K. A. R., Nelson, D., & Levesque-Bristol, C. (2015). A comparison of student attitudes, statistical reasoning, performance, and perceptions for web-augmented traditional, fully online, and flipped sections of a statistical literacy class. *Journal of Statistics Education, 23*(1). https://doi.org/10.1080/10691898.2015.11889723

Haerens, L., Aelterman, N., Van den Berghe, L., De Meyer, J., Soenens, B., & Vansteenkiste, M. (2013). Observing physical education teachers' need-supportive interactions in classroom settings. *Journal of Sport and Exercise Psychology, 35*(1), 3–17. https://psycnet.apa.org/doi/10.1123/jsep.35.1.3

Haras, C., Taylor, S. C., Sorcinelli, M. D., & von Hoene, L. (Eds.). (2017). *Institutional commitment to teaching excellence: Assessing the impacts and outcomes of faculty development*. American Council on Education.

Hardre, P. L., & Reeve, J. (2009). Training corporate managers to adopt a more autonomy supportive motivating style toward employees: An intervention study. *International Journal of Training and Development, 13*(3), 165–184. https://doi.org/10.1111/j.1468-2419.2009.00325.x

Harris, R. B., Mack, M. R., Bryant, J., Theobald, E. J., & Freeman, S. (2020, June). Reducing achievement gaps in undergraduate general chemistry could lift underrepresented students into a "hyperpersistent zone." *Science Advances, 6*(24). https://doi.org/10.1126/sciadv.aaz5687

Harter, S. (1981). A new self-report scale of intrinsic versus extrinsic orientation in the classroom: Motivational and informational components. *Developmental Psychology, 17*(3), 300–312. https://psycnet.apa.org/doi/10.1037/0012-1649.17.3.300

Head, A. J, Fister, B., & MacMillan, M., (2020). *Information literacy in the age of algorithms: Student experiences with news and information, and the need for change*. Project Information Literacy. https://files.eric.ed.gov/fulltext/ED605109.pdf

Heider, F. (1958). *The psychology of interpersonal relations*. Wiley.

Henderlong, J., & Lepper, M. R. (2002). The effects of praise on children's intrinsic motivation: A review and synthesis. *Psychological Bulletin, 128*(5), 774–795. https://psycnet.apa.org/doi/10.1037/0033-2909.128.5.774

Holgate, H. A. (2016). *Development and initial validation of a culturally responsive classroom climate scale*. Open Access Theses. 855. https://docs.lib.purdue.edu/open_access_theses/855

hooks, b. (1994). *Teaching to transgress: Education as the practice of freedom*. Routledge.

Hsu, H. K., Wang, C., & Levesque-Bristol, C. (2019). Reexamining the impact of self-determination theory on learning outcomes in the online learning environment. *Education and Information Technologies, 24*, 2159–2174. https://doi.org/10.1007/s10639-019-09863-w

Hunley, S., & Schaller, M. (2009). Assessment: The key to creating spaces that promote learning. *Educause Review, 44*(2), 27–34. https://doi.org/10.1007/978-94-6091-609-0_1

IMPACT Management Team and IMPACT Evaluation Team. (2013). *Annual IMPACT Report 2013: A report by the IMPACT Data Collection and Analysis Team*. IMPACT Reports. http://docs.lib.purdue.edu/impactreps/1

IMPACT Management Team and IMPACT Evaluation Team. (2017). *Annual IMPACT Report 2017: A report by the IMPACT Data Collection and Analysis Team*. IMPACT Reports. https://docs.lib.purdue.edu/impactreps/8/

IMPACT Management Team and IMPACT Evaluation Team. (2018). *Annual IMPACT Report 2018: A report by the IMPACT Data Collection and Analysis Team*. IMPACT Reports. https://docs.lib.purdue.edu/impactreps/10/

IMPACT Management Team and IMPACT Evaluation Team. (2019). *Annual IMPACT Report 2019: A report by the IMPACT Data Collection and Analysis Team*. IMPACT Reports. https://docs.lib.purdue.edu/impactreps/11/

IMPACT Management Team and IMPACT Evaluation Team. (2020). *Annual IMPACT Report 2020: A report by the IMPACT Data Collection and Analysis Team*. IMPACT Reports. https://docs.lib.purdue.edu/impactreps/12/

Iyengar, S. S., & DeVoe, S. E. (2003). Rethinking the value of choice: Considering cultural mediators of intrinsic motivation. In V. Murphy-Berman & J. J. Berman (Eds.), *Nebraska Symposium on Motivation: Cross-cultural differences in perspectives on self* (pp. 129–174). University of Nebraska Press.

Iyengar, S. S., & Lepper, M. R. (1999). Rethinking the value of choice: A cultural perspective on intrinsic motivation. *Journal of Personality and Social Psychology, 76*(3), 349–366. https://psycnet.apa.org/doi/10.1037/0022-3514.76.3.349

Jang, H., Reeve, J., & Deci, E. L. (2010). Engaging students in learning activities: It is not autonomy support or structure, but autonomy support and structure. *Journal of Educational Psychology, 102*(3), 588–600. https://psycnet.apa.org/doi/10.1037/a0019682

Johnston, M. M., & Finney, S. J. (2010). Measuring basic need satisfaction: Evaluating previous research and conducting new psychometric evaluation of the Basic Needs Satisfaction in General Scale. *Contemporary Educational Psychology, 35*, 280–296. https://doi.org/10.1016/j.cedpsych.2010.04.003

Kasser, V. G., & Ryan, R. M. (1999). The relation of psychological needs for autonomy and relatedness to vitality, well-being, and mortality in a nursing home. *Journal of Applied Social Psychology, 29*(5), 935–954. https://doi.org/10.1111/j.1559-1816.1999.tb00133.x

Kezar, A. (2017). Foreword. In C. Haras, S. C. Taylor, M. D. Sorcinelli, & L. von Hoene (Eds.), *Institutional commitment to teaching excellence: Assessing the impacts and outcomes of faculty development.* American Council on Education.

Klapp, A. (2015). Does grading affect educational attainment? A longitudinal study. *Assessment in Education: Principles, Policy, and Practice, 22*(3), 302–323. https://doi.org/10.1080/0969594X.2014.988121

Kuh G. D. (2018, July). *The impact of IMPACT: Evaluation of the Purdue University Instruction Matters: Purdue Academic Transformation (IMPACT) initiative.* Purdue University Office of the Provost.

Kuh, G. D., O'Donnell, K., & Schneider, C. G. (2017). HIPs at ten. *Change: The Magazine of Higher Learning, 49*(5), 8–16. https://doi.org/10.1080/00091383.2017.1366805

Lang, J. M. (2016). *Small teaching: Everyday lessons from the science of learning.* Jossey-Bass.

Lepper, M. R., Corpus, J. H., & Iyengar, S. S. (2005). Intrinsic and extrinsic motivational orientations in the classrooms: Age differences and academic correlates. *Journal of Educational Psychology, 97*(2), 184–196. https://psycnet.apa.org/doi/10.1037/0022-0663.97.2.184

Lepper, M. R., Greene, D., & Nisbett, R. E. (1973). Undermining children's intrinsic interest with extrinsic reward: A test of the "overjustification" hypothesis. *Journal of Personality and Social Psychology, 28*(1), 129–137. https://psycnet.apa.org/doi/10.1037/h0035519

Levesque-Bristol, C., Flierl, M., Zywicki, C., Parker, L. C., Connor, C., Guberman, D., Nelson, D., Maybee, C., Bonem, E., FitzSimmons, J., & Lott, E. (2019, February). *Creating student-centered learning environments and changing teaching culture: Purdue University's IMPACT program.* University of Illinois and Indiana University, National Institute for Learning Outcomes Assessment (NILOA).

Levesque-Bristol, C., Knapp, T. D., & Fisher, B. J. (2010). The effectiveness of service-learning: It's not always what you think. *Journal of Experiential Education, 33*, 208–224. https://doi.org/10.1177%2F105382590113300302

Levesque-Bristol, C., Maybee, C., Parker, L. C., Zywicki, C., Connor, C., & Flierl, M. (2019). Shifting culture: Professional development through academic course transformation. *Change: The Magazine of Higher Learning, 51*(1), 35–41. https://eric.ed.gov/?id=ED594392

Levesque-Bristol, C., Richards, K. A. R., Zissimopoulous, A., Wang, C., & Yu, S. (in press). An evaluation of the integrative model for learning and motivation in the college classroom. *Current Psychology*. https://doi.org/10.1007/s12144-020-00671-x

Levesque-Bristol, C., Sell, G. R., & Zimmerman, J. A. (2006). A theory-based integrative model for learning and motivation in higher education. In S. Chadwick-Blossey & D. R. Robertson (Eds.), *To improve the academy*, Vol. 24 (pp. 86–103). Anker.

Levesque-Bristol, C., Zuehlke, A. N., Stanek, L. R., & Ryan, R. M. (2004). Autonomy and competence in German and American university students: A comparative study based on self-determination theory. *Journal of Educational Psychology, 96*, 68–84. https://psycnet.apa.org/doi/10.1037/0022-0663.96.1.68

Lieberman, M. D. (2013). *Social: Why our brains are wired to connect*. Crown.

Locke, E. A., & Latham, G. P. (1990). *A theory of goal setting and task performance*. Prentice Hall.

Lott, E. A., & Nunes, L. (2018). Learning outcome transformation in course redesigns. *International Society for the Scholarship of Teaching and Learning (ISSoTL) Conference Toward a Learning Culture*. Bergen, Norway.

Lynch, D. R., Russell, J. S., Evans, J. C., & Sutterer, K. G. (2009). Beyond the cognitive: The affective domain, values, and the achievement of the vision. *Journal of Professional Issues in Engineering Education and Practice, 135*(1), 47–56. https://doi.org/10.1061/ ASCE 1052-3928 2009 135:1 47

Markus, H. R., & Kitayama, S. (2003). Models of agency: Sociocultural diversity in the construction of action. In V. Murphy-Berman & J. J. Berman (Eds.), *Nebraska Symposium on Motivation: Cross-cultural differences in perspectives on self* (pp. 18–74). University of Nebraska Press.

Markus, H. R., Kitayama, S., & Heiman, R. J. (1996). Culture and basic psychological principles. In E. T. Higgins & A.W. Kruglanski (Eds.), *Social psychology: Handbook of basic principles* (pp. 857–913). Guilford.

Maybee, C. (2018). *IMPACT learning: Librarians at the forefront of change in higher education*. Elsevier.

Maybee, C., Bruce, C. S., Lupton, M., & Pang, M. F. (2019). Informed learning design: Teaching and learning through engagement with information. *Higher Education Research & Development, 38*(3), 579–593. https://doi.org/10.1080/07294360.2018.1545748

Maybee, C., Bruce, C. S., Lupton, M., & Rebmann, K. (2017). Designing rich information experiences to shape learning outcomes. *Studies in Higher Education, 42*(12), 2373–2388. https://doi.org/10.1080/03075079.2016.1148684

Maybee, C., Doan, T., & Flierl, M. (2016). Information literacy in the active learning classroom. *The Journal of Academic Librarianship, 42*(6), 705–711. https://docs.lib.purdue.edu/

Maybee, C., & Flierl, M. (2017). Motivating learners through information literacy. In S. Kurbanoglu, J. Boustany, S. Spiranec, E. Grassian, D. Mizrachi, L. Roy, & T. Cakmak (Eds.), *Information literacy in the inclusive society (communications in computer and information science series),* Proceedings of the 4th European Information Literacy Conference (pp. 698–707). Springer.

McDavid, L., Parker, L. C., Burgess, W., Robertshaw, B., & Doan, T. (2018). The combined effect of learning spaces and faculty self-efficacy to use student-centered practices on teaching experience and student engagement. *Journal of Learning Spaces, 7*(1), 29–44. http://libjournal.uncg.edu/jls/article/view/1597

McMurtrie, B. (2018, October 21). How Purdue professors are building more active and engaged classrooms. *Chronicle of Higher Education, 2018 Innovators: 6 Programs to Change the Classroom Culture.* https://www.chronicle.com/article/how-purdue-professors-are-building-more-active-and-engaged-classrooms/

Mehaffy, G. (2018). Student success: It's not just for students. *Change: The Magazine of Higher Learning, 50*(2), 8–14. https://doi.org/10.1080/00091383.2018.1445912

Meyer, J. P., Cash, A. H., & Mashburn, A. (2011). Occasions and the reliability of classroom observations: Alternative conceptualizations and methods of analysis. *Educational Assessment, 16,* 227–243. https://doi.org/10.1080/10627197.2011.638884

Michael, J. (2007). Faculty perceptions about barriers to active learning. *College Teaching, 55,* 42–47. https://doi.org/10.3200/CTCH.55.2.42-47

Michaelsen, L. K., Knight, A. B., & Fink, L. D. (Eds.). (2002). *Team-based learning: A transformative use of small groups.* Praeger.

Michaelsen, L. K., Knight, A. B., & Fink, L. D. (Eds.). (2004). *Team-based learning: A transformative use of small groups in college teaching.* Stylus.

Middendorf, J., & Shopkow, L. (2018). *Overcoming student bottlenecks: Decode the critical thinking of your discipline.* Stylus.

Mitchell, M., Leachman, M., & Masterson, K. (2017). *A lost decade in higher education funding.* Center on Budget and Policy Priorities. https://www.cbpp.org/research/state-budget-and-tax/a-lost-decade-in-higher-education-funding

Moran, C. M., Diefendorff, J. M., Kim, T.-Y., & Liu, Z.-Q. (2012). A profile approach to self-determination theory motivations at work. *Journal of Vocational Behavior, 81*(3), 354–363. https://psycnet.apa.org/doi/10.1016/j.jvb.2012.09.002

Morris, R. C., Parker, L. C., Nelson, D., Pistilli, M. D., Hagen, A., Levesque-Bristol, C., & Weaver, G. (2014). Development of a student self-reported instrument to assess course reform. *Educational Assessment, 19,* 302–320. https://docs.lib.purdue.edu/cgi/viewcontent.cgi?article=1007&context=impactpubs

Mouratidis, A., Vansteenkiste, M., Lens, W., & Sideridis, G. D. (2008). The motivating role of positive feedback in sport and physical education: Evidence for a motivational model. *Journal of Sport and Exercise Psychology, 30*(2), 240–268. https://doi.org/10.1123/jsep.30.2.240

Nelson, D., Bonem, E. M., & FitzSimmons, J. (2019). Faculty perceptions of teaching in collaborative classrooms: A qualitative interview study [Manuscript in preparation].

Ogan, A., Aleven, V., & Jones, C. (2009). Advancing development of intercultural competence through supporting predictions in narrative video. *International Journal of Artificial Intelligence in Education, 19*(3), 267–288. https://www.semanticscholar.org/paper/Advancing-Development-of-Intercultural-Competence-Ogan-Aleven/40a5e34d0e964efdb4edc337940ec702aaaaa3a3

Oleson, A., & Hora, M. T. (2014). Teaching the way they were taught? Revisiting the sources of teaching knowledge and the role of prior experience in shaping faculty teaching practices. *Higher Education, 68*, 29–45. https://doi.org/10.1007/s10734-013-9678-9

Otis, N., & Pelletier, L. G. (2005). A motivational model of daily hassles, physical symptoms, and future work intentions among police officers. *Journal of Applied Social Psychology, 35*(10), 2193–2214. https://psycnet.apa.org/doi/10.1111/j.1559-1816.2005.tb02215.x

Pace, D., & Middendorf, J. (Eds.) (2004). Decoding the disciplines: A model for helping students learn disciplinary ways of thinking. In *Decoding the disciplines: Helping students learn disciplinary ways of thinking* (New Directions in Teaching and Learning, no. 98, pp. 1–12). Jossey-Bass.

Palmer, P. J. (1998). *The courage to teach: Exploring the inner landscape of teachers' life*. Jossey-Bass.

Pannells, T. C., & Claxton, A. F. (2008). Happiness, creative ideation, and locus of control. *Creativity Research Journal, 20*(1), 67–71. https://doi.org/10.1080/10400410701842029

Parker, L. C, Adedokun, O., & Weaver, G. C. (2015). Culture, policy, and resources: Barriers reported by faculty implementing course reform. In G. C. Weaver, W. D. Burgess, A. L. Childress, & L. Slakey (Eds.), *Transforming institutions: Undergraduate STEM education for the 21st century* (pp. 125–139). Purdue University Press.

Parker, L. C., & Nelson, D. (2019). Faculty autonomy in a large, trans-disciplinary faculty learning community focused on course redesign [Manuscript in preparation].

Patall, E. A., Cooper, H., & Robinson, J. C. (2008). The effects of choice on intrinsic motivation and related outcomes: A meta-analysis of research findings. *Psychological Bulletin, 134*(2), 270–300. https://doi.apa.org/doi/10.1037/0033-2909.134.2.270

Patall, E. A., Cooper, H., & Wynn, S. R. (2010). The effectiveness and relative importance of choice in the classroom. *Journal of Educational Psychology, 102*(4), 896–915. https://psycnet.apa.org/doi/10.1037/a0019545

Patall, E. A., Dent, A. L., Oyer, M., & Wynn, S. R. (2012). Student autonomy and course value: The unique and cumulative roles of various teacher practices. *Motivation and Emotion, 37*(1), 14–32. https://doi.org/10.1007/s11031-012-9305-6

Pelletier, L. G., Seguin-Levesque, C., & Legault, L. (2002). Pressure from above and pressure from below as determinants of teachers' motivation and teaching behaviors. *Journal of Educational Psychology, 94*(1), 186–196. https://psycnet.apa.org/doi/10.1037/0022-0663.94.1.186

Petersen C. I., & Gorman, K. S. (2014). Strategies to address common challenges when teaching in an active learning classroom. In D. C. Brooks, J. D. Walker, & P. Baepler (Eds.), *Active learning spaces* (New Directions for Teaching and Learning, no. 137, pp. 63–70). https://doi.org/10.1002/tl.20086

Piburn, M., Sawada, D., Turley, J., Falconer, K., Benford, R., Bloom, I., & Judson, E. (2000). *Reformed teaching observation protocol (RTOP) reference manual.* Arizona Collaborative for Excellence in the Preparation of Teachers.

Porter, L. W., & Lawler, E. E. (1968). *Managerial attitudes and performance.* Irwin.

Prince, M. (2004). Does active learning work? A review of the research. *Journal of Engineering Education, 93*(3), 179–263. https://doi.org/10.1002/j.2168-9830.2004.tb00809.x

Purdue University. (n.d.). *Exams and academic integrity considerations.* https://www.purdue.edu/innovativelearning/teaching-remotely/files/resources/Exams_and_Academic_Integrity_Considerations.pdf

Reeve, J. (2002). Self-determination theory applied to educational settings. In E. L. Deci & R. M. Ryan (Eds.), *Handbook of self-determination research* (pp. 183–203). University of Rochester Press.

Reeve, J., Bolt, E., & Cai, Y. (1999). Autonomy-supportive teachers: How they teach and motivate students. *Journal of Educational Psychology, 91*(3), 537–548. https://psycnet.apa.org/doi/10.1037/0022-0663.91.3.537

Reeve, J., Jang, H., Hardre, P., & Omura, M. (2002). Providing a rationale in an autonomy-supportive way as a strategy to motivate others during an uninteresting activity. *Motivation and Emotion, 26*(3), 183–207. https://doi.org/10.1023/A:1021711629417

Reeve, J., & Tseng, C.-M. (2011). Cortisol reactivity to a teacher's motivating style: The biology of being controlled versus supporting autonomy. *Motivation and Emotion, 35*, 63–74. https://doi.org/10.1007/s11031-011-9204-2

Reis, H. T., Sheldon, K. M., Gable, S. L., Roscoe, J., & Ryan, R. M. (2000). Daily well-being: The role of autonomy, competence, and relatedness. *Personality and Social Psychology Bulletin, 26*(4), 419–435. https://psycnet.apa.org/doi/10.1177/0146167200266002

Richards, K. A. R., Hemphill, M. A., & Templin, T. J. (2018). Personal and contextual factors related to teachers' experience with stress and burnout. *Journal of Teachers and Teaching Theory and Practice, 24*(7), 768–787. https://doi.org/10.1080/13540602.2018.1476337

Roth, G., Assor, A., Niemiec, C. P., Ryan, R. M., & Deci, E. L. (2009). The emotional and academic consequences of parental conditional regard: Comparing conditional positive regard, conditional negative regard, and autonomy support as parenting practices. *Developmental Psychology, 45*(4), 1119–1142. https://psycnet.apa.org/doi/10.1037/a0015272

Rotter, J. (1966). Generalized expectancies for internal versus external control of reinforcements. *Psychological Monographs, 80*(1), 1–28. https://doi.org/10.1037/h0092976

Ryan, R. M. (1995). Psychological needs and the facilitation of integrative processes. *Journal of Personality, 63*(3), 397–427. https://psycnet.apa.org/doi/10.1111/j.1467-6494.1995.tb00501.x

Ryan, R. M., & Connell, J. P. (1989). Perceived locus of causality and internalization: Examining reasons for acting in two domains. *Journal of Personality and*

Social Psychology, 57(5), 749–761. https://psycnet.apa.org/doi/10.1037/0022-3514.57.5.749

Ryan, R. M., Connell, J. P., & Deci, E. L. (1985). A motivational analysis of self-determination and self-regulation in education. In C. Ames & R.E. Ames (Eds.), *Research on motivation in education: The classroom milieu* (pp. 13–51). Academic Press.

Ryan, R. M., Connell, J. P., & Plant, R. W. (1990). Emotions in nondirected text learning. *Learning and Individual Differences, 2*(1), 1–17. https://psycnet.apa.org/doi/10.1016/1041-6080(90)90014-8

Ryan, R. M., & Deci, E. L. (2000). Self-determination theory and the facilitation of intrinsic motivation, social development, and well-being. *American Psychologist, 55*(1), 68–78. https://psycnet.apa.org/doi/10.1037/0003-066X.55.1.68

Ryan, R. M., & Deci, E. L. (2017). *Self-determination theory: Basic psychological needs in motivation, development, and wellness*. Guilford.

Ryan, R. M., & Grolnick, W. S. (1986). Origins and pawns in the classroom: Self-report and projective assessments of individual differences in children's perceptions. *Journal of Personality and Social Psychology, 50*(3), 550–558. https://psycnet.apa.org/doi/10.1037/0022-3514.50.3.550

Ryan, R. M., Mims, V., & Koestner, R. (1983). Relation of reward contingency and interpersonal context to intrinsic motivation: A review and test using cognitive evaluation theory. *Journal of Personality and Social Psychology, 45*(4), 736–750. https://psycnet.apa.org/doi/10.1037/0022-3514.45.4.736

Sawada, D., Piburn, M. D., & Judson, E. (2002). Measuring reform practices in science and mathematics classrooms: The reformed teaching observation protocol. *School Science & Mathematics, 102*, 245–253. https://doi.org/10.1111/j.1949-8594.2002.tb17883.x

Sawada, D., Piburn, M., Turley, J., Falconer, K., Benford, R., Bloom, I., & Judson, E. (2000). *Reformed teaching observation protocol (RTOP) training guide (ACEPT IN-002)*. Arizona Board of Regents.

Scott, W. E. (1976). The effects of extrinsic rewards on "intrinsic motivation": A critique. *Organizational Behavior and Human Performance, 15*, 117–129. https://doi.org/10.1016/0030-5073(76)90032-5

Seymour, E., Wiese, D., Hunter, A., & Daffinrud, S. M. (2000). *Creating a better mousetrap: On-line student assessment of their learning gains* [Paper presentation]. National Meeting of the American Chemical Society, San Francisco, California.

Sheldon, K. M., Elliot A. J., Ryan, R. M., Chirkov, V., Kim, Y., Wu, C., Demir, M., & Sun, Z. (2004). Self-concordance and subjective well-being in four cultures. *Journal of Cross-Cultural Psychology, 35*(2), 209–223. https://doi.org/10.1177%2F0022022103262245

Sheldon, K. M., & Hilpert, J. C. (2012). The balanced measure of psychological needs (BMPN). Scale: An alternative domain general measure of need satisfaction. *Motivation and Emotion, 36*, 439–451. https://doi.org/10.1007/s11031-012-9279-4

Sheldon, K. M., & Krieger, L. S. (2007). Understanding the negative effects of legal education on law students: A longitudinal test of self-determination theory. *Personality and Social Psychology Bulletin, 33*(6), 883–897. https://doi.org/10.1177%2F0146167207301014

Sheldon, K. M., Ryan, R. M., & Reis, H. (1996). What makes for a good day? Competence and autonomy in the day and in the person. *Personality and Social Psychology Bulletin, 22*(12), 1270–1279. https://doi.org/10.1177%2F01461672962212007

Sibley, J., & Ostafichuk, P. (2014). *Getting started with team-based learning.* Stylus.

Skinner, B. F. (1971). *Beyond freedom and dignity.* Knopf.

Skinner, B. F. (1974). *About behaviorism.* Knopf.

Skinner, E. A., & Belmont, M. J. (1993). Motivation in the classroom: Reciprocal effects of teacher behavior and student engagement across the school year. *Journal of Educational Psychology, 85*(4), 571–581. https://doi.org/10.1037/0022-0663.85.4.571

Stanny, C. J. (2016). Reevaluating Bloom's taxonomy: What measurable verbs can and cannot say about student learning. *Educational Science, 6*(4), 37. https://doi.org/10.3390/educsci6040037

Streb, J., Keis, O., Lau, K., Hille, L., Spitzer, M., & Sosic-Vasic, Z. (2015). Emotional engagement in kindergarten and school children: A self-determination theory perspective. *Trends in Neuroscience and Education, 4*(4), 102–107. https://doi.org/10.1016/j.tine.2015.11.001

Struthers, B., MacCormack, P., & Taylor, S. C. (2018). *Effective teaching: A foundational aspect of practices that supports student learning.* American Council on Education.

Sweet, M., & Michaelsen, L. K. (Eds.). (2012). *Team-based learning in the social sciences and humanities: Group work that works to generate critical thinking and engagement.* Stylus.

Talbert, R. (2014, April). Flipped learning skepticism: Is flipped learning just self-teaching? *Chronicle of Higher Education.* http://chronicle.com/blognetwork/castingoutnines/2014/04/28/flipped-learning-skepticism-is-flipped-learning-just-self-teaching/

Taylor, G., Jungert, T., Mageau, G. A., Schattke, K., Dedic, H., Rosenfield, S., & Koestner, R. (2014). A self-determination theory approach to predicting school achievement over time: The unique role of intrinsic motivation. *Contemporary Educational Psychology, 39*(4), 342–358. https://psycnet.apa.org/doi/10.1016/j.cedpsych.2014.08.002

Twigg, C. A. (2003, September/October). Improving learning and reducing costs: New models for online learning. *Educause Review*, 28–38.

U.S. Department of Education. (2006). *A test of leadership, 23.* https://www2.ed.gov/about/bdscomm/list/hiedfuture/reports/final-report.pdf

Vansteenkiste, M., & Deci, E. L. (2003). Competitively contingent rewards and intrinsic motivation: Can losers remain motivated? *Motivation and Emotion, 27*(4), 273–299. https://doi.org/10.1023/A:1026259005264

Vansteenkiste, M., & Ryan, R. M. (2013). On psychological growth and vulnerability: Basic psychological needs satisfaction and need frustration as a unifying principle. *Journal of Psychotherapy Integration, 23*(3), 263–280. https://psycnet.apa.org/doi/10.1037/a0032359

Vansteenkiste, M., Sierens, E., Goossens, L., Soenens, B., Dochy, F., Mouratidis, A., Aelterman, N., Haerens, L., & Beyers, W. (2012). Identifying configurations of perceived teacher autonomy support and structure: Associations with self-regulated learning, motivation, and problem behavior. *Learning and Instruction, 22*(6), 431–439. https://doi.org/10.1016/j.learninstruc.2012.04.002

Wang, C. (2019, October 17). *"Learning is not always fun, but it is fine": Effects of rationale generation on autonomous motivation and learning in uninteresting but required academic activities*. figshare. https://doi.org/10.25394/PGS.9955214.v1

Wang, C., Hsu, H. K., Bonem, E. M., Moss, J. D., Yu, S., Nelson, D. B., & Levesque-Bristol, C. (2019). Need satisfaction and need dissatisfaction: A comparative study of online and face-to-face learning contexts. *Computers in Human Behavior, 95*, 114–125. https://doi.org/10.1016/j.chb.2019.01.034

Wang, C., & Levesque-Bristol, C. (2019). "Learning is not always fun, but it is fine": Effects of rationale generation on motivation and learning in uninteresting but required academic activities. [Manuscript submitted for publication].

Wang, C., Zhang, Y., Moss, J. D., Bonem, E. M., & Levesque-Bristol, C. (2020). Multilevel factors affecting college students' perceptions of knowledge transfer: From the perspective of self-determination theory. *Research in Higher Education*, 1–25. https://doi.org/10.1007/s11162-020-09592-x

White, R. W. (1959). Motivation reconsidered: The concept of competence. *Psychological Review, 66*(5), 297–333. https://psycnet.apa.org/doi/10.1037/h0040934

Wiggins, G. P., & McTighe, J. (2005). *Understanding by design* (2nd ed.). Association for Supervision and Curriculum Development.

Wiles, B. (2020). *A motivation framework for the design and evaluation of learning environments in undergraduate mainstream calculus* [Doctoral dissertation, Purdue University].

Williams, G. C., & Deci, E. L. (1996). Internalization of biopsychosocial values by medical students: A test of self-determination theory. *Journal of Personality and Social Psychology, 70*, 767–779. https://psycnet.apa.org/doi/10.1037/0022-3514.70.4.767

Yu, S., Chen, B., Levesque-Bristol, C., & Vansteenkiste, M. (2016). Chinese education examined via the lens of self-determination. *Educational Psychology Review, 30*, 177–214. https://doi.org/10.1007/s10648-016-9395-x

Yu, S., & Levesque-Bristol, C. (2018). Are students in some college majors more self-determined in their studies than others? *Motivation and Emotion, 42*, 831–851. https://doi.org/10.1007/s11031-018-9711-5

Yu, S., & Levesque-Bristol, C. (2020). A cross-classified path analysis of the self-determination theory model on the situational, individual, and classroom levels in college education. *Contemporary Educational Psychology, 61*, https://doi.org/10.1016/j.cedpsych.2020.101857

Yu, S., Zhang, F., Nunes, L., & Levesque-Bristol, C. (2018). Self-determined motivation to choose college majors, its antecedents, and outcomes: A cross-sectional investigation. *Journal of Vocational Behavior*, 132–150. Advance online publication. https://doi.org/10.1016/J.JVB.2018.07.002

Zywicki, C., & Beaudoin, D. (2016). *Perspectives of successful IMPACT faculty.* Purdue University Office of Institutional Research, Assessment, and Effectiveness website. https://www.purdue.edu/idata/Products/Reports/whitePapers.html

ABOUT THE AUTHOR

Chantal Levesque-Bristol is a full professor of educational psychology and executive director of the Center for Instructional Excellence at Purdue University. Her research area is in human motivation, applied to a variety of contexts, specifically education and educational initiatives and programs. This is her first published book. She is an avid cyclist and enjoys being out in nature.

INDEX

Faculty Development books from Stylus Publishing

Advancing the Culture of Teaching on Campus
ow a Teaching Center Can Make a Difference
Edited by Constance Cook and Matthew Kaplan
Foreword by Lester P. Monts

Faculty Mentoring
A Practical Manual for Mentors, Mentees, Administrators, and Faculty Developers
Susan L. Phillips and Susan T. Dennison
Foreword by Milton D. Cox

Faculty Retirement
Best Practices for Navigating the Transition
Edited by Claire Van Ummersen, Jean McLaughlin and Lauren Duranleau
Foreword by Lotte Bailyn

The Prudent Professor
Planning and Saving for a Worry-Free Retirement from Academe
Edwin M. Bridges and Brian D. Bridges

Teaching Across Cultural Strengths
A Guide to Balancing Integrated and Individuated Cultural Frameworks in College Teaching
Alicia Fedelina Chávez and Susan Diana Longerbeam
Foreword by Joseph L. White

Why Students Resist Learning
A Practical Model for Understanding and Helping Students
Edited by Anton O. Tolman and Janine Kremling
Foreword by John Tagg

Student Affairs books from Stylus

Educating About Religious Diversity and Interfaith Engagement
A Handbook for Student Affairs
Edited by Kathleen M. Goodman,
Mary Ellen Giess and Eboo Patel

Debunking the Myth of Job Fit in Higher Education and Student Affairs
Edited by Brian J. Reece, Vu T. Tran,
Elliott N. DeVore and Gabby Porcaro

The Lives of Campus Custodians
Insights into Corporatization and Civic Disengagement in the Academy
Peter Magolda

Trans* Policies & Experiences in Housing & Residence Life
Insights into Corporatization and Civic Disengagement in the Academy
Edited by Jason C. Garvey, Stephanie H. Chang,
Z Nicolazzo and Rex Jackson

A Good Job
Campus Employment as a High-Impact Practice
George S. McClellan, Kristina L. Creager and
Marianna Savoca

Student Development books from Stylus Publishing

Advancing Black Male Student Success From Preschool Through Ph.D.
Edited by Shaun R. Harper and J. Luke Wood

The New Science of Learning Edition 2
How to Learn in Harmony With Your Brain
Terry Doyle and Todd D. Zakrajsek
Foreword by Kathleen F. Gabriel

Advancing Online Teaching
Creating Equity-Based Digital Learning Environments
Kevin Kelly and Todd D. Zakrajsek
Foreword by Michelle Pacansky-Brock

Real-Time Student Assessment
Meeting the Imperative for Improved Time to Degree, Closing the Opportunity Gap, and Assuring Student Competencies for 21st-Century Needs
Peggy L. Maki
Foreword by George D. Kuh

Successful STEM Mentoring Initiatives for Underrepresented Students
A Research-Based Guide for Faculty and Administrators
Becky Wai-Ling Packard
Foreword by Norman L. Fortenberry

Teach Students How to Learn
Strategies You Can Incorporate Into Any Course to Improve Student Metacognition, Study Skills, and Motivation
Saundra Yancy McGuire
With Stephanie McGuire
Foreword by Thomas Angelo

Teaching and Learning books from Stylus

Learner-Centered Teaching
Putting the Research on Learning into Practice
Terry Doyle
Foreword by Todd D. Zakrajsek

Of Education, Fishbowls, and Rabbit Holes
Rethinking Teaching and Liberal Education for an Interconnected World
Jane Fried With Peter Troiano
Foreword by Dawn R. Person

Creating Wicked Students
Designing Courses for a Complex World
Paul Hanstedt

Dynamic Lecturing
Research-Based Strategies to Enhance Lecture Effectiveness
Christine Harrington and Todd Zakrajsek
Foreword by José Antonio Bowen

Designing a Motivational Syllabus
Creating a Learning Path for Student Engagement
Christine Harrington and Melissa Thomas
Foreword by Kathleen F. Gabriel

Course-Based Undergraduate Research
Educational Equity and High-Impact Practice
Edited by Nancy H. Hensel
Foreword by Cathy N. Davidson

Also available from Stylus

Taking Flight

Making Your Center for Teaching and Learning Soar

Laura Cruz, Michele A. Parker, Brian Smentkowski, and Marina Smitherman

Foreword by Cher Hendricks

"*Taking Flight* is an amazing resource for everyone involved in educational development. Written in a friendly and supportive tone, the authors of this valuable resource have summarized the literature on educational development, provided examples of well-respected centers, created worksheets to help you develop your efforts, and infused their own decades of experience in this field. This book skillfully guides; it does not push. I am recommending this book to so many people."—***Todd D. Zakrajsek***, *Associate Professor, School of Medicine, University of North Carolina at Chapel Hill*

Taking Flight synthesizes research on best practices for running centers of teaching and learning, providing practical guidance and resources for educational developers who are looking to open new centers; revitalize an underperforming center; or sustain and enhance an effective center. The authors offer the necessary background, relevant examples, and practical exercises specifically designed to support the sustained vitality of educational development and its role in fostering organizational change. The book is practical in nature, with step sheets, diagrams, and similar materials designed to facilitate reflection and application.

Faculty Development in the Age of Evidence

Current Practices, Future Imperatives

Andrea L. Beach, Mary Deane Sorcinelli, Ann E. Austin and Jaclyn K. Rivard

"Overall, *Faculty Development in the Age of Evidence* is an essential resource for the field of faculty development and for the higher education sector. Beach and colleagues provide an updated examination of the status of the field, and create meaningful arguments in favor of continually strengthening faculty development. Beyond that, the book asks important questions for practitioners to reflect and act upon, in order to continue evolving the field of faculty development and the overall impact of higher education in society."—***Teachers College Record***

Building on their previous study of a decade ago, published under the title of *Creating the Future of Faculty Development*, the authors explore questions of professional preparation and pathways, programmatic priorities, collaboration, and assessment. Since the publication of this earlier study, the pressures on faculty development have only escalated—demands for greater accountability from regional and disciplinary accreditors, fiscal constraints, increasing diversity in types of faculty appointments, and expansion of new technologies for research and teaching. Centers have been asked to address a wider range of institutional issues and priorities based on these challenges. How have they responded and what strategies should centers be considering? These are the questions this book addresses.

Coming in from the Margins

Faculty Development's Emerging Organizational Development Role in Institutional Change

Connie Schroeder

With Phyllis Blumberg, Nancy Van Note Chism, Catherine E. Frerichs, Susan Gano-Phillips, Devorah Lieberman, Diana G. Pace and Tamara Rosier

"No doubt about, we have entered a new era in faculty development. As our institutions face a myriad of changes, faculty developers will increasingly need to look beyond traditional instructional development boundaries to emerging organizational development roles. The pressures put on faculty developers during this time of flux are immense. Luckily, this important new book, based on original research and state-of-the-art practice, provides a cogent range of insights into what we are all experiencing. Coming in from the Margins is an indispensable and timely addition to the field that takes a hard look at where we are right now, and provides a road map for the future."—***Mary Deane Sorcinelli***, *Associate Provost for Faculty Development, and Professor, Educational Policy, Research and Administration, University of Massachusetts Amherst*

The core argument of this book – that a necessary and significant role change is underway in faculty development – is a call for centers to merge the traditional responsibilities and services of the past several decades with a leadership role as organizational developers. Failing collectively to define and outline the dimensions and expertise of this new role puts centers at risk of not only marginalization, but of dissolution.

Adjunct Faculty Voices

Cultivating Professional Development and Community at the Front Lines of Higher Education

Edited by Roy Fuller, Marie Kendall Brown and Kimberly Smith

Foreword by Adrianna Kezar

"This book is a lucid analysis of the adjunct faculty crisis. It adds to the literature by updating the taxonomy of adjuncts in useful ways, but it is not just an academic exercise. Finally, a book that gives voice to contingent faculty themselves, their struggles and their accomplishments. The 4 areas for improvement identified—identification/ recruitment, community, equity, and development—are followed up with replicable models. A remarkable work, appealing to both adjunct faculty and administrators!"—***Michele DiPietro***, *Executive Director, Faculty Development and Recognition, Center for Excellence in Teaching and Learning, Kennesaw State University*

Teaching and Learning centers across the country are responding to the growing adjunct cohort in innovative and efficient ways. Administrators, deans, department chairs, and adjunct faculty will all benefit by hearing the voices of adjuncts as they express the challenges faced by adjunct faculty and the types of professional development opportunities which are most beneficial. Topics covered include:

- Best professional development practices that support and benefit adjunct faculty
- Faculty social isolation and community-building opportunities
- An overview of changes affecting the academic workforce
- An outline of issues and working conditions
- Current demographics and types of adjunct faculty
- Adjunct faculty narratives featuring their professional development and community experiences

22883 Quicksilver Drive
Sterling, VA 20166-2019

Subscribe to our e-mail alerts: www.Styluspub.com